Collins

Key Stage 3
Science

Student Book 2

Series editor: Ed Walsh
Authors: Tracey Baxter
Sunetra Berry
Pat Dower
Anne Pilling

William Collins' dream of knowledge for all began with the publication of his first book in 1819. A self-educated mill worker, he not only enriched millions of lives, but also founded a flourishing publishing house. Today, staying true to this spirit, Collins books are packed with inspiration, innovation and practical expertise. They place you at the centre of a world of possibility and give you exactly what you need to explore it.

Collins. Freedom to teach

Published by Collins
An imprint of HarperCollins*Publishers*
77 – 85 Fulham Palace Road
Hammersmith
London
W6 8JB

**Browse the complete Collins catalogue at
www.collins.co.uk**

10 9 8 7 6 5 4 3 2

ISBN 978-0-00-754021-1

Tracey Baxter, Sunetra Berry, Pat Dower and Anne Pilling assert
their moral rights to be identified as the authors of this work

British Library Cataloguing in Publication Data
A Catalogue record for this publication is available from the
British Library

Commissioned by Letitia Luff
Project managed by Jane Roth
Series editor Ed Walsh
Managing editor Caroline Green
Edited by Elizabeth Barker, Camilla Behrens, Hugh Hillyard-Parker,
John Ormiston and Ros Woodward
Proofread by Tony Clappison
Editorial assistance by Lucy Roth
Designed by Joerg Hartmannsgruber
Cover design by Angela English
Picture research by Amanda Redstone
Illustrations by Ken Vail Graphic Design
Typesetting by Ken Vail Graphic Design
Production by Emma Roberts
Printed and bound by L.E.G.O S.p.A, Italy

Contents

How to use this book

These tell you what you will be learning about in the lesson.

This introduces the topic and puts the science into an interesting context.

Each topic is divided into three parts. You will probably find the section with the blue heading easiest, and the section with the purple heading the most challenging.

Try these questions to check your understanding of each section.

Exploring diffusion

We are learning how to:

- Use the particle model to explain observations involving diffusion.

Diffusion is a process in which particles move and spread out. Unsurprisingly, gas particles diffuse much faster than particles in other states of matter. What make diffusion so special?

Examples of diffusion

Diffusion occurs because of the movement of particles in a gas or a liquid. There is hardly any diffusion in solids because the particles cannot move freely. Gas particles move faster and further than liquid particles, so diffusion in gases occurs faster than in liquids.

All smells spread as a result of diffusion. When particles of a gas, like air freshener spray or odours from smelly socks, are released into the air, they spread out as far away from each other as possible. These gas particles move through the air – when they reach your nose they are detected as a smell. This is why we can detect smells from a long distance away.

1. Give another example of diffusion in everyday life.
2. Why do smells become weaker the further you are from the source?

Diffusion and the particle model

Concentration is a measure of the number of particles packed in a certain volume.

Diffusion occurs because particles move from an area of high concentration to an area of low concentration, until there is no overall change in concentration. We call this the point of **equilibrium**. The difference in concentration is known as the **concentration gradient**. The higher the concentration gradient, the greater the rate of diffusion, and the quicker equilibrium is reached.

Temperature affects the rate of diffusion because it affects the energy of the particles. The higher the temperature, the higher the kinetic energy of the particles, and the faster they move in such a way as to reduce the concentration gradient.

FIGURE 2.3.14a: If a drop of coloured ink is added to water, after several hours the colour will have spread through the water so that it is of equal concentration throughout.

> **Did you know...?**
>
> The animal kingdom is full of amazing examples of how animals make use of diffusion to smell odours. Elephants can detect water sources up to 20 kilometres away.

Each topic has some fascinating extra facts.

3. If a drop of ink is added to some pure water, and a similar drop of ink is added to some dilute ink solution, in which solution would diffusion happen fastest? Explain your answer.

4. Think about these examples of diffusion. Which will reach equilibrium first and why?

   a) Placing a spoonful of coffee in 50 cm³ of hot water

   b) Adding a spoonful of cordial to 50 cm³ of cold water

3 .14

Explaining diffusion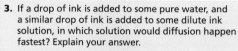

Look at Figure 2.3.14b. Concentrated ammonia is placed at one end of the tube and concentrated hydrochloric acid at the other end. Particles of ammonia are smaller than particles of hydrochloric acid. When the particles diffuse, they meet and react, forming a white cloud of ammonium chloride.

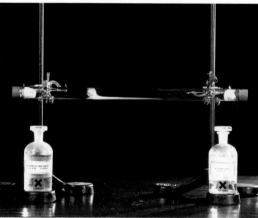

FIGURE 2.3.14b: How do the ammonia particles and hydrochloric acid particles reach each other to react?

5. What would happen if the concentrated solutions were replaced by dilute solutions of both ammonia and hydrochloric acid?

6. How else might the formation of the white ring be speeded up? Explain your answer.

7. Why doesn't the white ring in Figure 2.3.14b form in the centre of the tube?

Key vocabulary

diffusion

equilibrium

concentration gradient

These are the most important new science words in the topic. You can check their meanings in the Glossary at the end of the book.

SEARCH: diffusion **111**

Key this phrase into an internet search box to find out more.

The first page of a chapter has links to ideas you have met before, which you can now build on.

This page gives a summary of the exciting new ideas you will be learning about in the chapter.

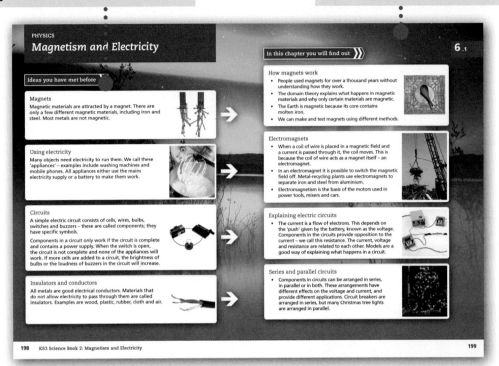

When you are about halfway through a chapter, these pages give you the chance to find out about a real-life application of the science you have been learning about.

The tasks – which get a bit more difficult as you go through – challenge you to apply your science skills and knowledge to the new context.

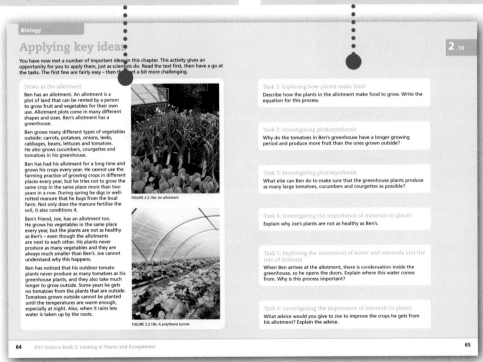

These lists at the end of a chapter act as a checklist of the key ideas of the chapter. In each row, the blue box gives the ideas or skills that you should master first. Then you can aim to master the ideas and skills in the orange box. Once you have achieved those you can move on to those in the purple box.

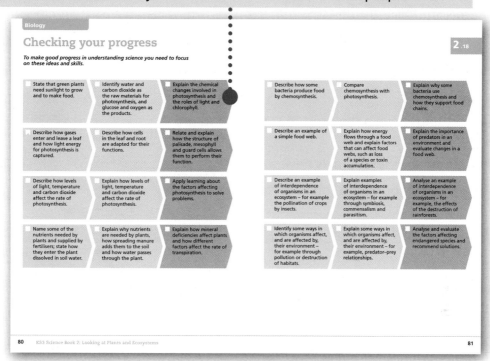

These end-of-chapter questions allow you and your teacher to check that you have understood the ideas in the chapter, can apply these to new situations, and can explain new science using the skills and knowledge you have gained.

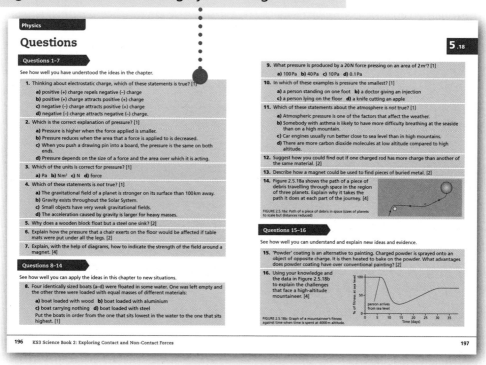

Getting the Energy your Body Needs

Movement

Some living things have a skeleton to support and protect them.

Humans and some other animals have a skeleton.

Animals with a backbone are called vertebrates.

Breathing

Breathing is the way that you get oxygen into your bodies and get waste carbon dioxide out.

The lungs are the main organs of the breathing system.

Oxygen breathed in is carried to the cells of the body by the blood.

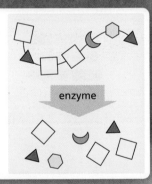

Nutrition

You eat to keep healthy and to give you energy.

During digestion, larger food molecules, such as starch, are broken down into smaller molecules, such as glucose.

Glucose from digestion is carried by your blood to the cells of your body.

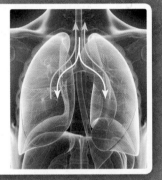

enzyme

Cells

Both animal and plant cells contain structures that have specific roles.

One of the largest of these organelles is the mitochondrion. It is a sausage-shaped organelle.

Energy is released in mitochondria.

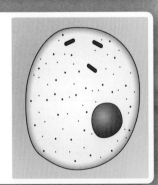

In this chapter you will find out

The skeleton

- The skeleton allows you to move at the joints.
- The skeleton also protects some organs.
- Blood cells are made inside bones.

Muscles

- Muscles contract to move some bones at the joints.
- Muscles can only contract and relax – they cannot push.
- Many muscles interact and work in pairs to bring about opposite movements.

Aerobic respiration

- Aerobic respiration uses glucose and oxygen to release energy.
- The energy released by respiration is needed for muscles to contract.
- Stamina sports rely mainly on aerobic respiration.

Anaerobic respiration

- Anaerobic respiration occurs when you do not have enough oxygen for aerobic respiration.
- Anaerobic respiration does not release as much energy as aerobic respiration.
- Brewing and baking are applications of anaerobic respiration.

Exploring the human skeleton

We are learning how to:

- Identify bones of the human skeleton.
- Explain why we have different shapes and sizes of bones.
- Communicate effectively to investigate the structure and function of bones.

There are 206 bones in the human skeleton. Each one contains calcium to make it strong. The smallest bone is found in your ear and is only approximately 3 mm long. The largest is found in your thigh. Why do bones vary so much?

The human skeleton

Bones make up the human **skeleton**. Without your skeleton you would flop!

Look at Figure 2.1.2a and answer these questions.

1. State the scientific name for the:

   a) skull

   b) collar bone

   c) shoulder blade

   d) funny bone.

2. Suggest why you cannot count 206 bones on the diagram of the skeleton in Figure 2.1.2a.

3. Explain why the name 'vertebrates' is so suitable for describing animals that have a backbone.

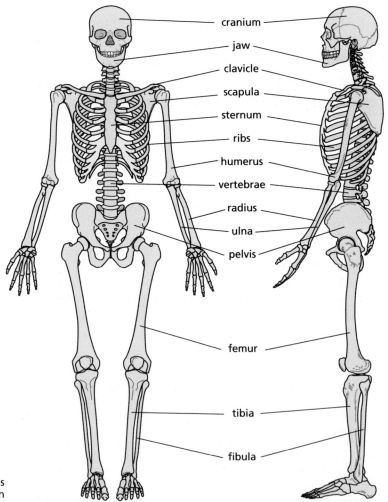

cranium
jaw
clavicle
scapula
sternum
ribs
humerus
vertebrae
radius
ulna
pelvis
femur
tibia
fibula

FIGURE 2.1.2a: The main bones of the human skeleton

Bones must be strong to support you. Most of a bone (approximately 70 per cent) is made up of hard minerals, such as **calcium**. The outside of a bone is smooth and hard to provide support. Inside this hard outer layer lies spongy, porous material. This spongy layer allows your bones to bend slightly. It also makes your bones lighter than if they were completely solid. At the centre of a bone is a softer substance called **marrow**.

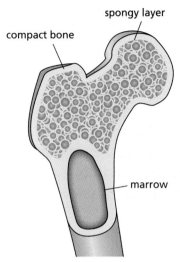

FIGURE 2.1.2b: Why is the outside layer of a bone hard?

4. **a)** Name the most common hard mineral in bones.

   b) Describe a food rich in this mineral.

5. Suggest why it is important that bones can bend slightly.

6. The spongy layer makes movement easier than if this layer was solid. Can you explain this?

Comparing bones 》》》

Some bones are long and narrow, such as those in your arms. Some bones are shorter, such as those in your feet. Other bones are flat and wide, such as the scapula (shoulder blade).

Each bone is adapted to suit its function. For example, the foot contains many small bones to allow flexibility.

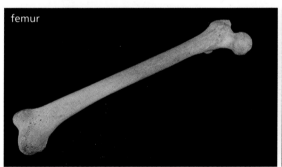 

FIGURE 2.1.2c: The femur is a long bone, whereas the scapula is a flat bone.

7. For each of the examples below, describe how the bone shape or structure is well adapted for its function in the body:

   a) femur (thigh bone)   **b)** bones of the hand   **c)** ribs.

8. Vertebrae are described as small and irregular bones.

   a) Explain what is meant by an 'irregular' bone.

   b) Suggest why all vertebrae are small and the same shape.

Did you know...?

Bones of flying birds are hollow to make the skeleton more lightweight. To increase the strength of the skeleton, more bones are fused together than in humans.

Key vocabulary

bone

skeleton

calcium

marrow

Analysing the skeleton

We are learning how to:

- Describe the roles of the skeleton.
- Explain the evidence for each of the roles of the skeleton.
- Estimate height using bone measurement calculations and suggest reasons for differences between people.

The role of the skeleton in giving support to your body is easy to see. However, the skeleton has several other important jobs. If you look carefully at the structure of a human skeleton, you may guess at these other roles.

FIGURE 2.1.3a: Jellyfish gain support from water, rather than from a skeleton.

Roles of the skeleton

The human skeleton has four main roles:

- **supports** the body
- **protects** the organs
- allows movement
- produces **blood cells**.

Without a skeleton you would not be able to sit, stand or hold yourself up.

The ribs are curved bones, forming a cavity inside the ribcage. The lungs are positioned inside the ribcage.

The many **joints** in your skeleton allow you to move. For example, the joint at the knee allows your leg to bend. Without joints, your skeleton would be rigid.

1. Describe the four main roles of the skeleton.

2. Explain which organ each part of the skeleton protects:

   a) ribs   **b)** cranium.

3. Describe three parts of the skeleton where joints are important.

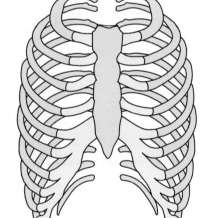

FIGURE 2.1.3b: The ribs are shaped to protect the lungs.

The importance of bone marrow

Bone marrow is in the centre of large bones. It is here where blood cells are made. There are three types of blood cells – red, white and platelets.

Patients with some medical conditions cannot make their own healthy blood cells. If a bone marrow transplant is carried out the patient may then make healthy blood cells again.

4. Describe the role of red blood cells.

5. Explain what is meant by a transplant.

Using bone measurements

Your skeleton has many symmetrical features. This helps you to balance and co-ordinate movements. Skeletons are usually made in similar proportions. For example, if you stretch your arms as wide as you can and measure their arm span, this will probably be similar to your height.

At an archaeological dig or a crime scene, only a few bones may be found. Yet scientists can predict the height of a person using only the length of the femur, humerus, or even the smaller bones in the arms and legs.

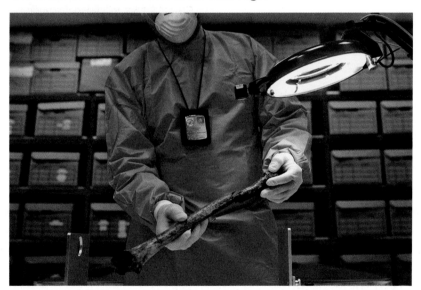

FIGURE 2.1.3d: A femur can be used to estimate the height of a person.

The calculation used to estimate height from the length of the femur is:

height (m) = (length of femur (m) × 2.6) + 65

6. A femur, 0.35 m in length, is found during a police investigation. Estimate the height of the victim. (Remember units.)

7. Estimate the arm span of the same victim.

8. Suggest why the calculation is not always accurate in people between 12 and 18 years of age.

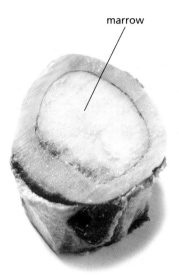

marrow

FIGURE 2.1.3c: Bone marrow makes blood cells. The red blood cells carry oxygen around the body.

Did you know…?

Your ears and the end of your nose do not contain bone. Instead, these body parts are given their shape by cartilage. **Cartilage** is softer than bone and does not contain blood vessels or nerve cells.

Key vocabulary

support

protect

blood cells

joint

cartilage

Understanding the role of skeletal joints

We are learning how to:

- Describe the roles of tendons, ligaments, joints and muscles.
- Compare different joints in the human skeleton.
- Collaborate effectively to interpret how we use joints.

Bones meet at joints. Some joints, such as those in your cranium, do not allow much movement. However, many joints allow a wide range of movement. Try moving your arm at your elbow, then try at your shoulder. Different joints allow you to move in different ways.

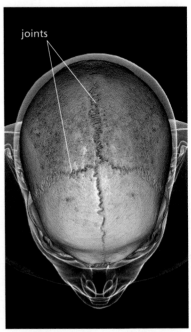

FIGURE 2.1.4a: Why are joints in the cranium fixed?

Tendons and ligaments

The bones of a skeleton are held together by **ligaments**. Bones are connected to **muscles** by **tendons**.

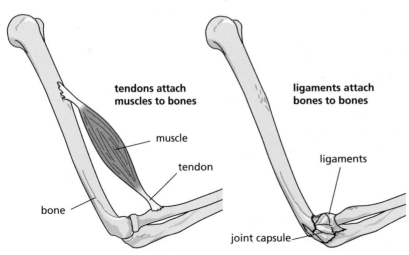

tendons attach muscles to bones

ligaments attach bones to bones

muscle

tendon

bone

ligaments

joint capsule

FIGURE 2.1.4b: Tendons join bone to muscle; ligaments join bone to bone.

Both ligaments and tendons are made of stretchy fibres called collagen. However, the fibres are arranged differently in each. In tendons, they are arranged so that the tendon can move easily as muscles contract. In ligaments, fibres are arranged more tightly to hold bones together securely.

1. Describe the roles of tendons and ligaments.

2. Explain why it is important that tendons are stretchy.

3. Sportspeople often damage ligaments. Suggest how this can happen.

We have three types of moveable joint. The range and type of movement that they allow varies.

Fixed joints, such as those in the skull, do not allow movement.

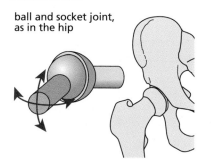
ball and socket joint, as in the hip

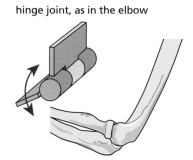
hinge joint, as in the elbow

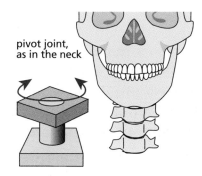
pivot joint, as in the neck

FIGURE 2.1.4c: Types of joints

Ball and socket joints allow forward, backward and circular movements. The shoulder joint is a ball and socket.

A hinge joint allows movement like the opening and closing of a door. This type of joint is found at the elbow.

A pivot joint allows rotation around an axis. This type of joint is found at the top of the neck and allows you to move your head from side to side.

4. List the four types of joint in order, starting with the type allowing least movement.

5. Suggest which type of joint is found in the:

   a) hip   **b)** knee.

6. Draw a table to summarise the types of joint and the movements they allow.

A team effort >>>

Most movements are more complex than simply moving at one joint. For example, throwing a ball could involve the shoulder joint to lift the ball, the elbow joint to bend the arm, and the finger joints to let go of the ball. You will co-ordinate movements of these joints without even realising it.

7. For each movement, list at least three joints that are involved:

   a) jumping into a swimming pool

   b) playing on a game console

   c) brushing your teeth.

8. Suggest how you co-ordinate the complex movements of joints.

Did you know...?

The lower jawbone is the only bone in your head that can move. It moves to enable you to talk and eat.

Key vocabulary

ligament

muscle

tendon

Investigating muscle strength

We are learning how to:

- Identify muscles used in different activities.
- Plan an investigation to compare the strengths of different muscles.
- Make a prediction about which muscles are stronger than others.

Muscles make up approximately 40 per cent of an adult's body. One type of muscle is skeletal muscle, attached to the skeleton. Athletes work hard to strengthen specific muscles and train them to tire less easily. Bodybuilders work on their muscles in a different way and train to make them bigger.

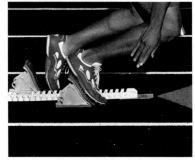

FIGURE 2.1.5a: Skeletal muscles allow you to move.

The main muscles of the body

There are three types of muscle – cardiac muscle in the heart, smooth muscle in the organs, and skeletal muscle attached to the skeleton. Skeletal muscles allow you to move. They are attached to bones by tendons. As the muscles contract, they pull on tendons causing the bones around a joint to move. You have over 600 skeletal muscles, which are all involved in moving parts of your body. You may not notice the movement caused by some of these muscles, such as tiny facial muscles that cause minor movements.

1. Name the three types of muscle and state where each is found.

2. Name three muscles of the arm.

3. Describe how muscles enable you to move.

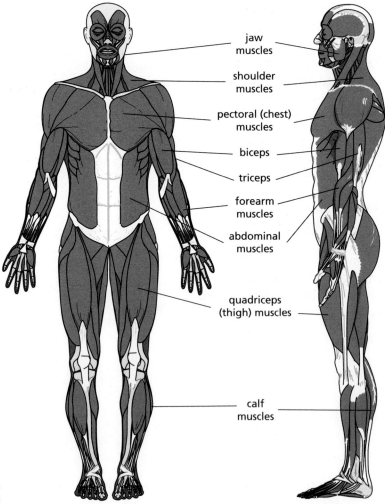

jaw muscles

shoulder muscles

pectoral (chest) muscles

biceps

triceps

forearm muscles

abdominal muscles

quadriceps (thigh) muscles

calf muscles

FIGURE 2.1.5b: The main skeletal muscles

Muscles in action ▶▶▶

Muscles can only pull – they cannot push. When a muscle pulls, it is **contracted**. This means the muscle gets shorter and fatter. When a muscle is not contracted, it is **relaxed**. When a muscle relaxes, it returns to its original size.

Most actions use many muscles. For example, when walking up stairs you use your calf muscles, quadriceps (thigh muscles) and abdominal muscles. If you move your upper body as you walk, you use many more muscles.

4. Describe the differences between a contracted and a relaxed muscle.

5. Explain how your calf muscle causes your heel to lift.

6. Suggest which muscles you use when climbing onto a bike.

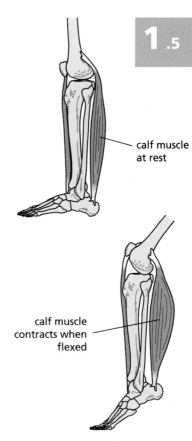

calf muscle at rest

calf muscle contracts when flexed

FIGURE 2.1.5c: The calf muscle relaxed and contracted

Measuring muscle strength ▶▶▶

By exercising you can increase the strength of muscles. Professional sportspeople consider their training very carefully to ensure that they target specific muscles.

They also test the strength of their muscles frequently to check their progress. These are scientific tests and must be carried out fairly so that measurements can be compared over time. Figure 2.1.5d shows a device to test the strength of the forearm and hand. The person squeezes the handle as hard as they can. The result is then displayed as a **force** (measured in **newtons**).

FIGURE 2.1.5d A handgrip strength tester

> **Did you know…?**
>
> The heart is made of muscle. But this is different to the muscles attached to your skeleton. Heart muscle (cardiac muscle) contracts approximately 70 times every minute for your entire life and it does not tire.

7. Describe how two rowers could compare hand and forearm strengths using a handgrip tester.

8. A basketball player wants to compare the strength of his forearm with that of a footballer. Predict who would have the most strength.

9. Suggest how you could test the strength of your quadriceps.

Key vocabulary

contracted

relaxed

force

newton

Analysing muscle strength

Strong muscles are important to a sportsperson's success. Some sportspeople even risk their health with illegal drugs to grow bigger, stronger muscles. Outside the sporting world, testing muscle strength has an important role in diagnosing certain disorders.

Who is the strongest?

Scientists have conducted muscle strength tests on large numbers of people. Using their results, they have calculated the average muscle strength for different groups of people for different muscles.

Six volunteers had the strength of their forearms and hands tested in a sports science laboratory, using a device like that shown in Figure 2.1.5d. The results are shown in Table 2.1.6. Muscle strength is a force and is measured in newtons.

TABLE 2.1.6: The strength of forearms and hands

Gender of volunteer	Age	Mass (kg)	Muscle strength (N)
A. Male	20	76	64
B. Male	55	76	50
C. Male	55	87	51
D. Female	20	64	38
E. Female	55	64	28
F. Female	55	76	20

FIGURE 2.1.6a: Gymnasts need high muscle strength.

1. Draw a graph to display these results.

2. The tester predicted that males have stronger muscles than females. Is this supported by the results?

3. The tester predicted that age affects the strength of men but not women. Does this data seem to support this idea?

Damage or disease? ≫≫

If a muscle strength test suggests that a volunteer has weak muscles, the first step is to repeat the test to ensure that the result is reliable. One cause of muscle weakness is injury. Muscles can be strained or torn. This can be very painful but the muscle repairs with rest.

Electromyography (EMG) tests if muscles are working properly by checking for electrical signals. In healthy people, muscles receive electrical signals to make them contract. EMG checks if the muscles are receiving these signals and whether they are contracting or not. Problems with the electrical signals to the muscles would need further treatment.

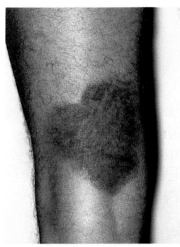

FIGURE 2.1.6b: A torn muscle can cause severe bruising.

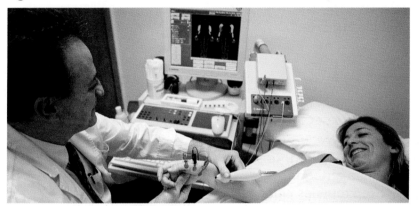

FIGURE 2.1.6c: An EMG test involves pricking the skin with needles to test for electrical signals.

4. Describe what electromyography (EMG) tests for.

5. Explain how repeating a test could tell us whether the result was reliable or not.

6. Suggest why a muscle tear is less serious than a problem with electrical signals getting to the muscles.

Give me strength ≫≫

Professional sportspeople are regularly tested to check that they have not taken performance-enhancing drugs. One type of these drugs are called **anabolic steroids**. These increase muscle mass. However, steroids can have serious side effects and can cause heart attacks and blood clots. Sportspeople who are found to have anabolic steroids in their blood also face a ban from the sport.

7. Suggest why sportspeople take anabolic steroids despite the well known side effects.

8. Apart from exercising, how else you can maintain healthy muscles?

Did you know...?

Muscle cramps are caused by involuntary contractions of one or more muscles – the muscles contract, but then do not relax. There are many causes of cramp but plenty of water and vitamins in the diet may help to prevent them.

Key vocabulary

electromyography (EMG)

anabolic steroid

Examining interacting muscles

We are learning how to:

- Describe antagonistic muscles and give examples.
- Explain how antagonistic muscles bring about movement.
- Evaluate a model of antagonistic muscles.

The majority of the 600 muscles of the human body work as pairs. As one muscle of the pair contracts, the other muscle relaxes and vice versa. Without muscles working together in this way we would not be able to move our joints freely.

Pairs of muscles

When muscles contract, they pull on both a tendon and bone. If the bone is at a joint, the bone will move. Muscles can only pull, they cannot push. If muscles just worked singly, the bone would simply stay in that position. To solve this problem, muscles work in pairs called **antagonistic muscles**. In the arm, the **bicep** and **tricep** muscles work as an antagonistic pair to control movement at the elbow. To move the forearm up, the bicep contracts and the tricep relaxes. To move the forearm down the tricep contracts and the bicep relaxes.

Other examples of antagonistic muscles include the **quadricep** and hamstring muscle in the thigh, which allow bending at the knee, and the shin and calf muscles, which allow movement at the ankle.

1. List some examples of antagonistic muscles.

2. Describe the changes in the bicep and tricep muscles as the forearm moves up and down.

3. Explain why some muscles need to work in pairs.

A muscles model

Scientists use models to explain their ideas. Models can be extremely useful to help us to visualise something that we cannot actually see.

Models are not usually a perfect representation of the real situation. Scientists must evaluate any model to decide how well it represents the real world.

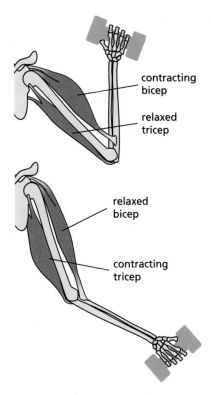

contracting bicep

relaxed tricep

relaxed bicep

contracting tricep

FIGURE 2.1.7a: Which way does the forearm move when the bicep contracts?

Did you know…?

Antagonistic muscles are at work in our eyes. Pairs of muscles in the coloured part of the eye, the iris, control how big the pupil is. This prevents the eye from being damaged by too much light entering it.

In the card and rubber band model of the arm (Figure 2.1.7b) the forearm moves up as the top rubber band is pulled and moves down as the bottom rubber band is pulled. This represents what happens in the body. However, the shoulder joint is fixed in the card model. This is a poor feature of the model because the shoulder joint is not fixed in the body.

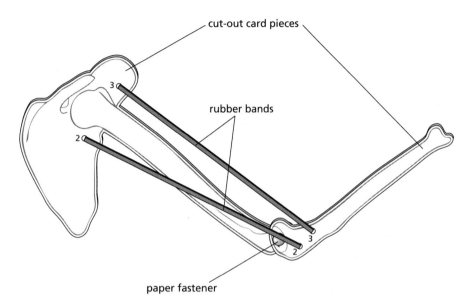

FIGURE 2.1.7b: A simple model of antagonistic muscles in the arm

4. Describe what the rubber bands represent in this arm model.

5. Summarise what is good and what is not so good about the model of the arm.

6. Suggest how the model could be adapted to show that the bicep muscle is bigger than the tricep muscle.

A nod of the head ⟫⟫⟫

A group of students were studying antagonistic muscles. One suggested that nodding of the head is caused by antagonistic muscles. The group tested the idea by nodding their heads back and forth and feeling around the neck as they did so.

FIGURE 2.1.7c: Is nodding caused by antagonistic muscles?

7. Describe what the students would feel in their neck as they nodded their heads:

a) down   b) up.

8. Explain whether or not you believe that nodding is caused by antagonistic muscles.

Key vocabulary

antagonistic muscles

bicep

tricep

quadricep

Exploring problems with the skeletal system

We are learning how to:

- Recall some medical problems with the skeletal system.
- Describe treatments for some skeletal system problems.
- Communicate effectively to learn how treatments have changed over time.

The skeletal system is made up of bones, tendons, ligaments, cartilage and muscles. Medical problems can arise with any of these components, ranging from fractures to genetic conditions that we inherit. The diagnosis and treatment of these problems have changed over time.

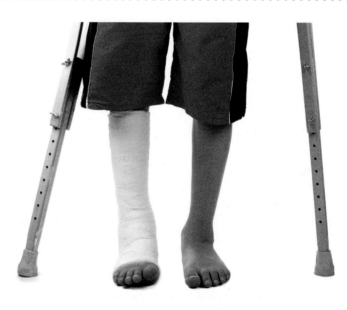

FIGURE 2.1.8a: Broken bones can heal in a cast.

Break a leg

With 206 bones in the human **skeletal system**, it is no surprise that bones are sometimes broken. Bones contain collagen, which allows them to bend a little. However, with a large enough impact bones can splinter, break or shatter.

Bone breaks, or **fractures**, can often be treated by covering the limb with a plaster cast of glass fibre. This holds the bones in place while new bone knits the broken ends together. More severe fractures require metal pins fastening through the broken bones to hold them in place while healing takes place. An open, or compound, fracture is one in which the skin is broken. This has a much higher risk of infection and usually requires surgery.

1. Suggest how a fracture may happen.

2. Describe how a fracture may be treated.

3. Explain why a compound fracture is often more serious than other fractures.

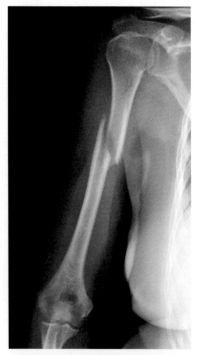

FIGURE 2.1.8b: Broken bones can be seen in an X-ray image.

From the age of approximately 35, the density of bones decreases naturally. In some people, the density drops below a healthy level and bones become fragile, making them prone to fractures. This condition is called **osteoporosis**. Treatment for osteoporosis includes taking drugs to strengthen the bones.

Arthritis is a condition that affects the joints. In one form of arthritis, the cartilage at the end of the bones wears away and bones rub together. This can be very painful. In severe cases, the worn joint is replaced with an artificial joint.

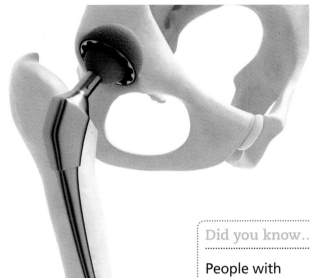

FIGURE 2.1.8c: An artificial hip joint

4. Explain why sufferers of osteoporosis are prone to fractures.

5. Explain why arthritis can be so painful.

6. Suggest why an artificial hip is the shape shown in Figure 2.1.8c.

Medical advances 〉〉〉

As technology improves, diagnosis of fractures by X-rays has become more precise. Surgical techniques have also improved recovery from serious fractures.

As scientists learn more about osteoporosis, they can advise on how to avoid this disease. In the past, all that could be done was to treat the fractures.

Scientists are also learning more about genes so that diagnosis of genetic conditions affecting the skeletal system is now possible. Genetic counselling allows parents at risk of passing on a condition to be informed of the risks and consequences.

7. Describe three improvements in treating skeletal system problems.

8. Suggest why improvements are likely to continue to be made.

Did you know...?

People with hypermobility syndrome are sometimes described as being 'double jointed'. In the past, people with this condition performed in circuses and sideshows as contortionists. The condition results in joint pain and dislocation of joints.

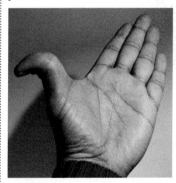

FIGURE 2.1.8d: Hypermobility syndrome causes hypermobile joints.

Key vocabulary

skeletal system

fracture

osteoporosis

arthritis

Applying key ideas

You have now met a number of important ideas in this chapter. This activity gives an opportunity for you to apply them, just as scientists do. Read the text first, then have a go at the tasks. The first few are fairly easy – then they get a bit more challenging.

The bare bones of space travel

The human body is very well adapted to live on Earth. If we take the body to a different environment, such as space, then body systems may suffer. This includes the skeletal system and its associated muscles.

Astronauts living in the International Space Station (ISS) are located approximately 250 km above the Earth. The pull of gravity here is approximately 90 per cent of that on Earth. However, because of the speed of the spacecraft, astronauts feel weightless. We call this a microgravity environment.

A loss of bone mass occurs in astronauts. This is particularly apparent in the lower half of the body. It is a similar effect to osteoporosis as seen on Earth. On Earth, untreated osteoporosis can typically lead to a loss of 1.5 per cent of bone mass in one year. Astronauts can lose 1.5 per cent of bone mass each month! Once back on Earth, the bone mass is gradually replaced but this can take up to three times the length of the mission.

The loss of mass leads to a weakening of the bones, which can then fracture more easily. As bone is broken down, calcium is released and absorbed into the blood. This increases the chance of making kidney stones.

Because astronauts do not work their muscles much in space, muscle wastage can occur. Activities are built into the daily routine of astronauts to try to maintain the muscle. The diet of the astronaut must also be carefully considered to ensure that they receive the nutrients they need to preserve healthy bone and muscle as far as possible.

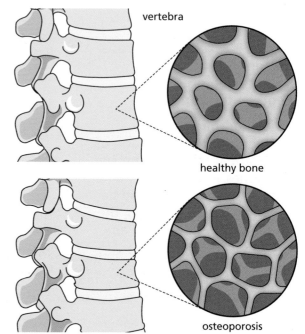

FIGURE 2.1.9a: Osteoporosis

FIGURE 2.1.9b: Exercising in space

Task 1: Identifying the problem areas

Suggest why the lower back and the legs may suffer the biggest bone and muscle loss during space travel.

Task 2: Thinking about the effects of space travel

Describe the effects of space travel on the bones and muscles.

Task 3: Calculating recovery time

Predict the percentage of bone mass lost during a 12 month mission. What assumption is made about the bone loss in this calculation?

How long would it take to replace the lost bone mass?

Task 4: Considering the consequences

Explain why it is important that we try to reduce the effects of space on astronauts' skeleton and muscles. Suggest why resistance training (with masses) may be more beneficial than cardiovascular training (such as cycling) during space travel.

Task 5: Researching osteoporosis

Would it help astronauts to have a calcium-rich diet, as is sometimes recommended for women thought to be at risk from osteoporosis? Find out more about osteoporosis including its causes and treatments.

Task 6: Planning a recovery

Patients who spend long periods of time in bed also suffer muscle and bone loss. Suggest a plan to build up patients once they are able to get out of bed. How would this compare to a plan for astronauts returning to Earth?

Understanding how muscles get energy

We are learning how to:

- Recall the equation for respiration and describe what it shows.
- Explain the importance of respiration.
- Apply what we know about respiration.

Your muscles need energy to contract and move bones. The food that you eat contains energy. But cells need to carry out a reaction to release this energy. This reaction takes place inside all your cells all the time, without you even thinking about it.

FIGURE 2.1.10a: You need energy to move.

How do you get energy?

You use **energy** in many ways, for example:

- to contract your muscles so that you can move
- to keep your body temperature at a suitable level and constant
- to grow.

You need to obtain this energy from your food. **Respiration** is the chemical reaction that releases energy from food that you have eaten.

Some of your food is digested in the intestines to convert it to **glucose**. The glucose travels in the bloodstream to all the cells of your body. Respiration takes place in the cells to release energy from the glucose.

1. State three ways in which you use energy.

2. From which food substance is energy released during respiration?

3. Suggest why you need energy even when you are asleep.

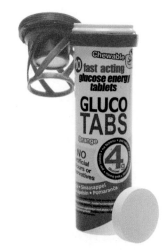

FIGURE 2.1.10b: Glucose is a type of sugar.

The respiration equation

Respiration takes place in the cells of animals and plants. The reaction can be shown by the equation:

glucose + oxygen → carbon dioxide + water (+ energy)

'Energy' is in brackets because it is not a substance.

This type of respiration, where oxygen is used, is known as **aerobic respiration**. Oxygen (from breathing) is carried from the lungs to all the cells of the body in the blood.

The waste products of respiration are carbon dioxide and water. These are taken away from the cells by the blood and breathed out from the lungs.

4. Explain what is meant by 'aerobic'.

5. Suggest why the circulatory system is so important for respiration.

6. Explain what the respiration equation tells us.

FIGURE 2.1.10c: Why is respiration sometimes compared with burning?

Building molecules

In order to grow bigger and to repair tissues, you need protein. Protein is made of complex molecules made of lots of smaller molecules, amino acids, joined together. When you eat protein, it is broken down into amino acids during digestion. Inside your body, you rebuild protein by joining amino acids back together. This process needs energy and that energy comes from respiration.

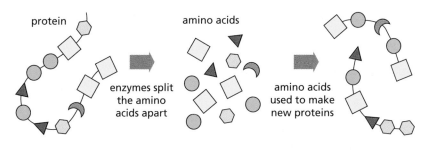

protein   amino acids

enzymes split the amino acids apart

amino acids used to make new proteins

FIGURE 2.1.10d: Amino acids join to make proteins.

Plant cells have a strong cell wall made from cellulose. Plants make cellulose by joining glucose molecules together. The energy to do this comes from respiration.

7. Describe the purpose of cellulose in plants.

8. Suggest why bodybuilders eat foods high in protein.

9. Suggest how your body could make different proteins.

> **Did you know...?**
>
> Any excess energy that you do not need from respiration is stored as fats. If you do not use the energy stored in these fats, they stay in your body.

Key vocabulary

energy

respiration

glucose

aerobic respiration

Investigating respiration

We are learning how to:

- Recall that respiration takes place in plants and animals.
- Describe some experimental evidence for respiration.
- Consider the quality of evidence for respiration.

Respiration is a process that releases energy. Every living cell in every living organism needs energy. Therefore, both plants and animals carry out respiration. The ways that plants and animals get the glucose needed for respiration vary.

Respiration in plants

Just as animals need energy, so do plants. Plants need energy to grow, to repair tissues, to reproduce and to absorb nutrients.

Respiration uses glucose and oxygen as the **reactants**. This is the same in both animals and plants. Animals use glucose from the food they eat in respiration. But plants make glucose by a process called **photosynthesis**. Photosynthesis only happens in plants. It does not occur in animals.

1. Describe what plants need energy for.

2. Describe a difference between respiration in plants and in animals.

3. Explain what is meant by a 'reactant'.

FIGURE 2.1.11a: Plants respire, as well as animals.

Where is the evidence?

You cannot see respiration happening. However, science experiments can provide evidence that respiration occurs.

When you breathe out onto a cold surface, such as a mirror or window, you see misting or droplets of water. This suggests that you produce water. Water is one of the **products** of respiration.

Figure 2.1.11b shows an experiment on **germinating** peas proving that carbon dioxide is given off by living things. The aspirator draws air through the tubes.

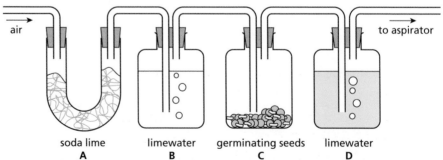

air → soda lime **A** | limewater **B** | germinating seeds **C** | limewater **D** | to aspirator →

FIGURE 2.1.11b: How does this show that living things produce carbon dioxide?

Soda lime absorbs carbon dioxide from the air around the seeds. The seeds produce carbon dioxide and this turns the limewater in flask D cloudy. Carbon dioxide is also a product of respiration.

4. Describe evidence for the release of water by animals.

5. Suggest how you could test if plants give off water.

6. Explain as fully as you can what the experiment in Figure 2.1.11b shows.

Respiration and photosynthesis

Photosynthesis and respiration are both vital for plants. We can compare the equations:

Photosynthesis:

carbon dioxide + water $\xrightarrow{\text{light energy}}$ glucose + oxygen

Respiration:

glucose + oxygen → carbon dioxide + water + (energy)

Plants photosynthesise using sunlight energy. This is a way of 'trapping' the energy. Respiration releases energy so that the plant can use it.

FIGURE 2.1.11c: Green plants use energy from sunlight to make glucose.

7. List the reactants and the products for both photosynthesis and respiration.

8. Explain why respiration and photosynthesis are dependent on each other.

9. Suggest whether respiration and/or photosynthesis are carried out by plants:
   a) during the day   b) at night.

Some plants, such as Venus fly traps and pitcher plants, trap insects and digest them. However, they only use these insects to gain nutrients, not for energy.

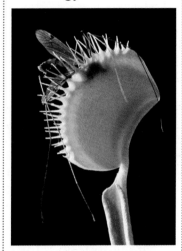

FIGURE 2.1.11d: The Venus fly trap is a carnivorous plant.

Key vocabulary

reactant

photosynthesis

product

germinating

Analysing adaptations for respiration

We are learning how to:

- Describe where in the cell respiration takes place.
- Explain how mitochondria are adapted for respiration.
- Compare and explain the numbers of mitochondria in different cells.

Cells contain several structures, each with a specific function – these are called organelles. An example is the mitochondrion. Mitochondria are described as 'powerhouses'. This is because they are the site of respiration, the process by which energy is released. The numbers vary in different cells depending on how much energy each cell needs.

Respiration powerhouses

Mitochondria are tiny sausage-shaped organelles found in most animal and plant cells. You can use a powerful microscope (such as an electron microscope) to see their complex structure.

Each mitochondrion has two **membranes**. The outer membrane surrounds the entire organelle. The inner one is highly folded – the tips of the folds are called 'cristae'. Respiration takes place on the cristae. Folding increases the number of cristae, maximising the amount of respiration that can take place. The fluid inside the mitochondrion is called the matrix. It contains the **enzymes** essential for respiration.

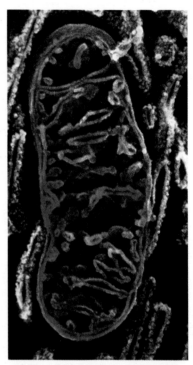

FIGURE 2.1.12a: Mitochondria are tiny organelles found in most cells. The magnification here is ×120 000.

1. Describe where mitochondria are found.

2. Explain why mitochondria are called 'powerhouses'.

3. Explain how folding of the inner membrane helps mitochondria to produce more energy.

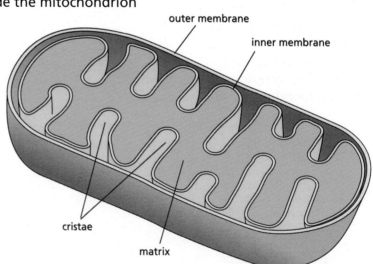

FIGURE 2.1.12b: How does the structure of mitochondria help with respiration?

The numbers of mitochondria vary in different types of cell.

TABLE 2.1.12: Numbers of mitochondria in different cells

Type of cell	Average number of mitochondria per cell
muscle cell	1900
red blood cell	0
liver cell	1300
skin cell	800
mucus cell	180

4. Explain what the data in the table shows as fully as you can.

5. At a different time, the muscle cell contained only 1400 mitochondria per cell. Suggest a reason for this difference.

6. Mitochondria can make copies of themselves if more are needed in a cell. Suggest when a cell may need more mitochondria.

FIGURE 2.1.12c: Why do muscle cells need lots of mitochondria?

What can go wrong? >>>

If mitochondria do not function properly, then cells do not get the energy that they need. When mitochondrial disease occurs, little or no respiration takes place in the mitochondria. The organs most affected are those needing most energy such as the heart (and other muscles), liver and brain. The symptoms are variable, depending on which mitochondria are affected. Mitochondrial disease is caused by a fault in inherited material.

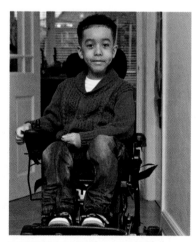

FIGURE 2.1.12d: Mitochondrial disease can lead to muscle degeneration.

7. Suggest why sufferers of mitochondrial disease are often exhausted.

8. Explain why it is wrong to think that we can 'catch' mitochondrial disease.

9. Explain why the most severe symptoms may be seen when mitochondria in the brain are affected.

Did you know...?

Some scientists believe that mitochondria are descended from bacteria. They think that bacteria similar to mitochondria once existed in their own right. These bacteria are thought to have entered cells. Over time, they evolved to exist within the cells and develop into mitochondria as we see them today.

Key vocabulary

mitochondria

membrane

enzymes

Examining links between respiration and body systems

We are learning how to:

- Describe some systems in animals and plants that are linked with respiration.
- Explain how some systems and respiration are dependent.
- Suggest the consequences of a failure in linked body systems.

Respiration is vital for living things. But respiration in your body relies on your body systems. Consider where the glucose used in respiration comes from and where the carbon dioxide formed during respiration goes to.

Respiration and body systems ❯❯

You have many systems in your body, each with a specific function. Three systems are shown in Figure 2.1.13a.

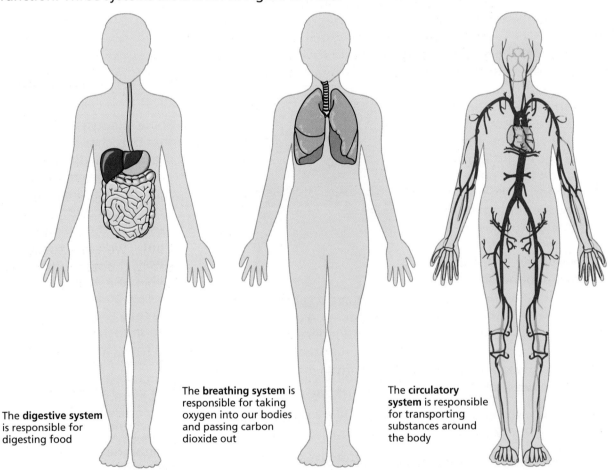

The **digestive system** is responsible for digesting food

The **breathing system** is responsible for taking oxygen into our bodies and passing carbon dioxide out

The **circulatory system** is responsible for transporting substances around the body

FIGURE 2.1.13a: Three body systems

The functions of all three body systems are linked with respiration. Glucose needed for respiration is produced by the digestion of carbohydrates in the **digestive system**. Oxygen needed for respiration is brought into the body by the **breathing system**. Also, carbon dioxide and water produced by respiration are removed by the breathing system. All these reactants and products are carried to and from cells by the **circulatory system**.

1. List the three body systems associated with respiration.

2. Describe where glucose is carried from and to by the circulatory system.

3. Suggest why carbon dioxide and water are sometimes described as waste products of respiration.

A weak link

Because respiration and some body systems rely on one another, there would be problems if either respiration or the body system did not function properly. For example, if the digestion of carbohydrates is inefficient, there may not be enough glucose for respiration. This results in insufficient energy being released. If the circulatory system is damaged this decreases the amounts of glucose and oxygen delivered to cells. Again, insufficient energy is released in the body.

4. Describe how a failure of the breathing system could affect respiration.

5. Explain why a decrease in the amount of respiration could negatively affect digestion.

6. Draw a table to explain how a failure in each system (breathing, digestive and circulatory) could negatively affect respiration.

What about plants?

Plants make the glucose needed for respiration in their leaves. The glucose is then dissolved and transported around the plant in a system of tubes called **phloem**. Phloem tubes are sometimes compared with blood vessels in animals. Oxygen enters a plant through pores on the underside of leaves. These pores are called **stomata**, shown in Figure 2.1.13b.

7. Suggest which system in animals corresponds to the transport system (by phloem) in plants.

8. Suggest how carbon dioxide leaves a plant.

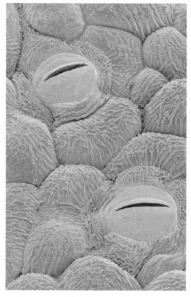

FIGURE 2.1.13b: Plants take in oxygen for respiration through stomata on the underside of a leaf (magnified ×750)

Did you know…?

Plants can store excess glucose as starch in their roots. So, when we eat root vegetables such as potatoes, carrots and turnip, we are actually eating the starch storage organ of a plant.

Key vocabulary

digestive system

breathing system

circulatory system

phloem

stomata

Exploring respiration in sport

We are learning how to:

- Describe what is meant by anaerobic respiration.
- Explain why some sports involve more aerobic or more anaerobic respiration.
- Explain what is meant by oxygen debt.

When athletes need to sprint, they cannot get enough oxygen to respire in the usual way. They need to work without oxygen for a short time, but also must release the energy that allows them to run. The body has mechanisms to manage without oxygen but there are consequences.

FIGURE 2.1.14a: When sprinting, the body is respiring without oxygen.

Respiration in sport

As sports have become more competitive and lucrative, sport science has emerged to help sportspeople to understand how their body works. When you exercise steadily, you gain enough oxygen to carry out aerobic respiration. So when jogging or swimming over a long distance, you respire in the normal way. However, when you exercise in short, energetic bursts the energy needed outweighs the oxygen that you can take in and you have to respire without oxygen. This type of respiration, without oxygen, is called **anaerobic respiration**.

Anaerobic respiration is important in sprinting and weightlifting. Other sports, which involve steady exercise as well as short bursts of high-energy exercise, rely on both aerobic and anaerobic respiration.

1. List some sports that involve:

   a) aerobic respiration

   b) anaerobic respiration.

2. Explain the main difference between aerobic and anaerobic respiration.

3. Suggest some sports or forms of exercise that rely on both aerobic and anaerobic respiration.

FIGURE 2.1.14b: Why does a circuit trainer need to use anaerobic respiration?

Anaerobic respiration can be shown in an equation:

glucose → lactic acid (+ energy)

Although anaerobic respiration does release some energy, it does not release as much as aerobic respiration does.

The **lactic acid** produced during anaerobic respiration builds up in muscles. This can be felt as an aching in muscles during or after exercise. After the short burst of vigorous exercise is over, you need to get rid of lactic acid using the oxygen that you breathe in. This oxygen is a 'payback' so that the body can rid itself of lactic acid – it is known as the **oxygen debt**. You may find yourself breathing deeply after exercise to repay this oxygen debt.

FIGURE 2.1.14c: Why do we breathe deeply after vigorous exercise?

4. Explain what is meant by 'oxygen debt'.

5. Suggest why anaerobic respiration can only be sustained for short periods of time.

6. Compare the word equations for aerobic respiration and for anaerobic respiration.

Energy stores >>>

Animals' bodies have developed ways of storing glucose. This means that they can slowly release energy as and when they need it.

Animals store energy in several ways:

- as **glycogen** in muscles
- as glycogen in the liver
- in fat reserves.

You can damage your body if you exercise too much without taking in sufficient energy as food. Once all other energy stores, such as glycogen and fat, have been used up, protein in the body can be used as a last resort.

7. Explain the benefits to an animal of storing glucose.

8. Suggest why using protein in your body as an energy source could be damaging.

Did you know...?

It takes 12 seconds for oxygen to be usable in respiration after you have breathed it in. So in a 100m sprint, athletes are respiring entirely anaerobically.

Key vocabulary

anaerobic respiration

lactic acid

oxygen debt

glycogen

Understanding anaerobic respiration

We are learning how to:

- Recall that plants and microbes carry out anaerobic respiration.
- Describe some evidence to show that anaerobic respiration can produce carbon dioxide.
- Construct a method to show what is produced in anaerobic respiration.

Plants and microbes, like animals, sometimes need to respire anaerobically. As in animals, this process uses glucose to release energy. But the products of anaerobic respiration in plants and microbes differ from the products in animals.

Anaerobic respiration in plants

Just like animals, plants respire anaerobically when oxygen is in short supply. However, the products of anaerobic respiration are different:

- In animals, lactic acid is produced.

- In plants, ethanol and carbon dioxide are produced.

The type of anaerobic respiration that produces ethanol and carbon dioxide is called **fermentation**. It can occur in the roots when a plant is growing in boggy or waterlogged soil.

FIGURE 2.1.15a: Why do these plants need to respire anaerobically?

1. Describe the soil conditions needed to make a plant respire anaerobically.

2. Name the type of anaerobic respiration that produces ethanol and carbon dioxide.

3. Write a word equation for fermentation.

Fermentation in microbes

Microbes are tiny organisms that we cannot see with the naked eye – they include bacteria, viruses and fungi. Microbes often respire by fermentation.

Some microbes are capable of both aerobic respiration and fermentation, and use fermentation only when oxygen levels fall. An example of a microbe that does this is the bacterium *Escherichia coli*. Some microbes are adapted to survive only in anaerobic conditions – bacteria that live far below the ocean's surface, for example. Other microbes respire only by fermentation even when oxygen is present. A microbe that does this is **yeast**. Yeasts are a type of fungus found all around us.

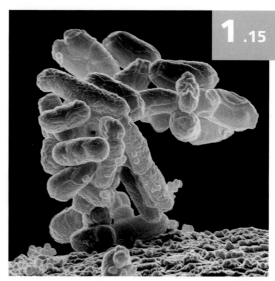

FIGURE 2.1.15b: Some bacteria, such as *E. coli*, can respire anaerobically when oxygen levels are low. The magnification here is approximately ×120 000.

4. Write a definition of 'microbes'.

5. Explain why it is an advantage for microbes to be able to respire both aerobically and anaerobically.

6. Suggest what would happen to microbes adapted to live without oxygen if they were suddenly exposed to oxygen.

Exploring anaerobic respiration >>>

You can show that a gas is given off by fermentation. Mix some dried yeast with warm water in a conical flask to activate it. Then give the yeast some sugar as a source of food. If the conical flask is then covered with a balloon, any gas given off will collect in the balloon.

7. Describe what process is taking place in Figure 2.1.15c.

8. Explain why sugar is added to the yeast.

9. Explain why the balloon inflates during the activity.

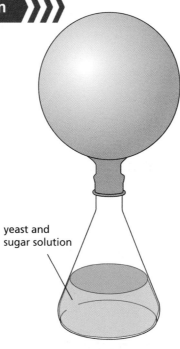

yeast and sugar solution

FIGURE 2.1.15c: Yeast is activated and sugar is added to the conical flask.

Key vocabulary

fermentation

microbe

yeast

Investigating fermentation

We are learning how to:

- Describe some applications of fermentation.
- Identify dependent, independent and control variables in an investigation.
- Analyse data and identify next steps.

Yeast is a simple organism that reproduces and ferments sugar rapidly. These features make it ideal to use in studies of fermentation. Fermentation by yeast has many applications – for example in baking and brewing.

FIGURE 2.1.16a: Yeast is a microscopic fungal organism. The magnification here is ×1000.

Applications of fermentation

Fermentation is used in **brewing** and the production of alcoholic drinks, as one of the products of fermentation, is ethanol (a type of alcohol). The type of alcoholic drink produced depends on the source of the sugar used in the process. For example, wine uses grapes whereas beer is made using hops and barley.

Fermentation is also important in baking. Yeast and sugar are included in bread recipes because the carbon dioxide produced during the fermentation causes the bread to rise. Another application of fermentation is in the production of 'gasohol' – a fuel containing a mixture of gasoline and alcohol. Mixing alcohol with a **fossil fuel** makes the non-renewable fossil fuel last longer.

FIGURE 2.1.16b: Fermentation is important in wine making, baking and brewing.

1. Describe three applications of fermentation.

2. Highlight an application of fermentation that relies on:

    a) carbon dioxide being produced

    b) alcohol being produced.

Investigating fermentation ▶▶▶

Some students investigated the effect of temperature on fermentation. They mixed dried yeast with warm water, to activate it, in a conical flask. Then they added some sugar so that the yeast could respire.

As the mixture fermented, carbon dioxide was produced. The gas formed bubbles in the conical flask. The students counted the bubbles for one minute. The experiment was repeated setting up identical flasks at different temperatures.

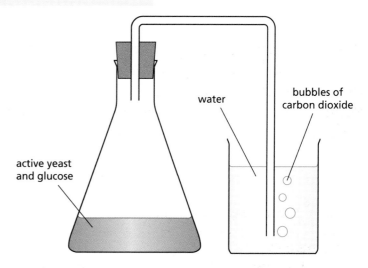

active yeast and glucose · water · bubbles of carbon dioxide

FIGURE 2.1.16c: Students counted the number of bubbles in one minute.

4. In the experiment, what was the:

    a) independent variable (that the students changed)?

    b) dependent variable (that the students measured)?

5. Suggest what the students might need to control (keep the same) in this experiment.

The effect of temperature on fermentation ▶▶▶

The students recorded the results of their investigation in a table.

TABLE 2.1.16: How temperature affects fermentation

Temperature (°C)	20	30	40	50
Number of bubbles per minute	14	26	60	16

6. Describe what the results show about the effect of temperature on fermentation.

7. Suggest how the students could improve the reliability of their results.

8. Suggest the temperature at which dough should be left to rise to ensure that the lightest bread is baked. Explain your answer.

Did you know...?

Fermentation has been used to preserve foods for about 10 000 years. It is likely that it was discovered with the observation that milk fermented naturally. Fermentation of milk results in the production of cheese or yogurt, for example. People then realised that the products of milk fermentation lasted longer.

Key vocabulary

brewing

fossil fuel

independent variable

dependent variable

Comparing aerobic and anaerobic respiration

We are learning how to:

- Describe some similarities and differences between aerobic and anaerobic respiration.
- Work responsibly within a team to summarise respiration.

The purpose of any respiration is to release energy in a form that an organism can use.

Aerobic and anaerobic respiration both release useful energy in cells. However, the amount of energy released is different from one situation to another.

FIGURE 2.1.17a: The energy contained in food is released by respiration.

Comparing energy

The energy contained in food needs to be converted so that cells can use it – this is the purpose of respiration. Aerobic respiration uses glucose and oxygen as the reactants.

In anaerobic respiration there is only one reactant, glucose. Aerobic respiration is 19 times more efficient at generating energy than anaerobic respiration. However, because anaerobic respiration generates energy more quickly, sometimes your body switches to this type of respiration. For example, when you sprint you need to generate energy quickly for your muscles. Even though there is still some oxygen in your body, it is better to respire anaerobically in this situation.

1. Compare the efficiencies of aerobic respiration and anaerobic respiration.

2. Explain why it is sometimes preferable to respire anaerobically, even if some oxygen is available.

3. Suggest another situation in which anaerobic respiration would be preferable, even if oxygen is available.

FIGURE 2.1.17b: Energy can be released more quickly by anaerobic respiration.

Anaerobic respiration takes place in the cytoplasm of cells. Many chemical reactions occur in the cytoplasm – the first stage of aerobic respiration is one of them. But the next stage continues in the mitochondria. It is during this mitochondrial stage that most energy is released so we usually say that aerobic respiration takes place in the mitochondria.

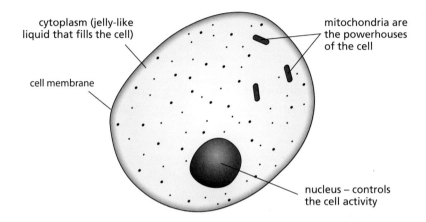

cytoplasm (jelly-like liquid that fills the cell)

mitochondria are the powerhouses of the cell

cell membrane

nucleus – controls the cell activity

FIGURE 2.1.17c: An animal cell

4. Draw a diagram of an animal cell and label where aerobic and anaerobic respiration take place.

5. Compare the amount of energy that is produced in the cytoplasm and in the mitochondria during aerobic respiration.

Respiration and enzymes >>>

Enzymes are protein molecules that speed up reactions – they are sometimes called biological **catalysts**. Enzymes are involved in both aerobic and anaerobic respiration – without enzymes neither would happen. Enzymes break up glucose molecules to release energy. There are more enzymes involved in aerobic respiration than in anaerobic respiration.

6. Explain why respiration would not happen without enzymes.

7. Suggest why more enzymes are involved in aerobic respiration than in anaerobic respiration.

8. Enzymes are involved in many reactions in living organisms. Suggest another process that requires enzymes.

Did you know…?

Carbon dioxide is toxic if it builds up in your body. This is because it takes the place of oxygen in the blood and you become starved of oxygen. Your breathing system is essential to remove the carbon dioxide produced during respiration.

Key vocabulary

catalyst

Checking your progress

To make good progress in understanding science you need to focus on these ideas and skills.

Identify the main bones of the skeleton.

Describe the functions of the skeleton.

Explain how different parts of the skeleton are adapted to carry out particular functions.

Describe the role of skeletal joints.

Identify some different joints and explain the role of tendons and ligaments in joints.

Compare the movement allowed at different joints and explain why different types of joints are needed.

Recall that muscles contract to move bones at joints.

Identify muscles that contract to cause specific movements.

Explain how muscles work antagonistically to bring about movement and evaluate a model.

Investigate the strengths of different muscles and draw a conclusion.

Plan and carry out an investigation to compare the strengths of muscles and analyse the results using a graph.

Plan and carry out a fair investigation, analyse the data and evaluate the procedure.

Describe some medical problems that can arise with the skeletal system.

Describe some treatments for a range of problems with the skeletal system.

Explain how diagnosis and treatment of problems with the skeletal system have changed over time.

Describe the purpose of respiration.

Describe and explain aerobic respiration using a word equation.

Explain the role of respiration in building up complex molecules.

Describe aerobic respiration in plants.

Identify evidence for aerobic respiration in plants and animals.

Evaluate the quality of evidence for aerobic respiration in plants and animals.

Describe where in a cell respiration takes place.

Explain how mitochondria are adapted for respiration.

Analyse data to compare and explain the numbers of mitochondria in different cells.

Define anaerobic respiration and give examples of sports that use anaerobic respiration.

Explain why some sports rely mainly on aerobic respiration while others require anaerobic respiration.

Describe and explain the effects on the body of anaerobic respiration and explain 'oxygen debt'.

Identify some living things that carry out anaerobic respiration and identify some applications.

Describe and explain some evidence to show the products of anaerobic respiration and plan an investigation into fermentation.

Plan an investigation to test a hypothesis about anaerobic respiration, analyse the data and evaluate the investigation.

Questions

See how well you have understood the ideas in the chapter.

1. Identify the femur in Figure 2.1.19a. [1]

2. Identify the bone that protects the brain in Figure 2.1.19a. [1]

3. What are the small bones that make up the backbone called? [1]

   a) ligaments
   b) joints
   c) vertebrae
   d) tendons

4. What is the function of joints? [1]

   a) to protect organs
   b) to make blood cells
   c) to hold the body up
   d) to allow movement

5. How does the ribcage protect the lungs? [2]

6. Explain how muscles cause bones to move. [2]

7. Describe the differences between aerobic and anaerobic respiration. [4]

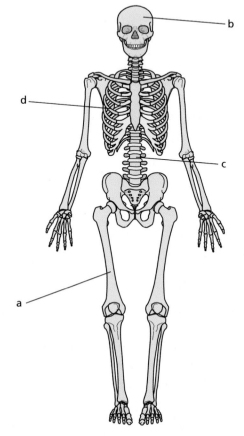

FIGURE 2.1.19a

See how well you can apply the ideas in this chapter to new situations.

8. We can prove that we produce carbon dioxide in our bodies by: [1]

   a) breathing on a cold mirror
   b) blowing through limewater
   c) growing yeast in a flask
   d) measuring our temperature with a thermometer.

9. During an uphill sprint, why does a runner use anaerobic respiration instead of aerobic respiration? [1]

    a) it releases energy more quickly   **b)** it releases more energy

    c) it forms lactic acid in animals   **d)** it releases energy more slowly

10. When a muscle underneath the toe contracts to move it down, its antagonistic muscle is: [1]

    a) contracting   **b)** relaxing

    c) neither contracting nor relaxing   **d)** pushing

11. Which row in Table 2.1.19 correctly matches the sport to the *main* type of respiration used? [1]

TABLE 2.1.19

	Sport	Type of respiration used
a)	long-distance swimming	anaerobic
b)	marathon running	aerobic
c)	weightlifting	aerobic
d)	sprinting	aerobic

12. Describe how movement at the elbow joint would be different if it was a ball and socket joint. Explain your answer. [2]

13. Explain why a student is not describing the full picture when she says that animals respire and plants photosynthesise. [2]

14. A bodybuilder has strained his tricep muscles and has been advised to rest his arm. He asks if he could carry on using hand weights to build up his bicep while still resting his tricep muscles. Explain why this is not possible. [4]

Questions 15–16

See how well you can understand and explain new ideas and evidence.

15. Imagine that a strange skeleton of an unknown animal is found at an archaeological dig. The backbone of the skeleton is one long bone. Suggest what this tells us about movement of the animal, compared to the movement of humans. [2]

16. Two types of microbe, A and B, are being considered for use by a brewing company. Microbe A respires aerobically and anaerobically, whereas microbe B only respires anaerobically. Suggest which microbe may be most useful based on this information, and suggest what other factors should be considered before choosing which microbe to use. [4]

Looking at Plants and Ecosystems

Plants

Green plants need water and nutrients from the soil in order to grow. They make food in their leaves by photosynthesis using light energy.

Flowers contain pollen. Pollination is the first stage in fertilisation. It occurs when pollen is transferred from the anther to the stigma.

Insects have an important role in pollination.

Cells

Cells are the basic building blocks of all plants and animals.

Plant cells have all the parts that animal cells have, but they also have chloroplasts containing chlorophyll, which capture light energy from the Sun for photosynthesis.

The environment

Animals and plants are adapted to the conditions of the habitats in which they live. Their adaptations help them to survive.

All living things also depend on one another to survive. A food chain shows how each living thing gets food and energy.

Humans can affect the environment both in positive ways, (for example, by creating nature reserves) and in negative ways (for example, by depositing huge quantities of rubbish and litter).

In this chapter you will find out >>>

Healthy plants

- Plants have adaptations that allow them to survive and grow, for example stomata in the leaves.

- Plants have a network of vessels that transport water and minerals to their leaves and flowers.

- Healthy plants need certain essential minerals. Without these minerals they show symptoms of mineral deficiency.

Producers

- Food chains usually start with a green plant, called a producer.

- The amount of photosynthesis that takes place in a plant is affected by various factors, including the levels of carbon dioxide, light, water and temperature.

- Some organisms that have no chlorophyll are also able to make their own food. They do this by chemosynthesis, using different chemicals in their environment.

Relationships in the environment

- All organisms are affected by the conditions in their environment and are dependent on one another.

- The relationships between organisms take different forms. In some relationships, both organisms benefit; in others, only one benefits or one even suffers harm.

- In any environment there are many interlinked food chains. These can be disrupted by factors such as toxins entering the food chain or disease.

- Some feeding relationships are very important to human survival, and we need to protect the organisms involved.

- Almost every human activity affects organisms in their habitats, very often in a negative way.

Understanding the importance of plants

We are learning how to:

- Identify the importance of plants to life on Earth.
- Use evidence to explain that plants do not use soil to grow.
- Evaluate secondary data to start to explain how plants make food.

A huge variety of plants grow on land and in water. Throughout the world humans plant, cut down and replant trees. They also cultivate many types of plant. Why do we grow plants? Why are plants so important to us?

Useful plants

Plants allow us to survive. We use plants every day for food. All food is either a plant or comes from an animal that has eaten plants. Some plants give us raw materials for fabrics, building and fuel; others are used in medicine. We even use plants as decoration in our gardens, homes and parks.

Plants:

- remove **carbon dioxide** from the atmosphere
- release **oxygen** into the atmosphere.

1. List the ways that we use plants.

2. Describe the ways that we use plants. Give at least one example for each use.

3. Explain why plants are essential to the survival of life on our planet.

Plants and soil

Small seeds grow over many years into very large trees. Up until the 1600s, most scientists thought that plants grew by taking in solid materials from the soil. The Belgian scientist Jan Baptist van Helmont (1580–1644) devised a plan to test this idea. He did an experiment that involved growing a willow tree in a large pot of soil.

Before the experiment, van Helmont measured the mass of the soil and the tree. He covered the soil with a transparent lid, but watered the plant regularly. After five years he again measured the mass of the soil and the tree. The results he obtained were similar to those in Figure 2.2.2b.

FIGURE 2.2.2a: How do we use these plants?

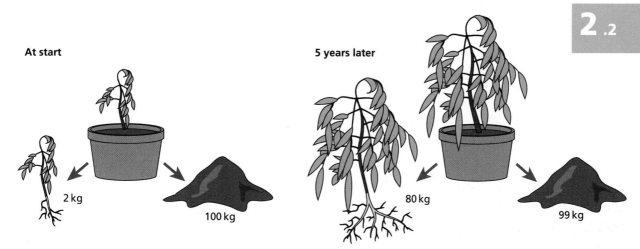

At start

5 years later

2 kg

100 kg

80 kg

99 kg

FIGURE 2.2.2b: Van Helmont's experiment

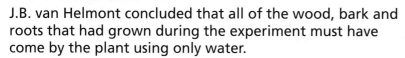

4. List five variables that might affect this experiment.

5. a) What was the change in the mass of the tree?

   b) What was the change in the mass of the soil?

6. Explain how this experiment suggested that plants did not grow by taking in solid materials from the soil.

7. a) What other explanations could there be for the results van Helmont found?

   b) How could van Helmont's experiment be improved?

Special plants 〉〉〉

J.B. van Helmont concluded that all of the wood, bark and roots that had grown during the experiment must have come by the plant using only water.

We now know much more about how plants grow. Look at the plants shown in Figure 2.2.2c, the water hyacinth. Its roots are not anchored in soil but are free-floating.

8. What conclusions can you draw from this information?

9. Is this sufficient information to support van Helmont's conclusion that plants do not use soil to grow?

10. Why did van Helmont cover the pot with a lid?

FIGURE 2.2.2c: Water hyacinths grow in fresh water.

Did you know...?

'Hydroponics' is a method of growing plants in water using mineral nutrient solutions. The roots are not kept in soil.

Key vocabulary

carbon dioxide

oxygen

Exploring how plants make food

We are learning how to:

- Identify the reactants and products of photosynthesis.
- Plan and predict the results of investigations.
- Evaluate the risks of a procedure.

Plants do not need to eat other plants or animals to get their food. They make food using materials around them. What do they use to make food? How do they do it?

Making food

Green plants use water from the environment and carbon dioxide from the air to make the sugar **glucose**. Light from the Sun provides the energy needed for the reaction. This process is called **photosynthesis**. The reaction also produces oxygen, which is released into the air during the daytime.

$$\text{carbon dioxide} \ + \ \text{water} \ \xrightarrow{\text{light}} \ \text{glucose} \ + \ \text{oxygen}$$

The plant uses the glucose for new growth and respiration and also stores unused glucose as a carbohydrate called **starch**.

1. **a)** Name the reactants in photosynthesis.

   b) Name the products of photosynthesis.

2. Why does photosynthesis not happen at night?

3. What will happen to the amount of carbon dioxide in the air during daylight?

4. Why is light not a reactant or a product in the reaction?

FIGURE 2.2.3a: These trees are giving out oxygen. Why is it important to conserve our trees?

Checking the evidence

You can show that a plant has photosynthesised by testing its leaves for starch. This is done using a chemical called **iodine**. Iodine is an orange colour, but it turns blue-black when added to starch.

First, the leaf needs to be boiled in ethanol and then rinsed in warm water. This kills the cells and removes the green colour. Iodine is then added. If the leaf become blue-black, then starch is present, showing that photosynthesis has taken place.

> **Did you know...?**
>
> 'Biomass' is the total mass of an organism. As plants photosynthesise and grow, their biomass increases.

leaf after extracting
green colour

leaf after iodine
is added

FIGURE 2.2.3b: Testing a leaf for starch: when a green leaf is boiled in alcohol the green colour is extracted. When iodine is added the leaf will turn blue-black if starch is present.

5. **a)** A leaf has been kept in the light for five days. What colour will it be when tested with iodine?

   b) The leaf is then kept in the dark for five days. Now what colour will it be when tested when with iodine? Explain your answer.

6. A leaf has been kept in a sealed jar without carbon dioxide for five days. What colour will it be when tested with iodine?

The importance of green leaves >>>

Leaves have a green colour because they contain a pigment called **chlorophyll** that absorbs light energy. Chlorophyll is found in the chloroplasts in plant cells. Look at the plant in Figure 2.2.3c. Some parts of its leaves are green and some parts are white.

FIGURE 2.2.3c: This plant has variegated leaves.

Think about the process for testing a leaf for starch. Like most activities, this process is not entirely free of risk. You have to judge which risks are greatest and reduce these to a level that can be managed by sensible, safe behaviour.

7. What do think would happen if you tested a leaf from the plant in Figure 2.2.3c for starch? Explain your answer.

8. What are the risks in the test for starch and how can they be controlled?

Key vocabulary

glucose

photosynthesis

starch

iodine

chlorophyll

Looking at leaves

We are learning how to:

- Relate the size of a leaf to the availability of light.
- Relate the function of the leaf to its structure and the types of cell.
- Evaluate the structure of a cell related to its function.

Leaves are one of the major organs in a plant. They have a complex structure that allows them to photosynthesise and make glucose. What is special about leaves? How are they able to capture the Sun's energy to make food for the plant?

FIGURE 2.2.4a: Leaves have many different shapes and sizes, but they all have some features in common with each other.

How are leaves adapted?

Leaves have features that allow them to photosynthesise efficiently. Typically, leaves are thin, flat, broad, green and have a network of veins. They all contain a pigment called chlorophyll, which absorbs the Sun's energy and enables the plant to photosynthesise. Scientists use a technique called chromatography to look at chemicals in the pigment. The leaves are ground up, and the pigments are separated using a solvent. The pigments in chlorophyll are green and different shades of yellow.

1. What features do leaves have in common?
2. Why do leaves have these features?
3. What cells have you studied that are found in leaves?

Observing leaves

Look at the photograph in Figure 2.2.4a. It shows different types of plants growing to different heights.

Water lilies (Figure 2.2.4b) grow in fresh water. Their leaves float on the surface of the water.

FIGURE 2.2.4b: Look at these leaves. How are they adapted to carry out their function?

The internal structure of a leaf is also adapted to allow it to photosynthesise efficiently. Look carefully at Figure 2.2.4c.

Leaves have:

- a waxy waterproof **cuticle**

- a transparent **epidermis**

- long, narrow **palisade cells** packed with chloroplasts, mainly at the top of the cells

- **spongy cells** that have a large surface area and large spaces between them.

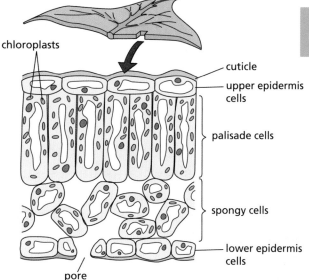

chloroplasts

cuticle

upper epidermis cells

palisade cells

spongy cells

lower epidermis cells

pore

FIGURE 2.2.4c: Section through a leaf showing the different types of cell

4. What do you notice about the size of the leaves growing at different heights in the forest?

5. Why is this important to the plants that grow to these heights?

6. What does this tell you about the leaves?

7. How do gases move in and out of a leaf?

8. Name the different types of cells in a leaf and describe their features.

Evaluating leaf adaptations ▶▶▶

Look closely at the different types of cells in the leaf section shown in Figure 2.2.4c. Each cell type has special adaptations to help it perform its function and maximise the amount of photosynthesis taking place.

- Light passes through the cuticle and epidermis until it reaches the palisade cells.

- The palisade cells absorb as much light as possible, to ensure that the rate of photosynthesis is as high as possible.

- The spongy cells capture the remaining light.

- Their surface area and the air spaces allow gases to diffuse through the leaf.

9. Evaluate the adaptations of each type of cell. How do these adaptations ensure that the cells perform their function efficiently?

Did you know... ?

Diatoms are microscopic plants that live in water all over the Earth. They are responsible for providing 20 per cent of the oxygen added to the atmosphere by plants.

Key vocabulary

cuticle

epidermis

palisade cell

spongy cell

Exploring the role of stomata

We are learning how to:

- Describe how stomata control gas exchange.
- Explain how gas exchange occurs in leaves.
- Analyse how stomata density is affected by different conditions.

Plants are found in a huge range of habitats. In order to photosynthesise, plants need a supply of carbon dioxide. How do plants get carbon dioxide? Why does oxygen, a product of photosynthesis, not build up in the leaf?

How do plants get the carbon dioxide they need?

Look again at Figure 2.2.4c. Land plants have **pores** (holes) on the underneath surface of their leaves. These pores can open and close to control materials that flow in and out of the leaf. You can see these in Figure 2.1.13c of Topic 1.13. These special structures are called **stomata** (the plural of **stoma**). When a plant needs carbon dioxide, the stomata open, allowing the gas into the leaf. Two **guard cells**, one on either side of each stoma, control the opening and closing of the stoma.

1. What are stomata and where are they found?

2. Describe how gases pass in and out of a leaf.

3. What is the name of the cells that control the size of the stomata?

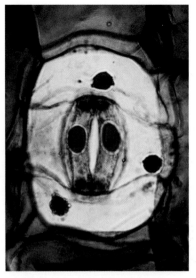

FIGURE 2.2.5a: Look at this picture. What shape are the guard cells?

Observing stomata

Guard cells have chloroplasts and can photosynthesise. When the guard cells are full of water, they open the stomata.

As the plant takes in carbon dioxide (CO_2) from the air, oxygen (O_2), a waste product of photosynthesis, is removed through the stomata. At the same time, water escapes from the plant. A stoma cannot stay open because the guard cells shrink back as the water escapes, and so the stoma closes.

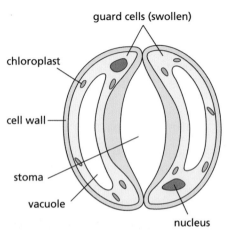
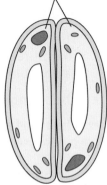

Stoma open — guard cells (swollen)

Stoma closed — guard cells (shrunken)

chloroplast

cell wall

stoma

vacuole

nucleus

FIGURE 2.2.5b: Open and closed stomata

4. Why must guard cells come in pairs?

5. Draw an annotated diagram to explain how stomata control the flow of substances in and out of the leaf.

6. Explain why stomata are found on the underside of leaves.

Density of stomata 〉〉〉

Look closely at the photographs of stomata from different plants in Figure 2.2.5c. The number of stomata varies depending on environmental factors, such as the concentration of carbon dioxide and the humidity of the air.

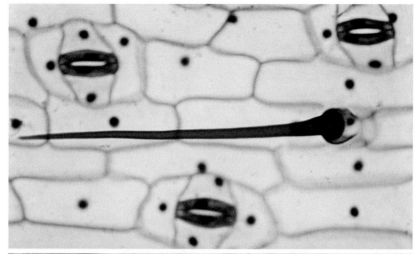

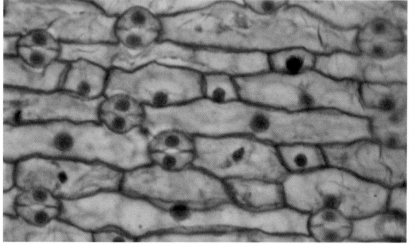

FIGURE 2.2.5c: Stomata from different plants: one with low stomatal density and one with high stomatal density

7. Suggest two other environmental factors that will affect the number of stomata

8. Describe how environmental factors would affect the number of stomata.

> **Did you know... ?**
>
> Plants respire just as animals do. They respire all day and all night, but only photosynthesise during the hours of daylight.

Key vocabulary

pore

stomata

stoma

guard cell

Investigating photosynthesis

We are learning how to:

- Identify the factors that can affect photosynthesis.
- Predict results of investigations.
- Interpret secondary data about photosynthesis.

Photosynthesis happens in all green plants. In this process the plant uses raw materials in the environment to make glucose. What factors can affect how fast a plant photosynthesises? How will these factors affect photosynthesis?

Photosynthesis ▶▶

Green plants all over the world use carbon dioxide and water from the environment to make glucose and then carbohydrates. Glucose is needed for the plants to grow and increase their biomass. Plants in some habitats grow at a much faster **rate** than others. For example, mosses growing in cold tundra habitats grow very slowly, whereas plants in the rainforest grow much more quickly.

FIGURE 2.2.6a: Will these trees photosynthesise at the same rate?

1. Write the word equation for photosynthesis.

2. What factors will affect how much photosynthesis takes place in a plant?

3. Look at Figure 2.2.6a. Will these trees photosynthesise at the same rate? Explain your answer.

Factors affecting photosynthesis ▶▶▶

The **concentration** of carbon dioxide in the air will affect the rate of photosynthesis. Carbon dioxide and water are the reactants in the reaction – the higher the amount of the reactants, the greater the amount of photosynthesis, as shown in Figure 2.2.6b.

Choloropyhll in the chloroplasts absorbs light energy. The more choroplasts a leaf has, the more light it can absorb to carry out more photosynthesis.

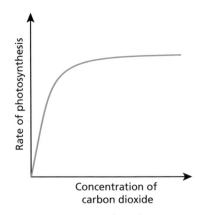

FIGURE 2.2.6b: How does the concentration of carbon dioxide affect photosynthesis?

A student is carrying out an investigation to see how the amount of light a plant receives affects the rate of photosynthesis. She uses some pondweed with the apparatus shown in Figure 2.2.6c. She counts how many bubbles of oxygen are given off by the pondweed in one minute, at different distances from a lamp.

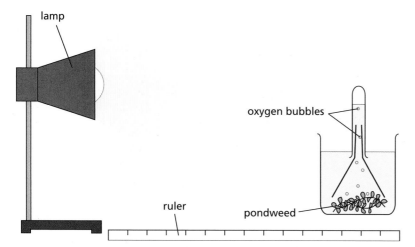

FIGURE 2.2.6c: Apparatus used in an investigation to see the effect of light on photosynthesis

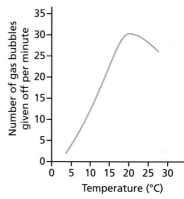

FIGURE 2.2.6d: Results of the investigation

4. How do we know that plants photosynthesise less in winter than in summer?

5. How does the amount of light available to a plant affect the rate of photosynthesis?

6. How does temperature affect the rate of photosynthesis?

7. a) Why does the student think that counting bubbles is a good way to measure photosynthesis?

   b) What variables does the student need to control?

   c) What errors might occur in the investigation?

Interpreting data ▶▶▶

A student's grandfather wants to grow tomatoes as quickly as possible in his greenhouse over the winter. The student carries out an investigation to find the temperature at which tomatoes photosynthesise the most.

8. Using the investigation results to help you, explain how the rate of photosynthesis changes from dawn to nightfall.

9. What is the best temperature for the student's grandfather to use in his greenhouse? Explain why.

Did you know...?

Rainforests produce over 20 per cent of the Earth's oxygen. This is why it is so important to look after them and stop the trees being destroyed.

Key vocabulary

rate

concentration

Exploring the movement of water and minerals in plants

We are learning how to:

- Identify how water and minerals move through a plant.
- Explain how water and minerals move through a plant.
- Evaluate the cell structures that allow the movement of water and minerals through a plant.

Water is needed in cells to support the plant and to photosynthesise. Minerals in the soil dissolve in water. How do plants get the water and minerals they need? How do they move through the plant?

Taking water in

Plants take in water and dissolved minerals through their roots. The roots grow downwards and can also spread out underground to absorb water and minerals from a large area. Roots anchor plants firmly in the ground.

Water and minerals move from the roots, up the stem or tree trunk to the leaves and flowers. Water in plant cells causes them to swell and become rigid.

1. Name two functions of the roots.

2. Look at Figure 2.2.7b. Why do these plants have differently shaped roots?

3. Why does water move to the leaves?

FIGURE 2.2.7a: The saguaro cactus

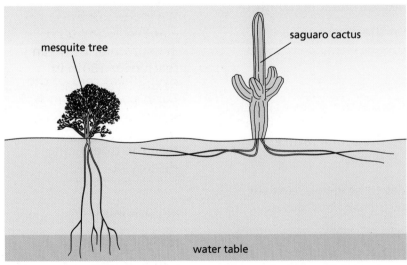

FIGURE 2.2.7b: Plants native to the Sonoran Desert in the Western USA. Why do these plants have differently shaped root systems?

mesquite tree

saguaro cactus

water table

FIGURE 2.2.7c: How is the saguaro cactus adapted to prevent water loss?

Plants can lose water from the leaves through the stomata, which let in carbon dioxide. Stomata close in hot conditions.

The loss of water from a leaf is called **transpiration**. Plants lose most water when it is dry, hot and windy. Leaves have a waxy cuticle to prevent water loss (see Figure 2.2.4c). The cuticles of desert plants are much thicker and waxier compared to other plants. Their leaves are often small or needle-like, which also prevents too much water loss.

Some plants have curled or folded leaves. The curl reduces the surface area of the leaf. It also traps moist air to help reduce transpiration further.

> **4.** What is transpiration?
>
> **5.** In what conditions will plants lose least water?
>
> **6.** Describe how plants can reduce water loss.
>
> **7.** Draw a diagram to show the movement of water through a plant.

FIGURE 2.2.7d: Some plants have curled or folded leaves to reduce water loss.

Looking at cells ▶▶▶▶

Water and minerals move from the roots up the plant, in a series of cells in the stem. These **xylem cells** form a pipeline through the plant.

The roots of the plant have special cells called **root hair cells**. These have long, hair-like extensions that penetrate between the soil particles. They have a large surface area through which they can absorb water.

The guard cells are also important for controlling water loss (see Topic 2.5). When the guard cells are swollen with water, they open the stomata to let excess water leave the leaf. When the guard cells contain little water, they close the stomata.

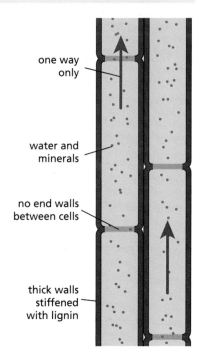

one way only

water and minerals

no end walls between cells

thick walls stiffened with lignin

FIGURE 2.2.7e: How are these xylem cells adapted to their function?

Key vocabulary

transpiration

xylem cells

root hair cell

> **8.** How effective are the adaptations of xylem, stomata and root cells for transpiration?

Investigating the importance of minerals to plants

We are learning how to:

- Identify the minerals essential to healthy plant growth.
- Explain the effects of a deficiency in essential minerals.
- Evaluate the limitations of evidence.

All plants require essential elements that are not supplied by photosynthesis – minerals that are found in soil and absorbed by the plant through its root system. What minerals do plants need? What happens if they do not get them? How can we help plants that we grow to get the minerals they need?

FIGURE 2.2.8a: Are these plants healthy? How do you know?

Mineral deficiency

Poor plant growth may be due to a deficiency, or shortage, of one or more minerals.

- Plants that do not have enough nitrates have poor growth and yellow leaves.
- Plants with too little magnesium cannot make chlorophyll.
- Phosphorus **deficiency** causes poor root growth and discoloured leaves.

1. What is a mineral deficiency?

2. Predict how a plant would grow if it had a lack of magnesium.

Essential minerals

When plants photosynthesise, they make glucose from carbon, hydrogen and oxygen. To convert these to protein, the element nitrogen must be added. Most plants obtain their nitrogen from the soil in the form of nitrates.

FIGURE 2.2.8b: What do plants need to be healthy?

Minerals are needed to make proteins, chlorophyll and energy-storage molecules. Not all minerals have the same importance for the plant. The major minerals that plants use in large quantities are called 'macroelements'. Phosphorous, potassium and nitrogen are the main macroelements. Others are sulfur, calcium and magnesium.

3. Explain how plants get the minerals they need.

4. What are macroelements?

5. Name the three main macroelements.

Putting it right ▶▶▶

Farmers grow many plants in specially selected fields. As the plants grow, they extract nutrients from the soil. Because the farmer harvests the crops from the fields, the soil becomes depleted of nutrients.

Tests can be done to establish which minerals are deficient, or a general purpose NPK **fertiliser** or **manure** can be added to the soil. (N, P and K are the symbols for the three macroelements:
N = nitrogen;
P = phosphorus;
K = potassium.)

FIGURE 2.2.8c: Fertilisers contain NPK.

FIGURE 2.2.8d: Why do farmers use fertilisers?

Commercial fertilisers release minerals quickly into the soil for the plants. However, they can get into waterways and cause algae in the water to grow very quickly. Many farmers prefer to use manure because it is natural, improves soil quality and releases the minerals much more slowly than commercial fertilisers. This means that manure has longer-term effects.

6. What is a fertiliser?

7. What is in an NPK fertiliser?

8. If farmers have fertile healthy soil, why do they need to use fertilisers?

9. Why do you think some farmers use manure and some use commercial fertilisers?

Did you know... ?

Many zoos sell elephant dung as manure. The nutrient-rich manure improves nutrient-depleted soils, helping farmers to ensure good soil for planting crops in.

Key vocabulary

deficiency

fertiliser

manure

Investigating chemosynthesis

We are learning how to:

- Describe how ocean vent communities survive.
- Describe the adaptations of tube worms.
- Compare and contrast chemosynthesis and photosynthesis.
- Evaluate models of chemosynthesis and photosynthesis.

Most living organisms depend on sunlight as their ultimate source of energy. Green plants use sunlight to make food by photosynthesis. In the darkness of the ocean depths there is no sunlight, but many organisms live there. How do living organisms survive in this environment?

Chemosynthesis

Scientists once thought that green plants were the only organisms able to make their own food (known as producers). Green plants use light energy to make food by photosynthesis.

Scientists now know that some bacteria are also able to make their own food. They can use energy from chemicals to make food by a process called **chemosynthesis**. Both methods involve an energy source, carbon dioxide and water and both produce sugars. Photosynthesis gives off oxygen gas as a byproduct, while chemosynthesis produces sulfur.

Chemosynthesis is the life-sustaining process in deep-sea communities where sunlight does not penetrate.

FIGURE 2.2.9a: In a hydrothermal vent, very deep in the ocean, communities of organisms survive without sunlight.

Photosynthesis:
carbon dioxide + water → glucose + oxygen

Chemosynthesis:
carbon dioxide + water + oxygen + hydrogen sulfide → glucose + sulfuric acid

1. Explain how chemosynthesis and photosynthesis are similar.

2. Explain how chemosynthesis and photosynthesis are different.

Hydrothermal vents form where there is volcanic activity on the ocean floor. Cold seawater (2 °C) seeps through cracks in the floor and is heated by molten rock (up to 400 °C). The hot fluid gushes out of the vent, carrying dissolved metals combined with sulfur to make metal sulfides.

The fluid also contains many bacteria adapted to live in very high temperatures. The bacteria absorb hydrogen sulfide, oxygen and carbon dioxide from the water. They break down the hydrogen sulfide to get energy, which they use to convert carbon dioxide into sugars. The bacteria are the producers – they are the food source on which all the other vent animals ultimately depend. Food chains and food webs are covered more fully in Topic 2.11.

Billions of chemosynthetic bacteria can be found living inside giant tubeworms. The tubeworms use some of the sugars produced by the bacteria as food, and they provide the bacteria with hydrogen sulfide and oxygen that they take up from the water. Both organisms benefit. The tubeworms have a coat made from chitin (a tough, protective substance derived from glucose).

3. Describe how bacteria near hydrothermal vents get the food and energy they need.

4. Why are these bacteria so important?

5. Explain how tubeworms and bacteria help each other to survive.

Life on Mars? »»»

Some scientists believe that life on Earth may have started in the sulfurous environment around the hydrothermal vents. They have proposed that many of the basic molecules needed to start life could have formed in vents just below the surface of the ocean floor (by the interaction of the rock and the circulating hot water).

This hypothesis has also helped space scientists to develop their ideas. They hope that they might find life elsewhere in the Solar System.

6. Explain why chemosynthesis may be more likely to support life on distant worlds than photosynthesis.

7. Explain how some scientists believe life on Earth may have started.

FIGURE 2.2.9b: A tubeworm.

Did you know...?

Our knowledge of chemosynthetic communities is relatively new. They were found during ocean exploration and first observed in 1977.

FIGURE 2.2.9c: What kind of life could exist on Mars?

Key vocabulary

chemosynthesis

hydrothermal vent

Applying key ideas

You have now met a number of important ideas in this chapter. This activity gives an opportunity for you to apply them, just as scientists do. Read the text first, then have a go at the tasks. The first few are fairly easy – then they get a bit more challenging.

Down at the allotment

Ben has an allotment. An allotment is a plot of land that can be rented by a person to grow fruit and vegetables for their own use. Allotment plots come in many different shapes and sizes. Ben's allotment has a greenhouse.

Ben grows many different types of vegetables outside: carrots, potatoes, onions, leeks, cabbages, beans, lettuces and tomatoes. He also grows cucumbers, courgettes and tomatoes in his greenhouse.

Ben has had his allotment for a long time and grows his crops every year. He cannot use the farming practice of growing crops in different places every year, but he tries not to grow the same crop in the same place more than two years in a row. During spring he digs in well-rotted manure that he buys from the local farm. Not only does the manure fertilise the soil, it also conditions it.

Ben's friend, Joe, has an allotment too. He grows his vegetables in the same place every year, but the plants are not as healthy as Ben's – even though the allotments are next to each other. His plants never produce as many vegetables and they are always much smaller than Ben's. Joe cannot understand why this happens.

Ben has noticed that his outdoor tomato plants never produce as many tomatoes as his greenhouse plants, and they also take much longer to grow outside. Some years he gets no tomatoes from the plants that are outside. Tomatoes grown outside cannot be planted until the temperatures are warm enough, especially at night. Also, when it rains less water is taken up by the roots.

FIGURE 2.2.10a: An allotment

FIGURE 2.2.10b: A polythene tunnel

Task 1: Exploring how plants make food

Describe how the plants in the allotment make food to grow. Write the equation for this process.

Task 2: Investigating photosynthesis

Why do the tomatoes in Ben's greenhouse have a longer growing period and produce more fruit than the ones grown outside?

Task 3: Investigating photosynthesis

What else can Ben do to make sure that the greenhouse plants produce as many large tomatoes, cucumbers and courgettes as possible?

Task 4: Investigating the importance of minerals to plants

Explain why Joe's plants are not as healthy as Ben's.

Task 5: Exploring the movement of water and minerals and the role of stomata

When Ben arrives at the allotment, there is condensation inside the greenhouse, so he opens the doors. Explain where this water comes from. Why is this process important?

Task 6: Investigating the importance of minerals to plants

What advice would you give to Joe to improve the crops he gets from his allotment? Explain the advice.

Understanding food webs

We are learning how to:

- Describe how food webs are made up of a number of food chains.
- Make predictions about factors affecting plant and animal populations.
- Analyse and evaluate changes in a food web.

Food chains show the feeding relationships between living organisms. If something happens to disrupt part of the chain, it can have serious knock-on effects through the whole chain.

The ups and downs of food chains

The organisms in a **food chain** are dependent on each other. For example, in Figure 2.2.11a, grass is eaten by rabbits, which in turn are hunted and eaten by foxes. The grass captures the energy from sunlight to photosynthesise and make glucose. The glucose provides energy for the plant to grow. When a rabbit eats grass, the energy left in the grass is transferred to the rabbit. The rabbit uses some of this energy to move and grow. When a fox eats a rabbit, the remaining energy in the rabbit is transferred to the fox.

Changes in the number of one organism in a food chain affects other organisms in the food chain.

- The number of plants in an ecosystem can be affected by the amount of rain, sunlight, minerals and space available to grow.

- The number of animals can be affected by the amount of food, habitats, mates, water and disease.

Look at Figure 2.2.11a again and then answer these questions.

1. What would happen to the numbers of rabbits and foxes if all the grass died out?

2. What would happen to the amount of grass and foxes if all the rabbits died out?

3. Why is it a good idea for an organism to have different sources of food?

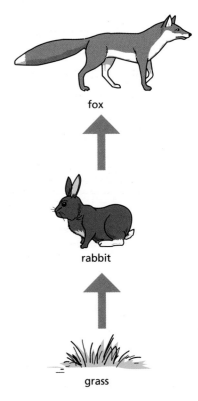

FIGURE 2.2.11a: A simple food chain

Did you know...?

Dugongs are marine mammals with important populations in the Arabian Gulf. They only eat seagrass. Building in the area has destroyed the seagrass beds, and the dugong is now endangered.

Food webs and trophic levels ▶▶▶

Most animals eat many different things and are involved in many different food chains. These food chains can be put together in a **food web**, which shows how the food chains are connected. Food webs can be complex.

In a food web:

*   producers make their own food
*   **primary consumers** eat producers
*   **secondary consumers** eat primary consumers
*   **tertiary consumers** eat secondary consumers.

These rankings are called **trophic levels**. The trophic level of an organism is the position it occupies in a food chain.

> **4.** What is a trophic level? Give an example of a trophic level.
>
> **5.** Looking at Figure 2.2.11b, give an example of an animal in each of the four trophic levels listed above.
>
> **6.** If the mice died, what could happen to the rabbits in the food web?

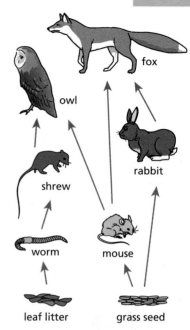

FIGURE 2.2.11b A simple food web. What do the arrows in the food web mean?

Knock-on effects ▶▶▶

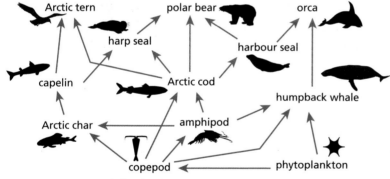

FIGURE 2.2.11c: An Arctic food web

Look at Figure 2.2.11c. Harbour seals, harp seals and Arctic terns all feed on Arctic cod. If the Arctic cod catch a disease and die, the Arctic tern and harp seals will eat more of their other prey. The harbour seal only eats Arctic cod, so they will die too. This means that the cod will not eat amphipods and copepods, so there will be more food for the humpback whale and Arctic char, and their populations will increase.

> **7.** Harp seal populations are controlled by killing them – this is called 'culling'. Analyse and evaluate the impact of culling the majority of harp seals.
>
> **8.** Explain how this food web shows that energy is transferred from the copepod to the Arctic tern.

Key vocabulary

food chain

food web

primary consumer

secondary consumer

tertiary consumer

trophic level

Exploring the importance of insects

We are learning how to:

- Describe the impact of low pollination on fruit production.
- Explain why artificial pollination is used for some crops.
- Evaluate the risks of monoculture on world food security.

Food security refers to the availability of food and the ability to obtain it. What is the role of bees and insects in our food security? How does agricultural practice impact on food security?

Fruit production and bees

Bees are vital in pollinating fruit crops. Pollination is successful when flowers receive healthy pollen at the best time. The better the pollination of apples and pears, the larger the fruits.

Anything that interferes with bee activity, such as disease or adverse weather, will reduce pollination. Bee colony numbers in Britain have fallen dramatically. The reduced pollination has lowered both fruit **yields** and the earnings of fruit growers – the apple harvest in 2012 was 50% lower than expected. This resulted in a higher cost of apples in the shops.

Recent research has found that the fall in wild bee populations, caused by habitat destruction, is having a greater impact than the fall in honeybee numbers. This is because wild bees are twice as effective as honeybees in pollinating orchards.

FIGURE 2.2.12a: Honeybee hives are placed in orchards to ensure pollination.

1. Why do fruit growers put beehives in their orchards?
2. How can we help wild bee colonies to survive and grow?

Ensuring pollination

In south west China, wild bees have become extinct because of overuse of **pesticides** and the destruction of their natural habitats. Apple and pear farmers now hand-pollinate their trees, using pots of pollen and paintbrushes to pollinate each flower individually.

Crops of cucumbers, tomatoes and peppers are also often hand-pollinated. Date palms have male and female plants; natural pollination therefore requires trees of both types.

FIGURE 2.2.12b: These women are hand-pollinating blossom on pepper plants.

By using hand-pollination, date farmers need only grow female trees and so avoid wasting space by growing male plants.

There are not enough humans in the world to pollinate all of our crops by hand. In addition, hand-pollinated fruits are often smaller than those pollinated by bees. Scientists are building a robotic bee that could one day be used to pollinate plants artificially and support the work of real bees.

3. Why is artificial pollination vital to fruit growers in China?

4. What are the advantages and disadvantages of artificial pollination?

Tackling food security >>>>

Evidence from around the world shows that yields of insect-pollinated crops are falling and are becoming ever more unpredictable. This is especially true in the areas with the most intensive farming. Where single crops are grown in vast fields – a practice called **monoculture** – there are not enough insects to go around.

FIGURE 2.2.12c: Monoculture is a modern agricultural practice that destroys the pollinators' natural habitats.

Almond orchards cover hundreds of square miles in California. Bees cannot survive naturally in these areas because the flowering time is too short and there are no other plants for them to feed on.

Some poor countries use monoculture to grow huge quantities of crops that they sell to richer countries, such as coffee, cocoa and bananas. Little fertile land is left to grow food crops for the local people who then suffer food insecurity.

5. Evaluate the practice of monoculture in agriculture.

6. Suggest how farmers can ensure pollination in monocultural systems.

Did you know...?

It has been suggested that 'travel stress' caused by bees being shipped from pollination site to pollination site is partly to blame for disorders in bee colonies that hugely reduce their population.

Key vocabulary

food security

yield

pesticide

monoculture

Looking at other examples of interdependence

We are learning how to:

- Describe examples of the interdependence of organisms.
- Explain how organisms help other organisms to survive.
- Explain ideas about habitat destruction.

Wherever you look in the world, you see habitats that support many different populations. The different species living in a particular habitat will all depend on others for their survival. What types of relationships occur? Are they always beneficial?

Niches and relationships

A **niche** is the role of an organism within a particular ecosystem. This includes what it eats; what eats it; its habitat; its nesting site, range and habits; what effect it has on the other populations; what effect it has on the environment.

The interdependence between organisms is called **symbiosis**. Types of symbiosis include:

- **commensalism** – one organism benefits, whereas the other does not. For example, clownfish live among the tentacles of sea anemones and are protected from their predators. The anemones do not benefit from this relationship.

- **mutualism** – both organisms benefit. For example, oxpeckers eat bugs that live on a rhinoceros.

- **parasitism** – one organism benefits, but the other is harmed. For example, fleas live on the skin of a dog. They feed on blood from the dog, which makes the dog weaker.

Other examples of interdependence are predator–prey relationships and decomposers (such as fungi and worms) that recycle nutrients from dead or decaying organisms.

1. Describe examples of the interdependence of organisms.

2. In the example of the oxpecker and the rhinoceros, how does the relationship benefit each animal?

3. What is an organism's 'niche'?

FIGURE 2.2.13a: The oxpecker eats bugs on the rhinoceros.

FIGURE 2.2.13b: There is a high level of interdependence between different organisms on a coral reef.

Competition

Competition is another example of interdependence. Organisms in every ecosystem are continually competing for the same resources. For example, if there are only ten trees with fruit and one animal is better at reaching the fruit than a shorter animal, then the shorter animal will not get any and may starve. However, if the tall animal kills all the trees with the high fruit and only low fruit is left, the shorter animal will survive at the expense of the larger.

Competition usually happens when there are limited resources. Sometimes, if everything is even, it can be a stalemate – both species compete, but both survive.

Some organisms co-exist by 'specialisation' – for example, plant roots may access water at different depths in the soil.

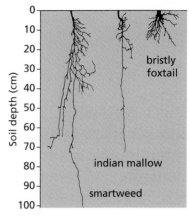

FIGURE 2.2.13c: Specialisation in plant roots

4. Give an example of:

   a) competition   **b)** mutualism

   c) parasitism   **d)** commensalism.

Problems in the rainforest

Rainforests are the oldest ecosystems on Earth. Nearly half of all animal species live in them. The high temperatures and abundance of water create an ideal environment for many organisms. The animals' long-term survival depends on a number of factors, such as their ability to adapt, their interdependence with other species and the actions of humans, e.g. hunting.

Loss of habitat is the biggest threat to animals inhabiting the rainforest. If animals lose their homes in a sudden way, they are likely to die. Large mammals, such as gorillas and leopards, rely on having large areas of suitable habitat in which to roam, hunt and find mates. It is difficult for them to survive if their habitat is cut back in size or is reduced to smaller, separated pockets.

5. Why are rainforests such important ecosystems?

6. What are the advantages and disadvantages of habitat destruction? Design a poster to communicate your ideas.

Did you know...?

Mountain gorillas are endangered. Fewer than 650 remain in the wild. A male mountain gorilla may stand as tall as six feet (two metres).

FIGURE 2.2.13d: Why are rainforest habitats being destroyed?

Key vocabulary

niche

symbiosis

commensalism

mutualism

parasitism

competition

Understanding interactions in the environment

We are learning how to:

- Describe some effects of human activity on the environment.
- Explain why many species are endangered.
- Analyse and evaluate secondary data and recommend solutions for species survival.

The 'environment' is a system of physical, chemical and biological factors that are in a dynamic equilibrium. This means that they are constantly changing, but overall the system stays in balance. If this balance is upset, species become endangered.

How humans affect the environment

Human actions and behaviours are major factors contributing to environmental change. We hunt animals for food, sport, medicines and to keep as pets. We use their fur, skin, horns and tusks for making clothing, bags, shoes and ornaments. We construct buildings, roads and other structures such as dams and reservoirs that destroy the habitats needed by plants and animals.

The human population is increasing rapidly as a result of factors such as better medical care and higher standards of living. This puts our planet at greater risk:

- More land is needed for farming, so natural habitats are being lost.
- More factories and power stations cause more pollution.
- Long-distance travel is easy, so plant and animal species can be transported around the world, sometimes with disastrous results.
- Many plants and animals all over the world are now becoming **endangered**.

Some people and communities make changes to their lifestyles that will reduce their impact on the environment. This helps to preserve **biodiversity** – the variety of living organisms found in an ecosystem.

1. Describe how humans interact with their environment.
2. Describe examples of human impact on the environment.
3. How can you help in protecting the environment?

FIGURE 2.2.14a: An example of our impact on the environment

Did you know...?

In December 2013, the US government's Fish and Wildlife Services reported 2143 species worldwide that are endangered or threatened, ranging from mammals and birds to flowering plants and ferns.

FIGURE 2.2.14b: Why is the Malagasy rainbow frog endangered?

A species is endangered when there are so few of its kind left that it could become **extinct**. Some animals are more threatened than others. Scientists categorise the level of risk to species. From most to least threatened, these levels are:

- critically endangered
- endangered
- **vulnerable**
- not threatened.

Some animals exist only in captivity, in wildlife parks. These animals are extinct in the wild – an example is the scimitar-horned oryx, which was once widespread across northern Africa.

Many countries have laws that protect endangered species from being captured, injured or killed.

4. Explain what an 'endangered species' is.

5. Explain why some species are more endangered than others.

FIGURE 2.2.14c: The scimitar-horned oryx is extinct in the wild.

Putting it right ⟫⟫⟫

Conservationists use various methods to identify species at risk and to measure their population size. Some of the methods include:

- observation
- surveys of nests and vegetation
- analysis of air, land and water
- identification of habitats
- collection of data, for example on pellets, fecal matter, feathers or scales.

These scientists also use methods to increase the numbers of animals, including **captive breeding**, re-introduction of animals, habitat creation and pest control. International agreements and the creation of protected areas also help to protect species and their habitats.

6. Explain the job of a conservationist.

7. Why do conservationists use captive breeding programmes?

FIGURE 2.2.14d: Environmentalists at work

Key vocabulary

endangered

biodiversity

extinct

vulnerable

captive breeding

Learning about ecological balance

We are learning how to:

- Describe ways in which organisms affect their environment.
- Explain why prey populations affect predator populations.
- Evaluate a model of predator–prey populations and explain the importance of predators.

Organisms are not isolated in their environment. They interact with other individuals of their own species, with other species and with their physical environment. The study of the interactions between organisms and their environment is called **ecology**. In what ways do organisms interact? How does one organism affect others?

FIGURE 2.2.15a: How can cows affect grass when they graze?

How organisms affect the environment

All organisms cause changes in the environment where they live. An organism's behaviour depends on the nature of its environment. This includes factors such as:

- the types and numbers of other organisms present
- the availability of food and resources
- physical characteristics of the environment.

Cattle that stay in one place for a long time will eat the plant life to death. Without plants to hold it, topsoil runs off into streams causing habitat loss for other organisms (in both the fields and the streams). Eventually there is a drop in the water supply, which can cause pollution of water resources. This then affects all the habitats that the water flows through, including surface water (such as lakes and rivers), groundwater and water found underground.

1. What is 'ecology'?
2. Describe examples of how organisms affect their environment.

Did you know...?

Big cats are examples of predators adapted for efficient hunting. One of the cheetah's best hunting skills is its ability to run at high speed. It can run faster than any other land animal, accelerating from 0 to 100 km/h (62 mph) in about three seconds.

FIGURE 2.2.15b

Predators and prey

The relationship between **predator** and **prey** is probably the most important interaction between organisms and their environment. Predators need to be adapted for efficient hunting to catch enough food to survive. Prey species must be well adapted to escape their predators to ensure their survival.

If the prey population grows, predator numbers will respond to the increased food supply and grow too. Increased predator numbers will reduce the food supply so that it can no longer supply the predator population.

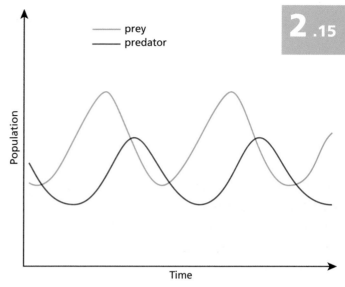

2 .15

FIGURE 2.2.15c: The relationship between predator and prey numbers

3. What variables affect the numbers of predators and prey in a population?

4. Explain how prey populations affect predator populations.

The importance of predators

The role of predators has been misunderstood by humans throughout time, and many predator species are now endangered.

Predators are an important part of the food web. They keep in check the negative impacts other animals have on the environment if they are too abundant. Predators keep prey moving around, which prevents population explosions and this gives plants time to grow. Predators also contribute to preserving biodiversity in environments.

Predators therefore play a vital role in maintaining the **equilibrium** in an environment. Humans need to understand this, or else they will remain in trouble. Ecologists now put more emphasis on studying and maintaining predator populations and their habitats.

Predators can be introduced to an ecosystem to control prey that are pests. For example, ladybirds (predator) can be used in greenhouses to control aphids (prey and pest).

FIGURE 2.2.15d: Ladybirds are used to control aphid populations.

Key vocabulary

ecology

predator

prey

equilibrium

5. How can predators be used to control a prey population? Why would you want to do that?

6. Explain why predators are important.

Understanding the effects of toxins in the environment

We are learning how to:

- Describe how toxins pass along the food chain.
- Explain how toxins enter and accumulate in food chains.
- Evaluate the advantages and disadvantages of using pesticides.

Otters nearly became extinct in the south of England in the 1960s. What caused this? Why were otters more affected than other animals? Why do we use chemicals in agriculture?

Why are chemicals used in agriculture?

In recent times, the global population has increased dramatically – food needs to be grown more quickly to feed the growing number of people. Soils are quickly depleted of the nutrients needed to grow healthy crops. Nowadays, farmers rarely mix keeping animals with growing crops, so they do not have the supplies of cattle manure to replace the nutrients naturally. Instead, artificial **fertilisers** and nutrients are used to replenish the soil.

Pesticides and **insecticides** are chemicals used to kill insect pests and small creatures that damage crops.

> 1. Why do farmers use chemicals in agriculture?
>
> 2. Why do most modern farms not use manure on their fields?

Chemicals entering the food chain

Toxins can enter the food chain in several ways.

- Fertilisers dissolve in water and are washed off the fields by rain into rivers and reservoirs.

- Pesticides, used by farmers to kill weeds or insects, contaminate small creatures that are eaten, or the chemicals are washed or blown into waterways.

- Water runs off urban streets into waterways.

- Soft mud acts like a sponge that slowly soaks up the toxins. Plants absorb these through their roots.

- Some chemicals fall from the air, such as mercury released by coal-burning power plants.

FIGURE 2.2.16a: Why is the farmer adding artificial fertiliser, not manure?

FIGURE 2.2.16b: Insects covered in insecticide are eaten by other animals.

Primary consumers eat the plants containing the toxins; secondary consumers eat the primary consumer; and so on up the food chain.

3. Give examples of a primary consumer and a secondary consumer that could be affected by pesticides used on farmland.

4. Explain how toxins enter the food chain.

Accumulation of toxins in the food chain ⟫⟫

Organisms at the start of a food chain can take up small amounts of toxins. The higher up the organism is in the food chain, the more concentrated the toxin will become – eventually it is so concentrated that it can kill the top predator.

A pesticide called DDT was used in the 1960s. It killed insects that were damaging crops, but it ran off into rivers and contaminated plants. The small animals and fish further up the food chain collected more and more of the toxin because it stayed in their bodies. This process is called **bioaccumulation**.

Otters that ate the fish were killed and almost became extinct in the south of England.

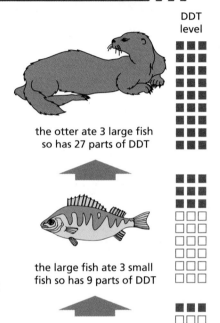

DDT level

the otter ate 3 large fish so has 27 parts of DDT

the large fish ate 3 small fish so has 9 parts of DDT

the fish ate 3 water weeds so has 3 parts of DDT

the water weed has 1 part of DDT

FIGURE 2.2.16d: Bioaccumulation of DDT in a food chain

FIGURE 2.2.16c: How does mercury released into the air get from here into an organism?

Did you know...?

In 2001, DDT was banned worldwide. The only remaining legal use of DDT is to control malaria-carrying mosquitoes. Modern insecticides do not accumulate in food chains.

Key vocabulary

fertiliser

insecticide

toxin

bioaccumulation

5. Explain why otters were in danger of extinction because of DDT.

6. If the otter population declined, how would this affect the river ecosystem?

Exploring how organisms co-exist

We are learning how to:
- Describe the role of niches.
- Explain the concept of resource partitioning.
- Analyse and evaluate the role of variation in enabling organisms to co-exist.

Living organisms all have basic needs that are vital to their survival. The world has finite resources. How do organisms ensure that they get what they need to survive?

Exploring niches

The ecological niche of an organism is the role it plays in a particular habitat. For example, a bee's niche is producing honey, pollinating flowers and drinking nectar, in its habitat of field or garden.

- **Specialists** have a narrow niche. They only survive in very specific environmental conditions and they have a very limited diet. For example, the giant panda lives only in the bamboo forests of China; bamboo shoots and leaves make up 99% of its diet.
- **Generalists** have a broad niche. They can live in a wide range of environmental conditions and eat many different types of food. Human beings are generalists.

Species with overlapping niches compete for resources – the greater the overlap, the greater the competition between the species.

1. Name two other examples of specialists.

2. Name two other examples of generalists.

3. Explain why competition arises.

Competition in detail

Animals and plants are constantly competing for resources. Animals compete for prey, water, mates, nest sites and so on. Plants compete for water, light, nutrients and space.

There are two main types of competition:
- Competition between organisms of the *same* species – for example, stags fighting for a mate
- Competition between organisms of *different* species – for example, lions and hyenas feeding on the same dead animal.

Did you know...?

Giant pandas have a 'sixth' finger – a small extension of the panda's wrist bone that helps them grasp the bamboo and pull the leaves and shoots off the stem easily. They have large jaws with smoother, wider and flatter premolars and molars to break down the hard bamboo.

FIGURE 2.2.17a: The niche of the panda is a herbivore active in the day in the bamboo forest.

Different species with similar needs use resources in different ways. They do not compete directly for the limited resource. This is called **resource partitioning**.

Anole lizards live in the Florida forests (USA). Seven species of anole live in the same community. They all feed on insects and other small invertebrates. These species **co-exist** because each one lives in a particular space in the forest and so has a different niche. Some anole lizards live in the tree canopy, some on the tree trunks and some live close to the ground or in the leaf litter.

> **4.** Explain what resource partitioning is in your own words.
>
> **5.** Explain how the different species of anole can co-exist.

Resource partitioning ▶▶▶

Variation helps the anoles survive in their chosen niche.

- Species living on tree trunks near the ground have long hind limbs for running and jumping.
- Species living on narrow twigs higher in the trees have very short legs and crawl slowly to capture prey and escape from predators.
- Species living in the vegetation high in the tree have very large toepads and are green for camouflage.

Animals can partition their niches by:

- feeding on different types of food
- feeding on different sizes of food – some feed on large seeds, others on small seeds
- feeding in different places
- feeding at different times – nocturnal foragers eat insects active at night; diurnal foragers feed on insects active during the day.

Robert MacArthur was an ecologist who studied how five species of warbler could live in one conifer tree without direct competition. He found that the birds occupied different niches in the habitat. They all fed on insects, but in different parts of the tree, at different times and with different preferences. By using these different behaviours they avoided competition and were able to co-exist.

> **6.** Explain how warblers avoid competing for resources.
>
> **7.** Using the information about how organisms partition their niches, explain how rabbits and cows can co-exist in the same field.

Anole insolitus usually perches on shady branches.

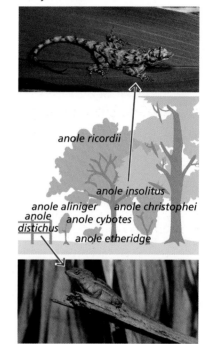

anole ricordii

anole insolitus

anole aliniger   anole christophei

anole distichus   anole cybotes

anole etheridge

Anole distichus usually perches on fence posts and other sunny surfaces.

FIGURE 2.2.17b: Different species of anole lizards live in the same forest.

Key vocabulary

specialist

generalist

resource partitioning

co-exist

variation

Checking your progress

To make good progress in understanding science you need to focus on these ideas and skills.

State that green plants need sunlight to grow and to make food.

Identify water and carbon dioxide as the raw materials for photosynthesis, and glucose and oxygen as the products.

Explain the chemical changes involved in photosynthesis and the roles of light and chlorophyll.

Describe how gases enter and leave a leaf and how light energy for photosynthesis is captured.

Describe how cells in the leaf and root are adapted for their functions.

Relate and explain how the structure of palisade, mesophyll and guard cells allows them to perform their function.

Describe how levels of light, temperature and carbon dioxide affect the rate of photosynthesis.

Explain how levels of light, temperature and carbon dioxide affect the rate of photosynthesis.

Apply learning about the factors affecting photosynthesis to solve problems.

Name some of the nutrients needed by plants and supplied by fertilisers; state how they enter the plant dissolved in soil water.

Explain why nutrients are needed by plants, how spreading manure adds them to the soil and how water passes through the plant.

Explain how mineral deficiencies affect plants and how different factors affect the rate of transpiration.

- Describe how some bacteria produce food by chemosynthesis.

- Compare chemosynthesis with photosynthesis.

- Explain why some bacteria use chemosynthesis and how they support food chains.

- Describe an example of a simple food web.

- Explain how energy flows through a food web and explain factors that can affect food webs, such as loss of a species or toxin accumulation.

- Explain the importance of predators in an environment and evaluate changes in a food web.

- Describe an example of interdependence of organisms in an ecosystem – for example the pollination of crops by insects.

- Explain examples of interdependence of organisms in an ecosystem – for example through symbiosis, commensalism and parasitism.

- Analyse an example of interdependence of organisms in an ecosystem – for example, the effects of the destruction of rainforests.

- Identify some ways in which organisms affect, and are affected by, their environment – for example through pollution or destruction of habitats.

- Explain some ways in which organisms affect, and are affected by, their environment – for example, predator–prey relationships.

- Analyse and evaluate the factors affecting endangered species and recommend solutions.

Questions

See how well you have understood the ideas in the chapter.

1. Where do plants get their food from? [1]

   a) Plants absorb food from the soil.
   b) Plants absorb nutrients from rain through their leaves.
   c) Plants make food in their leaves using carbon dioxide and water.
   d) Plants absorb nutrients from the soil and food is made from these in the roots.

2. Which of these does NOT affect the rate of photosynthesis? [1]

   a) temperature   b) light   c) chlorophyll   d) oxygen concentration.

3. Which of these is an important element needed for healthy plant growth? [1]

   a) cobalt   b) potassium   c) iodine   d) aluminium

4. Which of these organisms can make their own food without using sunlight? [1]

   a) tube worm   b) bacteria   c) seaweed   d) algae

5. Describe how palisade mesophyll cells are adapted to photosynthesise. [2]

6. Give two examples of the way that humans impact on the environment. [2]

7. What are the differences and similarities between photosynthesis and chemosynthesis? [4]

See how well you can apply the ideas in this chapter to new situations.

8. Stomata close when water is in short supply. Name a disadvantage of closed stomata. [1]

   a) Water is not lost.   b) Nutrient uptake is reduced.
   c) Photosynthesis increases.   d) Water is lost.

9. Look at this simple food web in a rainforest. What will happen to the number of red-eyed tree frogs if all the chimpanzees die from a disease? [1]

   a) They stay the same.
   b) They go up.
   c) They go down.
   d) They will die out too.

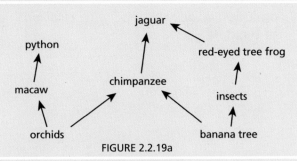

FIGURE 2.2.19a

10. What is the niche of the jaguar in the food web in Figure 2.2.19a? [2]

11. Look at the food web in Figure 2.2.19a. The jaguar and the python are predators. What will happen if both predators die out? [4]

82   KS3 Science Book 2: Looking at Plants and Ecosystems

12. What effect will increasing the light intensity have on transpiration? [1]

    a) It will stay the same. **b)** It will drop. **c)** It will rise. **d)** It will stop completely.

13. Harmful algal blooms (HABs) produce toxins in the sea. Oysters are animals that filter food particles like plankton from the water. How could dining on oysters during an HAB affect a person's health? [1]

14. Look at Figure 2.2.19b. This single-celled organism lives in pond water. How does it get food? Explain how you know this. [2]

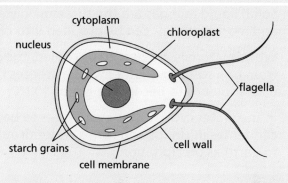

FIGURE 2.2.19b: Chlamydomonas – a unicellular organism

Questions 15–16

See how well you can understand and explain new ideas and evidence.

15. Marram grass grows on sand dunes. It has rolled leaves. Why do you think it has:

    a) sunken stomata and rolled leaves?
    b) a thick, waxy cuticle? [2]

FIGURE 2.2.19c: The leaf blade of the marram grass is rolled towards the mid vein.

16. Figure 2.2.19d shows how the populations of lynx and hares change over time. Analyse and evaluate the data to explain why the populations rise and fall when they do. Do you think this pattern is still happening today? Explain your answer. [4]

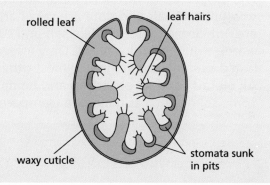

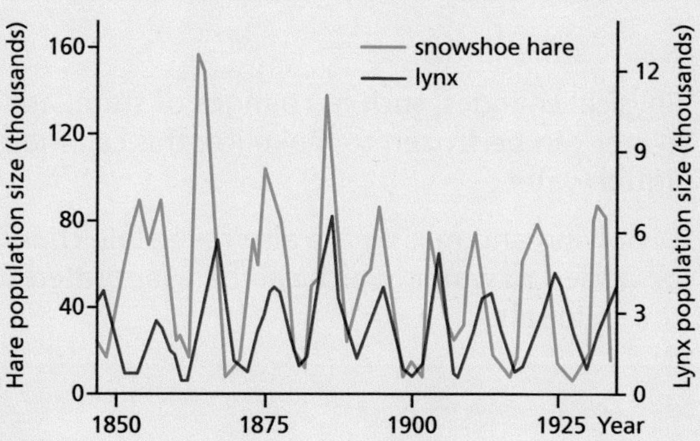

FIGURE 2.2.19d: Lynx and hare population data

Explaining Physical Changes

Ideas you have met before ⟫

States of matter

Solid, liquid and gas are the three main states of matter and most materials can be grouped into one of these.

When materials are heated or cooled, they may change from one state to another. Water freezes to become ice at 0 °C, and boils to becomes a gas at 100 °C.

In the water cycle, water evaporates to become a gas, condenses in clouds and forms water droplets. It falls back to Earth as precipitation.

Properties of materials

The properties of different materials affect their use. Some solids like metals and slate are very hard; paper and fabric are not. Some materials, like salt and sugar, dissolve in water; flour and talc do not. Only a few metals, such as iron and steel, are magnetic; most other metals are not. All metals conduct electricity and heat; non-metals do not. Some solids, such as glass, are transparent.

Reversible changes

Physical changes, such as changes of state, are reversible. Water can be frozen to make ice; this can melt to form liquid water.

Dissolving and mixing are also reversible changes – salt can be added to water, which can be evaporated to recover the solid salt.

In this chapter you will find out

Using the particle model to explain the states of matter

- The particle model explains why solids have a fixed shape and cannot flow, and why liquids and gases do not have a fixed shape, and can flow.

- Particles in solids, liquids and gases have their own internal energy – the energy of particles in a gas is far higher than the energy of particles in liquids and solids.

- The effect of temperature can be explained using the particle model. It can explain how changes of state take place and how solids, liquids and gases expand on heating.

Using the particle model to explain properties

- Brownian motion was the first description of how liquid particles move. From this observation, the theory of how particles behave was developed.

- Properties of materials can be explained in terms of the strength of the forces between the particles.

- Foams, gels and emulsions are different types of mixtures, involving different states of matter. They have special properties that can be explained using the particle model.

- We can explain differences in density, concentration and pressure using the particle model. These differences can account for why perfume spreads in a room and why astronauts need to wear space suits in space.

Particles in physical and chemical changes

- The particle model can be used to show how mass is conserved in physical and chemical changes. Using particles, we can explain why physical changes are reversible and why it is very difficult to reverse chemical changes.

Using particles to explain matter

We are learning how to:

- Recognise differences between solids, liquids and gases.
- Describe solids, liquids and gases in terms of the particle model.

Have you ever wondered why it is possible to put your hand through a liquid such as water, or a gas, such as air, but not through a solid wooden door? The answer lies in how the particles are arranged in these states of matter.

Particle arrangement

Anything that takes up space and mass is called 'matter'. All matter is made from **particles**. Particles vary in the ways they are arranged and behave. These are known as different states of matter. Figure 2.3.2a shows how particles are arranged in the three most common states of matter – solids, liquids and gases.

1. Name three solids, three liquids and three gases you are familiar with.

2. Describe how the arrangements of particles in solids, liquids and gases differ from each other.

Particles and internal energy

All particles above the temperature known as absolute zero (–273 °C) have internal **energy**. Particles in solids, liquids and gases have different amounts of energy.

- In solids, the particles vibrate in their fixed positions.
- Particles in liquids can move slowly from their positions, but are always in contact with other particles.
- Particles in a gas move about very fast, colliding with other particles.

Temperature affects how fast particles move. At higher temperatures, particles in a solid vibrate faster, while in liquids and gases particles move around faster.

3. Draw a cartoon to describe how the energies of the particles in solids, liquids and gases vary.

4. In which of the following do the particles have the most internal energy – ice, oxygen at room temperature or steam (over 100 °C)?

solid

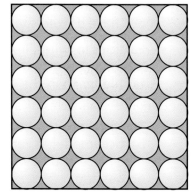

liquid

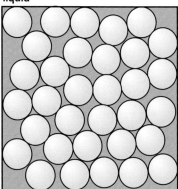

gas

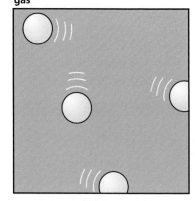

FIGURE 2.3.2a: Solid – particles are in fixed, regular positions.

Liquid – particles are close together and touching. They can move from their position.

Gas – particles have no fixed position and are far away from each other. They can move very fast.

The particles in a solid have very strong, attractive **intermolecular forces** between them, which hold the particles in their positions. Between particles in liquids, the intermolecular forces are still strong, but not as strong as in a solid. This is why the particles are able to move about. The intermolecular forces between the particles of a gas are very weak.

FIGURE 2.3.2b: Which particles here have the strongest intermolecular forces?

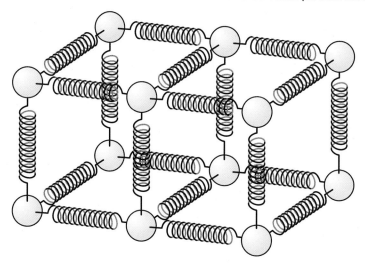

FIGURE 2.3.2c: Forces between particles can be represented by springs. How would you modify this particle model to show a solid with strong intermolecular forces and one with weak intermolecular forces?

Some solids, like metals, have very strong intermolecular forces between the particles – others, like paper, are not nearly as strong.

5. Use ideas about intermolecular forces to explain why you can put your hand through air but not through wood.

6. What can you say about the intermolecular forces between the particles of jelly compared with those of a metal?

7. Describe the relationship between the energy of the particles and the intermolecular forces holding them together.

8. What do you think is in between the particles of a gas?

Did you know...?

The most common state of matter in the Universe is called 'plasma'. It is known as the fourth state of matter, and is a form of gas.The Sun and space are made of plasma. We can make tools from plasma to cut strong metals.

Key vocabulary

particles

energy

intermolecular forces

Understanding solids

We are learning how to:

- Describe the properties of solids.
- Relate the properties and behaviour of solids to the particle model.

Some properties are common to all solids and help to define them. Differences between solids can be explained using the particle model.

General properties of solids

Except for mercury, all metals are solid at room temperature. They have high melting and boiling points, and all conduct heat and electricity well. A few non-metallic solids share these properties, but many others have very different properties.

Flow

Some solids appear as if they can flow, like sand. Seen under a microscope, such a solid is made up of many individual grains. None of the individual solid grains can flow – they do, however, flow over each other.

Changing shape

Some solids are **malleable** – they can be hammered into shape without being broken. Solids such as plastic are brittle – they will snap if hit. Metals are ductile – the layers of atoms are able to slide past each other, so they can be pulled into extremely thin wires.

Strength

Strength is the ability of a solid to withstand a force. Metals are generally very strong, but waxy solids are easily squashed.

Hardness

Hardness is a measure of how easy it is to scratch a solid – it is not the same as strength. Slate and concrete are very strong solids, but are easily scratched so they are not as hard.

Solubility

Some solids, salt for example, dissolve readily in water – they are **soluble**. Others, such as sand, do not dissolve and some, such as sodium, react chemically with water.

Conduction of heat and electricity

Metals will readily **conduct** heat and electricity, whereas non-metal solids, like plastic and rubber, will not. The only exception is graphite, which conducts electricity even faster than metals.

FIGURE 2.3.3a: The hardest and strongest material in the world

> **Did you know...?**
>
> Diamond has the strongest intermolecular forces of all solids. This makes it the strongest, hardest material in the world. Drills that cut through rock are tipped with diamonds.

TABLE 2.3.3: Put these solids in order of hardness.

Substance	Hardness
aluminium	3
carbon (diamond)	10
iron	4
silver	2.5
tin	1.5
copper	3

1. Which property is responsible for making copper wires?

2. Use the data in Table 2.3.3 to explain which material you would use on the end of drill.

What are alloys? >>>

Alloys, such as brass, bronze and chrome, are mixtures of metals. They are often stronger than the individual metals they are made from. Different shapes and colours can be used to represent the different types of atoms in the particle model.

3. Duralumin is an alloy made from 96 per cent aluminium (very light) and 4 per cent copper (heavy). What might the particle model look like?

4. Use the particle model to explain why some alloys are less ductile than the metals they are made from.

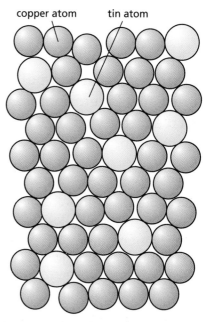

copper atom   tin atom

FIGURE 2.3.3b: Bronze is made up of 85 per cent copper and 15 per cent tin.

Explaining properties >>>

Strength, shape and hardness all depend on the strength of the intermolecular forces between the particles in a solid.

Solubility also depends on intermolecular forces. In solids which dissolve, forces between the particles of the solid are weaker than the forces between the particles of the solid and the particles of the liquid. In insoluble solids, the forces between the particles of the solid are too strong to be overcome.

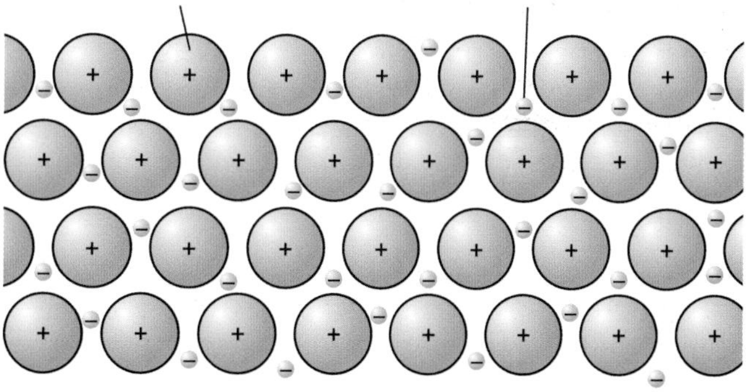

The arrangement of particles in metals is special, accounting for their ability to conduct heat and electricity. This is shown in Figure 2.3.3c.

metal particle with positive charge – stays in position

electron with negative charge – free to move

FIGURE 2.3.3c: Metals can conduct heat and electricity because they have negative particles that move freely.

5. How would you modify the particle model to show a solid with strong intermolecular forces and one with weak intermolecular forces?

6. Explain as many differences in the properties of copper and wax as you can using appropriate particle models.

Key vocabulary

malleable

strength

hardness

soluble

conduct

alloy

Exploring Brownian motion

We are learning how to:

- Describe how theories develop.
- Describe and explain Brownian motion in terms of particles.

Particles are very small and cannot be seen except with special equipment. How did we first discover that matter was made from particles that can move in liquids?

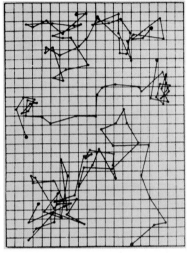

FIGURE 2.3.4a: Brownian motion

Making observations

Scientific theories are developed as a result of making observations, developing a **hypothesis** and testing this in further investigations. An important part of this process is 'peer review' – other scientists perform similar experiments to confirm the initial observations, or debate the findings of investigations based on their own research. The idea that particles move was developed in this way, but over many years.

In 1785 Jan Ingenhauz first noticed a random movement of charcoal dust in alcohol. In 1827, the Scottish botanist Robert Brown was studying pollen grains in water under a microscope. He observed that particles from the grains moved around in a random motion – this came to be called '**Brownian motion**'. He did not know what caused the movement and carried out further investigations to develop a hypothesis.

1. What is a hypothesis?
2. Why is it important for other scientists to confirm experimental observations?

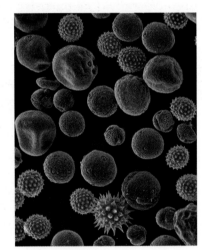

FIGURE 2.3.4b: Pollen grains can be seen to perform Brownian motion.

Developing hypotheses

Brown tested other pollen grains and found that smaller, more spherical grains had even more vigorous motion. He suspected that Brownian motion could have been produced because the pollen grains were living.

He then tested pollen from dead plants and found the same result. He wondered if there was some mysterious 'life force' at this miscroscopic level. He tested fossilised wood and dust from a stone that had been part of the Sphinx, an ancient Egyptian statue. Any material, dead or alive, produced this same random motion under the microscope. He could not explain this motion with the ideas established during his time.

3. Identify one hypothesis Robert Brown that had developed concerning his obeservations.

4. How did he test this hypothesis?

Using models and analogies to connect ideas ⟫⟫

Fifty years later, scientists were developing the **kinetic theory**, which included the idea that matter was made of particles. The theory attempted to explain the properties and motion of particles in solids, liquids and gases. Scientists deduced that the Brownian motion shown by pollen in water was caused by the particles of the liquid colliding with the pollen grains – however, this conflicted with some existing ideas.

The kinetic theory was important to all chemists and physicists of the late 1800s. Albert Einstein was determined to resolve the problems. If Brownian motion could not be explained, the kinetic theory was in trouble.

Because individual particles could not be seen, the only **evidence** of them was from observations of their behaviour. Mathematical calculations were made from this and predictions developed.

In 1905, Einstein wrote an article in which he developed an analogy, comparing Brownian motion with osmosis. He found that the mathematical predictions between Brownian motion and his analogy were identical, proving that Brownian motion was due to the movement of the liquid particles colliding with the pollen grains. Amendments were made to the kinetic theory to fit this new evidence.

5. Why is it important for observations to fit in with an existing theory?

6. Why is it important to use models and analogies in developing theories?

7. Do you think a theory should be established by the evidence that supports it, or by the evidence that refutes it? Explain your answer.

FIGURE 2.3.4c: Albert Einstein: a brilliant scientist and mathematician

> **Did you know...?**
>
> Einstein's 1905 article on Brownian motion is his most cited work by researchers. It has been instrumental in use by scientists working on aerosols and in investigating the properties of milk and paint.

Key vocabulary

hypothesis

Brownian motion

kinetic theory

evidence

Understanding liquids and gases

We are learning how to:

- Compare different properties of liquids and gases.
- Relate the properties and behaviour of liquids and gases to the particle model.

Oxygen cylinders, fish tanks, oil pipes and bicycle pumps all rely on important properties of liquids and gases.

Viscosity

Liquids and gases can be poured and can flow. This ability to flow is known as **viscosity**. Some liquids flow more easily than others. This is because the intermolecular forces holding the particles of a liquid in place are quite strong, but not strong enough to keep the particles in position. They are able to slide over and roll around each other.

Liquids in which the intermolecular forces are stronger do not flow as easily because it is more difficult for the particles to slide past each other. Think of oil and water – oil flows more slowly than water; it is more viscous.

1. Give three applications of liquids and gases that rely on their ability to flow.

2. You want to oil your bike. You decide to investigate three different brands to find out which spreads most easily in the cold.

   a) Which variables must you control?

   b) What values should you select for these control variables for this investigation?

Volume and compression

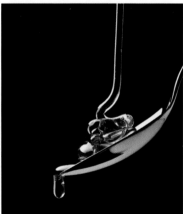

FIGURE 2.3.5a: Which material has particles with the stronger intermolecular forces?

'Volume' is defined as the amount of space that matter takes up. A liquid will take up the same space, no matter which container it is placed in. There is no space between the particles in a liquid, so it cannot be **compressed**.

In a gas, the particles continue to move in a straight line, until they collide with the sides of the container or with other gas particles. This enables them to fill the space they occupy.

There is literally *nothing* in between the gas particles. They can, therefore, be easily pushed closer together, or compressed. When they are compressed a lot, the particles

> **Did you know...?**
>
> In the longest experiment ever, scientists left tar pitch to drop from a funnel. After 70 years, one drop of tar pitch, finally, fell!

are forced very close together. If the gas is cool, the intermolecular forces become strong enough to change the gas into a liquid.

3. What is the advantage of compressing gases into liquids to fill containers?

4. Figure 2.3.5c shows a bicycle pump in operation. Use ideas about particles to explain what happens when the piston is lifted up and pushed down.

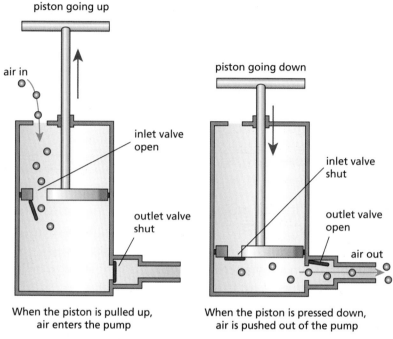

When the piston is pulled up, air enters the pump

When the piston is pressed down, air is pushed out of the pump

FIGURE 2.3.5c Which properties of a gas enable this device to work?

FIGURE 2.3.5b: The cylinders contain gas which has been liquefied. When released, the change in pressure causes the liquid particles to become gas particles again.

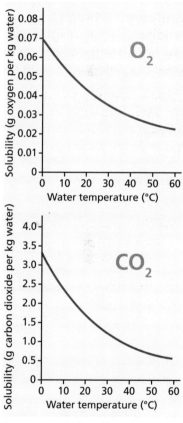

FIGURE 2.3.5d: The effect of temperature on the solubility of oxygen and carbon dioxide

Effect of temperature on solubility >>>>

Figure 2.3.5d shows the effect of temperature on the **solubility** of different gases in water. When the intermolecular forces between particles of the gas and the water particles are stronger than those between the gas particles, then the gas will dissolve in the water. It is the same for liquids dissolving in water – a liquid will dissolve in water if the intermolecular forces between the liquid and the water particles are stronger than the intermolecular forces between the particles of the liquid.

5. Explain the differences between the graphs.

6. Develop a hypothesis for why temperature affects the solubility of gases in this way.

7. Use the graph to explain why environmental scientists monitor the temperature of rivers near factories.

Key vocabulary

viscosity

compressed

solubility

Changing state

We are learning how to:

- Recognise changes of state as being reversible changes.
- Use scientific terminology to describe changes of state.
- Explain changes of state using the particle model and ideas about energy transfer.

When you make ice or melt the frost from a windscreen, you are making use of changes of state. What is actually happening to the particles in these processes?

FIGURE 2.3.6a: Solid carbon dioxide is known as 'dry ice'.

Reversible changes

Have you ever seen 'dry ice'? It is solid carbon dioxide that is turning straight into a gas – there is no liquid state. This is a process called **sublimation**. Iodine is another example of a substance that sublimes. If the gas is cooled sufficiently, it turns directly into a solid.

Turning solids into liquids or gases, and liquids into or gases or solids, are reversible changes. They are called physical changes.

Figure 2.3.6b summarises the processes by which substances change their state.

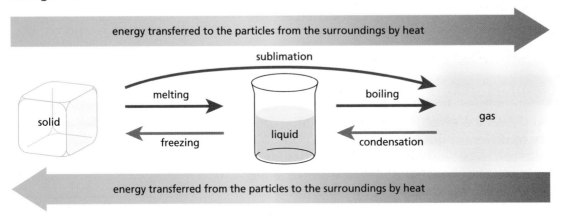

FIGUE 2.3.6b: The changes of state

1. Describe how you could show that making water freeze is a reversible change.

2. Use Figure 2.3.6b to describe the meaning of the following words:

   a) melting   **b)** condensing   **c)** boiling

   d) freezing   **e)** sublimation.

Changing state ⟫⟫

The temperature at which a pure substance melts or freezes is fixed – it is called the **melting point** or freezing point, depending on the change taking place.

When a pure substance boils or condenses, this also occurs at a fixed temperature called its **boiling point**.

Different substances have different melting points and boiling points. These points depend on the strength of their intermolecular forces.

> **3.** Aluminium melts at 660 °C but copper melts at a 1064 °C. Explain why.
>
> **4.** At 0 °C, hydrogen is a gas, mercury is a liquid and water is a solid. What can you infer from this data? Explain your answer.

> **Did you know...?**
>
> Helium has the lowest melting point of all substances at –272 °C, whereas diamond has the highest melting point of 3500 °C.

Latent heat ⟫⟫⟫

When a solid is heated, its temperature increases until it reaches its melting point. Here, all the energy transferred by heat is used to overcome the strong intermolecular forces between the particles, until the solid changes state. There is no increase in temperature until all the solid has changed state, even though energy is still being transferred by heat. This 'extra heat' is known as the **latent heat**.

This concept also applies to a liquid. Latent heat energy is used to overcome the intermolecular forces between the particles of the liquid, changing it into a gas. The temperature remains constant until all the liquid turns into a gas.

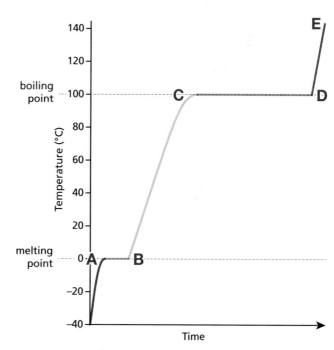

FIGURE 2.3.6c: How the temperature of ice changes with time

> **5.** Look at the graph of heating ice (water). Identify what state the water is in:
>
> **a)** between A and B   **c)** between B and C
>
> **d)** between C and D   **e)** between D and E.
>
> **6.** Why is there no temperature increase between C and D?
>
> **7.** Do you think the latent heat energy will be the same for all substances? Explain your answer with two examples.

Key vocabulary

sublimation

melting point

boiling point

latent heat

Understanding evaporation

We are learning how to:

- Investigate factors affecting evaporation.
- Explain the differences between boiling and evaporation using the particle model.

Have you ever thought about what happens to the water particles when a puddle is left in the sunshine, or to the water produced when you sweat? The answer is the water has evaporated. What does this actually mean and how is it different from boiling?

Examples of evaporation

If you spill some water on a surface and leave it in the sunshine, after a few hours the water particles will no longer be present and there is no sign of the spill. The water has evaporated. The water particles have gained sufficient energy from their surroundings to become a gas.

When clothes are hung out to dry, the air particles in the wind transfer energy by movement (kinetic energy) to the water particles in the clothes. These gain enough energy to change from a liquid into a vapour.

Smells from perfumes are also an example of **evaporation**. The perfume particles gain enough energy by heat from the body, or by kinetic energy from air particles, to become a vapour.

1. Describe one other example of evaporation.

2. When we sweat, water evaporates from the surface of our skin. Where does the energy needed for evaporation to take place come from?

Differences between boiling and evaporation

Evaporation occurs at any temperature between the melting point of a liquid and its boiling point. It occurs only at the surface of the liquid. Some of the surface particles gain enough energy from the surroundings from heat, or from kinetic energy, to leave the surrounding particles in the liquid and become a vapour. Over time, all the particles at the surface will evaporate.

Boiling, however, occurs only at the boiling point, and the whole liquid changes into a gas. The water particles gain sufficient energy from their surroundings to leave the liquid.

FIGURE 2.3.7a: How is evaporation different from boiling?

3. Is evaporation more likely to take place at temperatures near the boiling point or near the melting point? Explain your answer.

4. What are the main differences between boiling and evaporation?

Factors affecting evaporation

Four factors that affect evaporation are:

Wind speed: in faster winds, air particles have more kinetic energy. More energy can therefore be transferred to the evaporating particles of the liquid.

Temperature: at higher temperatures, more energy can be transferred to the particles of the liquid by heat.

Surface area: evaporation occurs at the surface of a liquid. With a larger **surface area**, more energy can be transferred to the particles in the liquid from the surroundings.

FIGURE 2.3.7b: Salt being made in La Palma, one of the Canary Islands.

Strength of the intermolecular forces: some liquids, such as alcohol, have weaker intermolecular forces than others, such as water. Therefore, with the same amount of energy transferred from the surroundings, more alcohol particles than water particles will escape as a gas.

5. Look at the photo of salt production in Figure 2.3.7b. Explain the factors that affect the rate of evaporation in this process.

6. Which of the factors above are likely to have the biggest effect on the rate of evaporation? Explain your answer.

> **Did you know...?**
>
> Evaporation from oceans accounts for 80 per cent of water delivered as precipitation (rain, snow).

Key vocabulary

evaporation

boiling

surface area

Exploring thermal expansion

We are learning how to:

- Identify how heat affects the arrangement and movement of particles.
- Use the particle model to explain the effects of heat on expansion.

Heat has a significant effect on the particles in solids, liquids and gases. It causes materials to expand. Should the temperature of the seas and oceans increase by only 0.5 °C, the worldwide sea level would rise by 30 cm!

Examples of expansion

Heat causes solids, liquids and gases to expand. This means that they take up more room when they are hot than when they are cold.

The photos in Figure 2.3.8a show a brass ball before and after heating it. After heating, it will no longer fit through the ring. This is because the metal has expanded.

Think of a mercury thermometer. The liquid level rises when the temperature increases because the mercury particles move around more and become further apart. This causes the silvery liquid to take up more space overall, meaning that the level of the liquid rises.

Gases expand more than solids and liquids. If a balloon is placed over a bottle full of air (Figure 2.3.8b) and the air is warmed, the air particles will soon begin to fill the balloon as the air expands.

Expansion of gases is also made use of in steam engines, car engines and rockets.

before heating the ball

after heating the ball

FIGURE 2.3.8a: What do these photos tell you about the particles in the metal when it is heated?

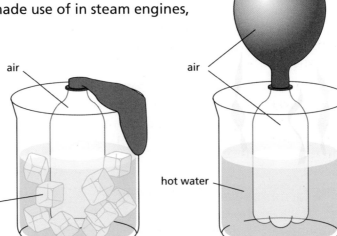

air

air

ice

hot water

FIGURE 2.3.8b: If the air in the bottle was replaced with water, would the effect be the same?

1. Why might heating the lid of a jam jar make the jar easier to open?

2. Explain why an inflated party balloon might pop if placed over a heater.

Expansion in different materials

Different solids and liquids vary in how much they expand for a given increase in temperature. Also, the more particles there are in a material, the bigger the expansion will be.

All gases expand by the same extent depending only on the temperature rise, not on the type of gas.

TABLE 2.3.8: Expansion of different solids

Material	lead	steel	aluminium	copper	glass
Expansion of 100 cm bar at 100 °C (cm)	0.29	0.11	0.23	0.17	0.09

3. Use the data from Table 2.3.8 to write the materials in order of which expands most to which expands least.

4. Copper is often used in making hot water pipes. What precautions should be taken when using this metal for this purpose?

Explaining the effect of heat

The particles in a solid are always vibrating. Transferring more energy by heat increases the frequency and amplitude of the vibration. As the particles vibrate more, each takes up more room. The amount of space increased by individual particles is very small, but over billions and billions of particles the overall expansion becomes measurable and significant.

The same is true for liquids. Because they have more kinetic energy than solids to start with, **thermal expansion** in liquids is significantly greater than in solids.

All gases expand to the same extent. This is because the intermolecular forces between the gas particles are very weak and do not play any significant role in the extent of expansion. Temperature is the only factor affecting the expansion of gases.

5. Why is a thermometer filled with a liquid and not a solid or gas?

6. Explain how global warming might increase flooding caused by the sea.

> **Did you know...?**
>
> The Eiffel Tower in Paris can grow in height by as much as 15 cm in very hot summer weather.
>
>
>
> FIGURE 2.3.8c: The Eiffel Tower expands in the heat and contracts in the cold.

Key vocabulary

thermal expansion

Making sense of models

We are learning how to:

- Describe the concept of a 'good enough' model.
- Link the particle model to elements and compounds.
- Evaluate the strengths and weaknesses of the particle model.

A model is a way of representing something that cannot be seen. Particles are too small to be seen – so the particle model is a useful tool, allowing us to understand the properties and observations of solids, liquids and gases. However, it does not provide us with the full picture.

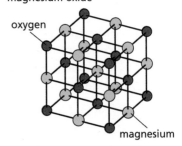

FIGURE 2.3.9a: Popcorn popping is a model of a change of state.

A good enough model

You already know about **atoms, elements** and **compounds**. All matter is made from atoms.

More advanced models are used to represent elements and compounds, compared with the model used to represent solids, liquids and gases. This is because the simplified **particle model** is 'good enough' for the purposes of explaining states of matter and changes of state.

1. List all the properties of solids, liquids and gases that the standard particle model can explain, making it a 'good enough' model.

2. Popcorn (Figure 2.3.9a) can be used as a model for explaining states of matter and changing states. How is this a 'good enough' model? Can you identify any problems with it?

Developing models further

Each element is made of only one type of atom. Compounds are made of two or more elements chemically bonded together.

Figure 2.3.9b shows the structures of two different solid compounds – aluminium oxide (Al_2O_3) and magnesium oxide (MgO). These adapted models can now explain more than just the state of matter a material is in. As you can see from the diagrams, both are solids but the atoms are organised in different ways.

FIGURE 2.3.9b: What differences can be picked out between these two solids?

Look at the model of carbon dioxide gas and helium gas in Figure 2.3.9c. By adapting the model to show the relative sizes of the atoms, you can see why carbon dioxide is much heavier than helium.

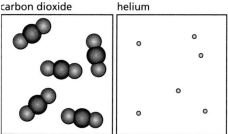

FIGURE 2.3.9c: Compare the molecules of carbon dioxide with helium gas. What does this model reveal that the model in Topic 3.2 does not?

3. Draw a model to show liquid water (H_2O) and liquid hydrochloric acid (HCl).

4. What does this model show that the standard particle model cannot?

Evaluating models ⟩⟩⟩⟩

Figure 2.3.9d shows diagrams of water in the solid, liquid and gaseous states.

solid water (ice)   liquid water   gaseous water (steam)

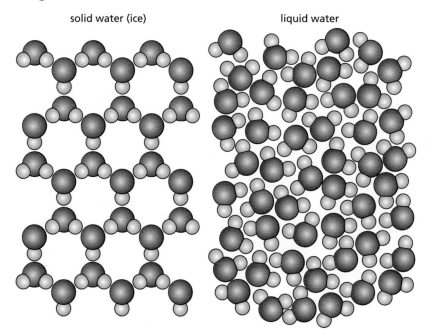

FIGURE 2.3.9d: The molecular structure of water in three states

The model shown here and the model in Topic 3.2 may be used to explain particular observations. You can compare how well they do this by evaluating the models. You need to be clear, when using models, about what they can explain and what their limitations are.

5. Which model can explain why steam diffuses faster than liquid water?

6. Which model is unable to explain the observed phenomenon that the same number of ice particles takes up *more* space than the same number of liquid water particles? Explain your answer.

Did you know...?

John Dalton was the first person to propose a model for particles. Today, scientists are still adapting and changing their ideas about particles as they learn more.

Key vocabulary

atom

element

compound

particle model

Applying key ideas

You have now met a number of important ideas in this chapter. This activity gives an opportunity for you to apply them, just as scientists do. Read the text first, then have a go at the tasks. The first few are fairly easy – then they get a bit more challenging.

Explaining heat packs

Self-heating packs have been around since about 1912. Electricity was used in early versions to transfer heat and help with pain relief. Since then, different chemical versions have been invented. An iron and charcoal pack relies on the heat produced from the reaction between iron and air. Unfortunately once used this has to be discarded because the iron is changed into iron oxide.

Calcium chloride produces heat when it is dissolved in water. Two separate compartments have to be built into self-heating coffee cups, and these must be completely sealed off from the drink to avoid contamination. Again, once used this cannot be used again.

Using changes of state to release heat has several advantages – the most important being that packs can be used over and over again.

Sodium acetate hot packs

Figure 2.3.10a shows a chemical called sodium acetate. It is dissolved in water until no further amount can be dissolved, forming a saturated solution. If the saturated solution is heated, the water expands creating more gaps into which more sodium acetate particles can be dissolved. This is known as a supersaturated solution.

The supersaturated solution needs particles to trigger a change, converting from a liquid to a solid. This is done is by clicking a metal disc, which releases tiny particles of metal into the solution, on which new crystals can form. The sodium actetate solution changes visibly throughout, converting it from a liquid to a solid. Figure 2.3.10b shows this happening. It is a different process from freezing, but has the same effect.

FIGURE 2.3.10a: Sodium acetate can be used to warm your hands.

Particles in a liquid have more energy than particles in a solid. When they change state, energy from the heat pack is transferred to the surroundings by heat, over an hour or so. This is a useful energy transfer enabling you to warm your hands. Once the heat pack has completely solidified, there is no more transfer of energy by heat. The sodium acetate must be re-dissolved to become a liquid again by heating it up. None of the sodium acetate has been lost or changed in any way. It can be used again and again.

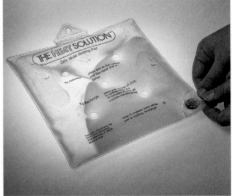

FIGURE 2.3.10b: Changing from liquid to solid

Task 1: Solids and liquids

Compare the particles of the sodium acetate hand warmer when it is a solid and when it is a liquid. Use ideas about energy to help you.

Task 2: Drawing particle diagrams

Draw particle diagrams to show particles of sodium acetate changing from a liquid to a solid.

Task 3: Explaining changes of state

a) Use ideas about changing state to explain how the hand warmer is able to warm your hands.

b) Why does it need to be reheated in order to work again?

Use particle diagrams to support your explanation.

Task 4: Comparing hand warmers

a) Use your own particle diagrams to explain how heat is transferred from an iron–oxygen hand warmer and a calcium chloride hand warmer. Use the information from the text to help you. Include the term 'reversible change' in your explanation, where appropriate.

b) Discuss the advantages and disadvantages of iron–oxygen, calcium chloride and sodium acetate hand warmers.

Explaining the density of solids and liquids

We are learning how to:

- Use the particle model to explain density differences between solids and liquids.
- Use the particle model to explain anomalies between ice and water.

The particle model is very useful for explaining what density is. By understanding how to change density, we make it possible to explore the deepest ocean trenches and to float massive tankers on our seas.

What is density? 》

Density is defined by:

$$density = \frac{mass}{volume}$$

The units of density are g/cm³.

Solids are usually more dense than liquids and gases – there are more particles (and hence more mass) packed in the same volume. However, some liquids are more dense than some solids because of how the particles are arranged in a solid.

1. Use Table 2.3.11 to explain what would happen if you put the following materials together:

   a) paper and syrup　　**b)** iron and alcohol

   c) brick and honey　　**d)** baby oil and water

2. Much smaller amounts of sweeteners are needed in soft drinks than sugar. How does this explain why a can of sugar-free drink is less dense than a can of normal drink?

Factors affecting density 》》

Temperature: as a solid or liquid is heated, the particles move about more because they have more kinetic energy, and can move further apart. The volume of the solid or liquid increases. The mass of the particles remains unchanged. The density of a hot liquid will, therefore, be lower than that of a cooler one, enabling it to **float** on top of the colder one.

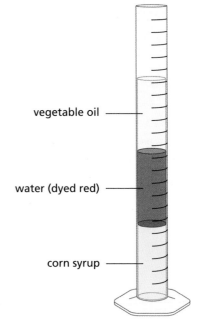

vegetable oil

water (dyed red)

corn syrup

FIGURE 2.3.11a: Which is the most dense and which the least dense substance?

TABLE 2.3.11: The density of a selection of substances

Substance	Solid or liquid	Density (g/cm³)
brick	solid	1.4
paper	solid	0.7
ice	solid	0.9
iron	solid	7.9
alcohol	liquid	0.79
baby oil	liquid	0.8
water	liquid	1.0
syrup	liquid	1.3
honey	liquid	1.4

Dissolved salts: if some salt is dissolved in water, the volume change is very small. This is because the salt particles fill the spaces between the liquid particles, so the overall volume does not change very much. In this way, more mass is added with little change in volume, so the density increases.

3. When a saucepan of liquid is heated, the hotter liquid at the bottom rises. Use ideas about density to explain why this happens.

4. The Dead Sea has a salt concentration ten times greater than in normal seas. It is possible for people to just lie and float on top of it, without effort – see Figure 2.3.11b. Explain why this is possible.

Density anomalies: ice and water >>>

Figure 2.3.11c shows the density of water at different temperatures. Ice and water are not typical in the way the density changes with temperature.

FIGURE 2.3.11b: Floating in the Dead Sea

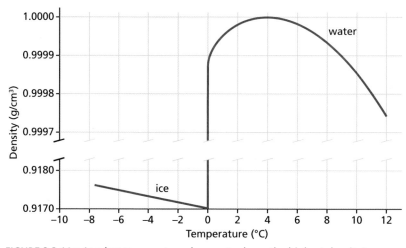

FIGURE 2.3.11c: At what temperature does water have the highest density?

Ice, instead of being more dense than cold water, is in fact less dense. Ice is made of water molecules. The bonds between the atoms of the molecules are very strong. However, *between* the water molecules, there are weak intermolecular forces which account for the spaces in the crystal structure shown in Figure 2.3.9d of Topic 3.9.

5. Look at the graph in Figure 2.3.11c.

   a) At what temperature does water have its maximum density?

   b) At what temperature does ice have its minimum density?

6. How is it possible for fish to survive at the bottom of a frozen lake?

> ### Did you know...?
>
> The world's largest floating iceberg is 295 km long and 37 km wide; it is larger than the island of Jamaica.

Key vocabulary

density

mass

volume

float

Explaining the density of gases

We are learning how to:

- Use the particle model to explain differences in the densities of gases.
- Evaluate a method of measuring density.

Have you ever wondered why helium balloons float or why carbon dioxide gas sinks? The answer lies in understanding the density of gases.

How dense are gases?

As for solids and liquids, the **density** of gases depends on the **mass** of the gas particles and the **volume** they occupy.

Table 2.3.12a shows the densities of different gases. All gases less dense than air will float in it, while gases with a density higher than that of air, like carbon dioxide, will sink in it.

TABLE 2.3.12a: Densities of different gases

Gas	Density (mg/cm³)
hydrogen	0.089
helium	0.18
air	1.28
carbon dioxide	1.977
ammonia	0.73
chlorine	3.2

FIGURE 2.3.12a: How are more modern balloons adapted to be safer, so that the flames can burn for longer?

1. Draw a graph to show how the densities of the gases in the table vary.

2. Which gases will sink in air?

Applications of gases based on density

Gases, just like solids and liquids, become less dense when heated. This principle was used in the development of hot-air ballooning. The air has to remain hot for the balloon to stay afloat. This led to many fires because early balloons were made from paper.

TABLE 2.3.12b: Density of air at different temperatures

Air temperature (°C)	Air density (g/l)
20	1.20
99	0.95
120	0.90

Nowadays air ballons use nylon (melting temperature 250 °C) and air at 120 °C. Most modern balloons use helium instead of air (density 0.18 g/l).

Carbon dioxide gas is nearly twice as dense as air. When it is released, it sinks to the floor, causing any air (and oxygen) to rise up above it. This is a useful property for fighting fires.

3. Why is it preferable to use helium in a balloon rather than hot air?

4. Look at Table 2.3.12a. Chlorine damages the lungs. It was used as a chemical weapon in World War I by firing it into the trenches. Why was this an effective method?

Working out density

We can work out the mass of different elements and compounds using the Periodic Table. We do this by finding the atomic mass of the element, multiplying it by the number of atoms of that element in one unit of the compound, and adding all the masses together.

For example, the atomic mass of N = 14 and the atomic mass of H = 1.

So the mass of one unit (one molecule) of the compound ammonia (NH_3) is $(1 \times 14) + (3 \times 1) = 17$ in atomic mass units.

Scientists discovered that if you work out the atomic mass of any gaseous element or compound, and scale it up from atomic mass units to grams, all gases occupy very nearly the same volume of 22.4 litres (at standard temperature and pressure).

So if you had 17 g of ammonia gas, it would have a volume of 22.4 litres. The approximate density can then be calculated as:

$$\text{density} = \frac{\text{mass}}{\text{volume}} = \frac{17}{22.4} = 0.8 \, \text{g/l}$$

5. Use the Periodic Table to work out the approximate density of the following gases:

   a) oxygen (O_2)   b) carbon dioxide (CO_2)

   c) sulfur dioxide (SO_2)   d) camping gas – butane (C_4H_{10})

Did you know...?

The first human flight in a hot-air balloon took place in 1783 by the Montgolfier brothers in France.

Montgolfiers Luftballon, 1783.

FIGURE 2.3.12b

Key vocabulary

density

mass

volume

Explaining concentration and pressure

We are learning how to:

- Describe what is meant by concentration and pressure.
- Use the particle model to explain differences in concentration and pressure.

What is the difference between a strong drink of cordial and a weak one? Why can't we dive with ease to the bottom of the ocean? Why would our bodies explode if we went into space without a space suit? Ideas about concentration and fluid pressure can help to explain such things.

What is concentration? 〉〉

Concentration is a term that generally applies to solutions. It is a measure of the number of solute particles in a given volume of solvent. When there are a high number of solute particles, we say the solution is **concentrated**. When the number is low, the solution is said to be **dilute**.

To increase the concentration of a solution, you would need to either add more solute or reduce the volume of solvent.

1. Look at the particle diagrams in Figure 2.3.13a. Rank the diagrams in order of concentration, with the highest first.

2. How would you decrease the concentration of a cordial drink? Explain your answer using a particle diagram.

Working out concentration 〉〉〉

We need to work out concentrations so we can determine the strengths of particular solutions for making medicines or chemical solutions. Concentration can be calculated according to how much solute is dissolved in a given volume of solvent. It is a measure of the mass of solute particles in a given volume.

For solids dissolved in liquids:

$$\text{concentration} = \frac{\text{mass of solute}}{\text{volume of solvent}}$$

The units for concentration are g/cm^3.

(a)
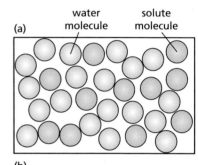

(b)
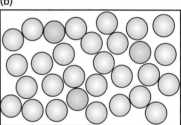

(c)
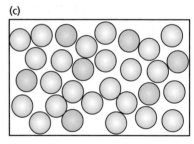

FIGURE 2.3.13a: What are the differences between these particle diagrams?

So if 30 g of salt were added to 100 cm³ of water, we can calculate the concentration as:

$$\text{concentration} = \frac{30\,g}{100\,cm^3} = 0.3\,g/cm^3$$

Concentration can also be measured by 'volume per cent', which is more suitable for liquids dissolved in other liquids.

$$\text{concentration} = \frac{\text{volume of solute}}{\text{volume of solution}} \times 100\%$$

The units for concentration in this case are % volume.

So if 20 cm³ of alkali were dissolved in 200 cm³ of water:

concentration = 20 ÷ 200 × 100% = 10%

> **3.** Calculate the concentration of a solution of 25 g of sodium chloride added to 100 cm³ of water.
>
> **4.** Calculate the concentration of 10 cm³ of acid in 90 cm³ of water.

FIGURE 2.3.13b: How can the concentration of a solution be determined?

Explaining pressure in liquids and gases ⟫⟫

When gas particles or liquid particles move, they have collisions between themselves and also with the sides of the container they occupy. The **pressure** is a measure of the average force of these collisions over the area of the container's sides. The standard units of pressure are **kilopascals** (kPa).

Higher pressure are applied when there are more particles and, therefore, more collisions with the sides of the container. Also, increasing the temperature causes the particles to move faster. The force of the collisions against the sides of the container is larger and the pressure is higher. The pressure of a gas is proportional to its temperature, as long as the volume remains constant.

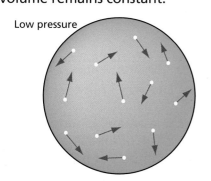 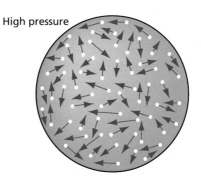

Low pressure   High pressure

FIGURE 2.3.13c: What do we mean by pressure?

> **5.** Suggest one reason why atmospheric pressure is lower on top of a mountain than at sea level.
>
> **6.** Sketch a graph to show the relationship between pressure and temperature.

Did you know...?

The most toxic substance is called botulinum toxin. A concentration of just 0.000 000 0015 g in 1 kg of body weight will kill a person. One sugar-bag size of this toxin would wipe out the human race!

Key vocabulary

concentration

concentrated

dilute

pressure

kilopascal

Exploring diffusion

We are learning how to:

- Use the particle model to explain observations involving diffusion.

Diffusion is a process in which particles move and spread out. Unsurprisingly, gas particles diffuse much faster than particles in other states of matter. What make diffusion so special?

Examples of diffusion

Diffusion occurs because of the movement of particles in a gas or a liquid. There is hardly any diffusion in solids because the particles cannot move freely. Gas particles move faster and further than liquid particles, so diffusion in gases occurs faster than in liquids.

All smells spread as a result of diffusion. When particles of a gas, like air freshener spray or odours from smelly socks, are released into the air, they spread out as far away from each other as possible. These gas particles move through the air – when they reach your nose they are detected as a smell. This is why we can detect smells from a long distance away.

1. Give another example of diffusion in everyday life.

2. Why do smells become weaker the further you are from the source?

Diffusion and the particle model

Concentration is a measure of the number of particles packed in a certain volume.

Diffusion occurs because particles move from an area of high concentration to an area of low concentration, until there is no overall change in concentration. We call this the point of **equilibrium**. The difference in concentration is known as the **concentration gradient**. The higher the concentration gradient, the greater the rate of diffusion, and the quicker equilibrium is reached.

Temperature affects the rate of diffusion because it affects the energy of the particles. The higher the temperature, the higher the kinetic energy of the particles, and the faster they move in such a way as to reduce the concentration gradient.

FIGURE 2.3.14a: If a drop of coloured ink is added to water, after several hours the colour will have spread through the water so that it is of equal concentration throughout.

Did you know...?

The animal kingdom is full of amazing examples of how animals make use of diffusion to smell odours. Elephants can detect water sources up to 20 kilometres away.

3. If a drop of ink is added to some pure water, and a similar drop of ink is added to some dilute ink solution, in which solution would diffusion happen fastest? Explain your answer.

4. Think about these examples of diffusion. Which will reach equilibrium first and why?

   a) Placing a spoonful of coffee in 50 cm³ of hot water

   b) Adding a spoonful of cordial to 50 cm³ of cold water

Explaining diffusion

Look at Figure 2.3.14b. Concentrated ammonia is placed at one end of the tube and concentrated hydrochloric acid at the other end. Particles of ammonia are smaller than particles of hydrochloric acid. When the particles diffuse, they meet and react, forming a white cloud of ammonium chloride.

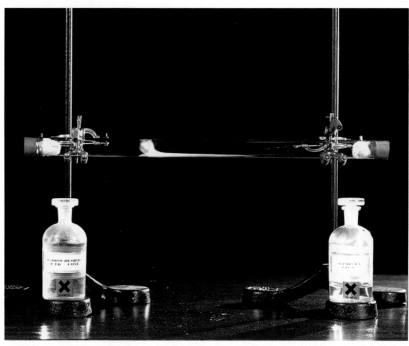

FIGURE 2.3.14b: How do the ammonia particles and hydrochloric acid particles reach each other to react?

5. What would happen if the concentrated solutions were replaced by dilute solutions of both ammonia and hydrochloric acid?

6. How else might the formation of the white ring be speeded up? Explain your answer.

7. Why doesn't the white ring in Figure 2.3.14b form in the centre of the tube?

Key vocabulary

diffusion

equilibrium

concentration gradient

Conserving mass

We are learning how to:

- Use the particle model to explain the Law of Conservation of Mass.

When a given amount of water is frozen to make ice, or boiled to make steam, what happens to the mass?

The Law of Conservation of Mass

In 1789, Antoine Lavoisier, a French chemist, first proposed the **Law of Conservation of Mass**. To do this, he had to carry out thousands of experiments, making very careful measurements. He found that in any **chemical reaction** or **physical change**, the total mass after the reaction was exactly the same as the mass before. His law can be summarised as follows:

'Matter cannot be destroyed, or created, just transformed.'

Notice the similarity between this and the conservation of energy – energy is never lost or created, only transferred by different processes to different places. Much later, Albert Einstein saw a fundamental link between mass and energy.

1. If 100 g of water was placed in a freezer overnight, how much ice will be made?

2. When water is boiled to make steam, why do the mass of the saucepan and its contents decrease over time?

FIGURE 2.3.15a: Antoine Lavoisier first stated the Law of Conservation of Mass.

Conservation of mass and solutions

When 50 cm³ of water is added to 50 cm³ of alcohol, you would expect the total volume to be 100 cm³ – it is in fact less. When you weigh the liquids, you find that the mass of the water and alcohol before is exactly equal to the mass of the water and alcohol afterwards. What is going on?

Look at the particle diagrams in Figure 2.3.15b. You can see that exactly the same numbers of particles of water and alcohol are present before and after they are mixed. However, the mixture takes up less room. This is because the aclohol particles occupy the spaces between the water molecules. The total volume of the mixture is, therefore, less than their combined volumes. Mass, however, is conserved in the change.

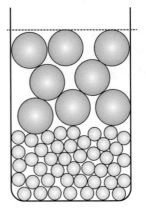
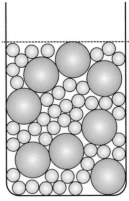

FIGURE 2.3.15b: Volume changes but mass is conserved.

3. You add 20 cm³ of sugar and 80 cm³ of hot water to a measuring cylinder. What is the total volume of the sugar solution formed? Explain your answer.

4. 20 cm³ of sugar has a mass of 14 g. 80 cm³ of water has a mass of 80 g. What is the total mass of the sugar solution? Explain your answer.

Efficiency of a process ⟫

Gold is found chemically uncombined in rocks. Many physical changes are involved in separating the gold from the rock. Figure 2.3.15c gives a simplified summary of these processes.

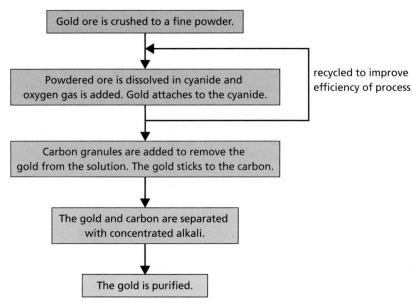

Gold ore is crushed to a fine powder.

↓

Powdered ore is dissolved in cyanide and oxygen gas is added. Gold attaches to the cyanide. → recycled to improve efficiency of process

↓

Carbon granules are added to remove the gold from the solution. The gold sticks to the carbon.

↓

The gold and carbon are separated with concentrated alkali.

↓

The gold is purified.

FIGURE 2.3.15c: Different processes in extracting gold

FIGURE 2.3.15d: Gold ore and purified gold

The Law of Conservation of Mass makes it possible to caculate how much gold you should be able to theoretically make.

We calculate the **efficiency** of a process as follows:

$$\text{efficiency} = \frac{\text{actual yield}}{\text{theoretical yield}} \times 100\%$$

The processes used in the extraction are not 100 per cent efficient. This is because some of the gold particles remain in the rock, or in the cyanide, or on the machinery. It is very difficult to make a separation process perfectly efficient.

5. The overall process is thought to be 95 per cent efficient. What does this mean?

6. Dissolving gold in cyanide is about 50 per cent efficient. If 10 kg of gold ore were put through this process, how much gold would come out?

Did you know...?

As early as 490 BCE, Greek philosphers had formed the idea that 'nothing comes from nothing'. They believed, from observations, that matter could not just be created or destroyed, but must be just transformed.

Key vocabulary

Law of Conservation of Mass

chemical reaction

physical change

efficiency

Deciding between physical and chemical changes

We are learning how to:

- Use the particle model to explain the differences between physical and chemical changes.
- Recognise that mass is conserved in all changes.

The particle model can help to decide whether a physical change or a chemical change has occurred. What other signs are there of these changes?

Signs of a change

All changes of state are called **physical changes** because the atoms and molecules within do not change.

All physical changes are easily **reversible**, which means the orginal state can be achieved by reversing the change. The nature of the atoms and molecules involved in a physical change is not altered – chemically they are the same.

A few physical changes, like dissolving certain solutes, result in a temperature change, but most physical changes do not have an energy change associated with them.

All **chemical changes** are difficult to reverse. They occur as a result of a reaction between reactant chemicals to make new products – they can be summarised by an equation.

Observations that a chemical change has occurred include:

- There may be a colour change.
- A new substance may be formed that has a different state from the reactants. For example, a solid may be formed from two liquids or a gas may be released from reacting a solid and a liquid.
- There may be an energy change. Energy may be given out – this is an **exothermic** process, and there is an increase in temperature. Energy may be taken in – this is an **endothermic** process, and the temperature decreases. Energy transfers can also be caused by light.

FIGURE 2.3.16a: A physical change

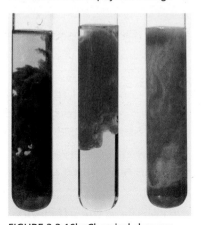

FIGURE 2.3.16b: Chemical changes

1. Identify three common physical changes and three common chemical changes.

2. When colourless acid and alkali are mixed, a colourless solution remains. If indicator is added, there is a colour change. Is this a physical or chemical change?

Did you know...?

Some chemical changes are reversible. The production of ammonia from hydrogen and nitrogen is an example. Under the right conditions, ammonia is made.

Figure 2.3.16c shows some particle diagrams of different changes.

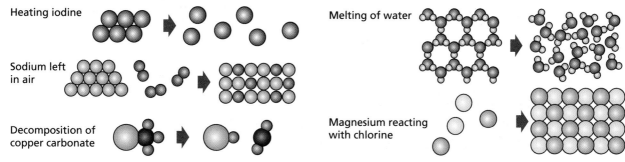

Heating iodine

Melting of water

Sodium left in air

Decomposition of copper carbonate

Magnesium reacting with chlorine

FIGURE 2.3.16c

3. Look at the changes in Figure 2.3.16c. Explain, using ideas about particles, whether a physical or chemical change has taken place in each diagram.

4. Draw two annotated particle diagrams to show a physical change and a chemical change. Write a word equation for your reaction.

Ambiguous changes ➤➤➤

Some changes cannot easily be identified as a physical change or a chemical change – they show signs of both.

Adding ammonium nitrate to water gives a marked temperature decrease – it is an endothermic process. However, the ammonium nitrate is just dissolving. If the mixture is heated, the salt can be recovered – it has not changed chemically.

An alloy has different physical properties from both of its component metals. This might lead you to believe that making an alloy is a chemical change. However, the particles within the alloy have not been changed. Brass is made from 60 per cent copper and 40 per cent zinc. There is no such thing as a brass molecule, and the copper and zinc atoms have not formed chemical bonds.

5. Heating rubber causes changes in its physical properties, making it harder and more rigid. The mass of the rubber does not increase or decrease on heating. Is the change physical or chemical?

6. When sodium chloride is added to water, the solution is able to conduct electricity. Solid sodium chloride cannot conduct. Explain why adding sodium chloride to water is still considered to be a physical change.

FIGURE 2.3.16d: The oxidation of sodium left in air

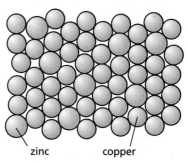

zinc   copper

FIGURE 2.3.16e: Why might you think making an alloy is a chemical change?

Key vocabulary

physical change

reversible

chemical change

exothermic

endothermic

Explaining the properties of mixtures

We are learning how to:

- Use the particle model to explain the properties of mixtures.

Making mixtures is a physical process. This means that the atoms and molecules in the mixture are the same as before they were mixed. However, some of the physical properties of a mixture can be different from the original substances, resulting in useful applications.

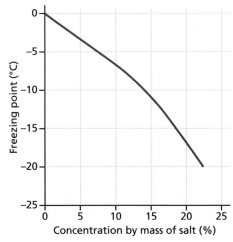

FIGURE 2.3.17a: How the freezing point of water changes with sodium chloride concentration

Changes to boiling point and melting points

Pure water freezes at 0 °C and boils at 100 °C. If salt, sodium chloride, is added to liquid water, the temperatures at which water freezes and boils changes. Figure 2.3.17a shows a graph of how the freezing point is affected by the concentration of salt.

1. What is the freezing point of a 15 per cent salt solution?

2. How does this help to explain why salt is added to roads in the winter?

Emulsions

An **emulsion** is a mixture of two liquids (one water-based, the other oil-based) which do not normally mix. An emulsifier can be added to the mixture to change its properties. The emulsifier has a structure with a water-loving end and an oil-loving end. It allows the two different liquids to be in contact with each other, and they become evenly spread throughout the mixture. This is an important quality in many food products such as mayonnaise, milk, ice cream and salad cream – also in many other products such as paints, moisturising creams, butter and margarine.

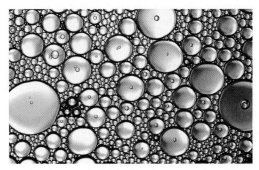

FIGURE 2.3.17b: An emulsion

3. What would happen if the emulsifier was not present in Figure 2.3.17b?

4. Why is it important to use emulsifiers?

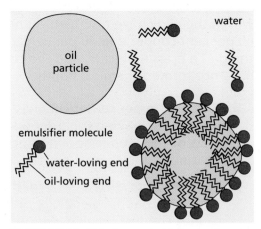

FIGURE 2.3.17c: This shows what is happening at a particle level in an emulsion

When different states of matter are dispersed together, this is known as a **colloid**. For example, in an aerosol there may be particles of liquid or solid spread about in a gas. When an aerosol is sprayed, the gas particles help to move the liquid or solid particles to where they need to be applied.

Foams are a mixture of gas bubbles trapped inside a liquid. Blowing bubbles is an example of making a foam.

Figure 2.3.17d shows some soap that has been made into a foam by heating it in a microwave. The particles of the soap have not been changed, but air and water vapour have been added to the soapy mixture.

FIGURE 2.3.17d: How are the soap foam and the bar of soap different?

Foaming changes the properties of the original liquid by making it much less dense and increasing the surface area. This has many useful applications. Foams filled with carbon dioxide gas are effective at preventing oxygen getting to a fire, because carbon dioxide is more dense than oxygen. Oil spill fires are treated using special foams.

FIGURE 2.3.17e: Fighting a fire with foam

A **gel** is a mixture of liquid particles floating in a solid. Examples include hair gel, jelly and gelatin. The liquid particles make the solid structure less rigid, and easier to spread more accurately. Some eye ointments are in the form of gels – they are easier to apply and do not run.

> **5.** Describe two other uses each of foams, gels and aerosols.
>
> **6.** Draw a particle model of a foam, an aerosol and a gel.

Did you know...?

'Aerofoam' is a gas–solid colloid. It was first made in the 1930s. It is the lightest solid known, and is the best solid thermal insulator.

FIGURE 2.3.17f: With a blow torch underneath, the flower on top of the aerofoam does not burn.

Key vocabulary

emulsion

colloid

foam

gel

Using particle models

We are learning how to:

- Use 'good enough' particle models to explain different observations.

You have learnt that the particle model is a 'good enough' model for explaining most changes of state. How good is it at explaining other phenomena and observations related to physical and chemical changes?

Explaining separation processes

You may remember using different separation techniques like filtration, chromatography and distillation. The **particle model** can be used to explain how these work, but some adaptations may be needed because it has some limitations.

The particle model cannot:

- distinguish between different types of particles, unless they are given different colours
- show what kinds of atoms are in the molecules
- show different intermolecular forces between particles.

The particle model needs to be adapted to explain particular phenomena – so it can be a 'good enough' model.

Figure 2.3.18a shows the process of distillation, which separates liquids. The particle model has been adapted to explain distillation.

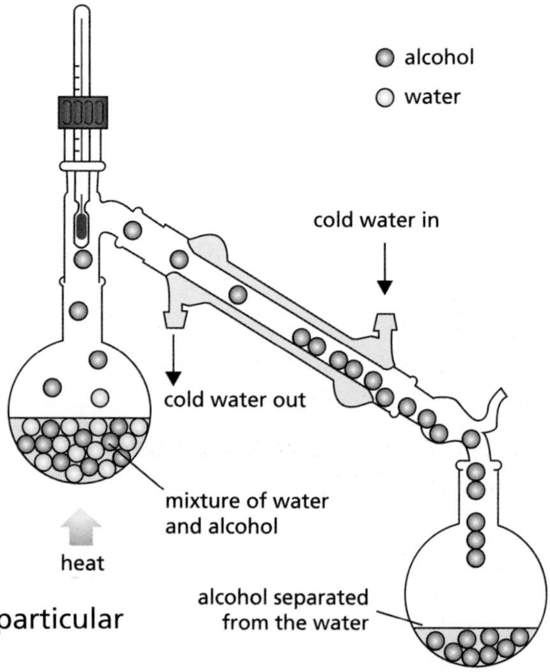

FIGURE 2.3.18a: Explanation of distillation using the particle model

1. How has the particle model been adapted to make it a 'good enough' model?

2. Use a 'good enough' model to explain how filtration works.

Explaining solubility

It is clear that some substances are more soluble than others. As it stands, the particle model is not a 'good enough' model to explain this and needs adapting.

Solute particles have forces of attraction between themselves and between the solvent particles. When the forces of attraction between the solute and solvent are stronger than between the solute particles, then the solute will dissolve. The solute particles fill the spaces between the solvent particles. When all the spaces are filled up, the solution is said to be saturated, because no more solute can be dissolved.

If the temperature is increased, the solvent particles move with more energy, moving further apart and creating more space. More solute can be dissolved at the higher temperature because as there are more gaps that can be filled.

3. Adapt the particle model to explain why some solids are more soluble than others.

4. Can the particle model be used to show how temperature affects solubility? What are the strengths and limitations of the model?

Explaining chemical changes »»»

When calcium carbonate is added to hydrochloric acid, a gas, carbon dioxide, is formed. A chemical change takes place. Models that involve representations of the atoms must be used to explain this. Notice that the same number of atoms must be on both sides of the equation, ensuring that mass is conserved.

Certain standard colours can be used for particular elements as shown in Table 2.3.18.

| calcium carbonate | + | hydrochloric acid | → | calcium chloride | + | carbon dioxide | + | water |
| $CaCO_3$ | + | $2HCl$ | → | $CaCl_2$ | + | CO_2 | + | H_2O |

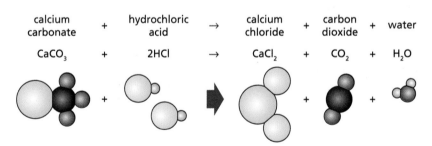

FIGURE 2.3.18b: This shows a 'good enough' particle model to demonstrate the changes when calcium carbonate is added to hydrochloric acid.

5. Use particle model colours from the table to show what would happen when magnesium metal is added to hydrochloric acid (HCl), making magnesium chloride ($MgCl_2$) and hydrogen (H_2). Write a word equation for the reaction first. Think about the conservation of mass.

6. Lead nitrate ($Pb(NO_3)_2$) solution reacts with potassium iodide (KI) solution to make lead iodide (PbI_2) and potassium nitrate (KNO_3). Write a word equation for the reaction. Think about the conservation of mass and use a particle model to show the reaction.

TABLE 2.3.18: Colours for elements in the particle model

Common elements	Colour for atom
hydrogen	white
oxygen	red
carbon	black
chlorine	green
nitrogen	blue
bromine	brown
sulfur	yellow
iodine	purple
metals, e.g. sodium, calcium	grey

Key vocabulary

particle model

Checking your progress

To make good progress in understanding science you need to focus on these ideas and skills.

- Compare the properties of solids, liquids and gases.

- Draw circle diagrams to demonstrate the differences between the arrangement of particles in solids, liquids and gases, and describe their different properties.

- Use particle diagrams to explain the differences in energy and forces between the particles in different states of matter, accounting for differences in their properties.

- Recognise how theories are developed.

- Use observations to develop hypotheses.

- Change hypotheses in the light of new evidence and use this evidence to develop theories.

- Use correct terminology and the particle model to describe changes of state, including evaporation.

- Interpret and explain data relating to melting and boiling points.

- Use the particle model to explain latent heat and how impurities affect melting and boiling points.

- Describe how solids, liquids and gases behave when heat is applied to them.

- Describe applications and problems caused by thermal expansion.

- Use the particle model to explain expansion in solids, liquids and gases.

- Describe a model that can be used to represent particles.

- Apply and adapt models to make them more suitable for use.

- Evaluate the strengths and limitations of particle models.

- Make predictions about floating and sinking using ideas about density.

- Use the particle model to explain density differences between gases and calculate the density of solids.

- Use the particle model to explain factors relating to density.

- [ ] Make predictions about floating and sinking using ideas about density.

- [ ] Use the particle model to explain the density differences between gases and calculate the density of solids.

- [ ] Use the particle model to explain factors relating to density.

- [ ] Describe what is meant by the terms 'concentration' and 'pressure'.

- [ ] Calculate concentrations of solutions.

- [ ] Use ideas about particles to explain the effects of pressure.

- [ ] Describe how diffusion occurs in liquids and gases.

- [ ] Explain observations relating to diffusion in terms of particles.

- [ ] Make predictions, using ideas about particles, about factors affecting the rate of diffusion.

- [ ] Describe features of physical and chemical changes, recognising how mass is conserved.

- [ ] Use ideas about particles to describe separation processes.

- [ ] Apply the particle model to explain physical and chemical changes, taking conservation of mass into account.

- [ ] Describe different types of colloids.

- [ ] Explain the properties of different colloids using the particle model.

- [ ] Evaluate the particle model in its ability to explain colloids and their properties.

- [ ] Use particle models to describe different separation processes.

- [ ] Use particle models to explain how the solubility of solids and gases changes with temperature.

- [ ] Evaluate the effectiveness of the particle model in explaining physical changes.

Questions

See how well you have understood the ideas in the chapter.

1. Which of the following statements is true? [1]

    a) Particles in a solid have more energy than particles in a liquid.

    b) Particles in a gas have weaker intermolecular forces than particles in a liquid.

    c) Particles in a liquid have more internal energy than particles in solids and gases.

    d) Particles in a solid do not have any internal energy because they do not move.

2. What does diffusion depend on? A difference in: [1]

    a) temperature   b) state   c) concentration   d) mass

3. Which of these relates to a physical change and not a chemical change? [1]

    a) The change is reversible.   b) New chemicals are made.

    c) Colour changes are seen.   d) Mass is conserved.

4. A foam is a mixture of: [1]

    a) a liquid and a solid   b) two solids

    c) two liquids   d) a gas and a liquid

5. Describe the evidence that Robert Brown collected which led to the theory of Brownian motion. [2]

6. Describe, using ideas about particles, how temperature affects the viscosity of liquids. [2]

7. Explain, using ideas about particles, what is unusual about the change in density of water as it freezes. [4]

See how well you can apply the ideas in this chapter to new situations.

8. Iron has a melting point of 1535 °C and a boiling point of 2750 °C. At which temperature will iron be a liquid? [1]

    a) 2752 °C   b) 2751 °C   c) 1534 °C   d) 1536 °C

9. The density of water is 1 g/cm³ and that of syrup is 1.3 g/cm³. Which of the following statements is false? [1]

    a) In a mixture of syrup and water, the water will float on top.

    b) The syrup is more dense than the water.

    c) In a mixture of syrup and water, the syrup will float on top.

    d) There is more mass per unit volume in syrup than in water.

10. Figure 2.3.20a shows the particles of different substances. Which particle diagram represents a shaving foam aerosol? [1]

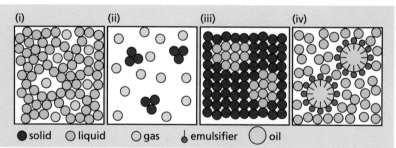

FIGURE 2.3.20a   ● solid   ○ liquid   ○ gas   ⦙ emulsifier   ○ oil

11. Which of the following is *not* a reason for using carbon dioxide gas in fire extinguishers? [1]

    a) It is more dense than air.   **b)** It is not flammable.

    c) It sublimes.   **d)** It can flow.

12. A particular type of hand warmer uses calcium chloride and water. Energy is transferred in the process by heat. How would you prove this is a physical change and not a chemical change? [2]

13. Ammonium nitrate and water can be used to make fertiliser. Tomato plants require a concentration of 20 mg/l. You have 250 cm³ of water. How much ammonium nitrate should you add? [2]

14. Aerosol cans have a warning on them to prevent their use on fires. Explain reasons for this, using ideas about particles. [4]

Questions 15–16

See how well you can understand and explain new ideas and evidence.

15. Butane (C_4H_{10}) is camping fuel. Its boiling point is –1 °C. Hydrogen (H_2) is also a fuel, with a boiling point of –252 °C. Both fuels are transported under pressure, turning them into a liquid so that more particles can be carried. Explain which fuel will be easier to transport in this way and why. [2]

16. Figure 2.3.20b shows how the temperature changes over time for a new substance called xmenium.

    a) What information about this new material does the graph provide?

    b) Xmenium is going through trials to see if it can be used in a heat pack (see Topic 3.10). Use the graph to explain whether it is suitable or not, and what could be done to improve its properties. [4]

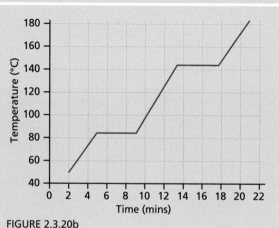

FIGURE 2.3.20b

Explaining Chemical Changes

Ideas you have met before

The particle model

Matter is made of particles, and we can describe these particles in terms of atoms and molecules.

We can represent atoms and molecules in particle pictures.

During a chemical change, atoms and molecules are rearranged. This can be shown using particle pictures.

Chemical changes

Changes can occur when materials are mixed. Some of these changes are non-reversible – these are called chemical changes, or chemical reactions.

Mixing bicarbonate of soda with vinegar and making toast are chemical changes – you cannot get the original materials back.

The new materials made in chemical changes can be useful.

Burning

Burning materials (such as wood, wax and gas) produces new materials.

Burning is usually a chemical change. Burning is also known as combustion.

In this chapter you will find out

Acids, alkalis and indicators

- We use acids in our everyday lives, such as in food and batteries.

- We use alkalis in our everyday lives, such as in cleaning products and medicines.

- Some acids and alkalis are hazardous.

- We can make and use indicators to show how acidic or alkaline a substance is.

- The pH scale is an important measure of the level of acidity and alkalinity of a substance.

Reactions of acids and alkalis

- Acids react with metals, with carbonates and with alkalis.

- In these reactions the particles are rearranged – we can show this using diagrams, equations and other models.

- A neutral substance is one with pH 7. It is made when an acid and an alkali exactly neutralise one another.

- Neutralisation reactions can be useful for our health.

Combustion

- We can control combustion by understanding what is needed for substances to burn.

- Combustion changes the atmosphere because of the new products that are formed.

- Air pollution from combustion can cause rain to become acidic and cause environmental problems.

Exploring acids

We are learning how to:

- Recognise acids used in everyday life.
- Describe what all acids have in common.
- Identify the hazards that acids pose.

Acids are often thought of as dangerous substances. Indeed, many acids *are* dangerous and we must take precautions when handling them. However, we come across many acids in our daily life that are useful and not dangerous at all.

Useful acids

If you look around your kitchen, you may find some **acids** to eat or drink.

Citrus fruits such as lemons and oranges contain citric acid. Vinegar, which is used to pickle foods or to flavour chips, contains ethanoic acid. Fizzy drinks contain carbonic acid. Tea contains tannic acid.

Acids also have industrial uses. Sulfuric acid is used in car batteries and in making fertilisers. Nitric acid can also be used in making fertilisers and in paints.

1. List some examples of acids that we have in our homes.

2. Describe two acids that may be used to make fertilisers.

3. Suggest what taste acids have in common.

FIGURE 2.4.2a: Which acid is found in each of these?

Considering the hazards

Concentrated acids, such as concentrated sulfuric acid, are extremely dangerous. These acids are **corrosive** – this means that the acid can destroy skin and attack metals if spilled.

The types of acid that are often used in science lessons are dilute acids – this means that they have had water added to them. Dilute acids are not as dangerous as concentrated acids. They are not corrosive but may be an **irritant** to the skin. Your skin might become red and blistered if some acid was spilled on it.

Acids that are found in food and drink, such as in lemons and vinegar, are extremely weak and dilute. This is why they are safe to eat and drink, whereas dilute hydrochloric acid is not. However, they may still sting if they get into a cut.

4. Explain why is it better to use images on hazard labels, rather than words.

5. Suggest why you usually use dilute acids in school practical experiments, rather than concentrated acids.

6. Describe the precautions that you should take when working with an acid that displays the hazard symbol.

7. Explain why concentrated acids are more dangerous than dilute acids.

What do acids have in common? >>>

Some acids taste sour. Some acids are weak enough that we can eat or drink them. Some acids would burn your skin. However, one thing that *all* acids have in common is that they contain the element **hydrogen**. We can show this by looking at the chemical formulas of acids:

Hydrochloric acid, HCl – this shows that the acid contains hydrogen and chlorine.

Sulfuric acid, H_2SO_4 – this shows that the acid contains hydrogen, sulfur and oxygen.

FIGURE 2.4.2b: 'Corrosive' hazard sign

FIGURE 2.4.2c: 'Harmful' hazard sign, which is used for substances that are not corrosive but are irritants.

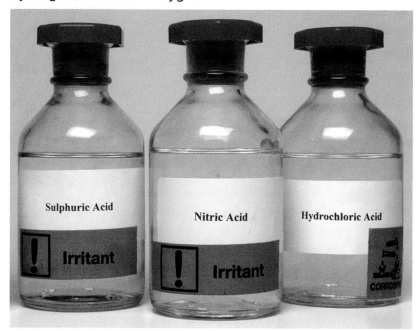

FIGURE 2.4.2d: Which element do all of these acids contain?

8. The chemical formula for nitric acid is HNO_3. Which elements does nitric acid contain?

9. A sour-tasting substance is found to contain the elements oxygen, sulfur and hydrogen. Suggest whether or not this is an acid and explain your reasoning.

Did you know…?

Your stomach contains hydrochloric acid, which helps to digest food and kill bacteria. You can feel this acid burning your throat slightly when you vomit.

Key vocabulary

acid

corrosive

irritant

hydrogen

Exploring alkalis

We are learning how to:

- Recognise alkalis used in everyday life.
- Describe what all alkalis have in common.
- Identify the hazards that alkalis pose.

Many of the cleaning products that we use have something in common – they all contain an alkali. It is the alkali that gives soap, shampoo and washing powder a soapy feeling. We have alkalis all around us and life would be very different without them.

Useful alkalis

Some **alkalis** are harmful. However, many alkalis are harmless and are very useful.

Many cleaning products – such as bleach, oven cleaner, disinfectant and washing powder – contain alkalis. Toiletries such as soap, shampoo and toothpaste also contain an alkali. Even some medicines such as indigestion remedies contain alkalis.

When you bake a cake, you use baking powder to ensure that the cake is light and fluffy. Baking powder contains an alkali called sodium hydrogencarbonate (sodium bicarbonate). Without it, your cakes would be like biscuits!

FIGURE 2.4.3a: Many cleaning products contain an alkali.

1. Name some alkaline cleaning products.

2. Name two alkalis that are safe to put in your mouth and two that are not.

3. Suggest how your life would change if there were no alkalis.

What do alkalis have in common?

Most alkalis feel **soapy** to touch. Soap forms because the alkali reacts with fats on your skin. However, some alkalis are too harmful to put on your skin. The common feature of all alkalis is that they contain **hydroxide** particles (chemical symbol OH).

Sodium hydroxide, NaOH, is the alkali used in many cleaning products, such as oven cleaners. Calcium hydroxide, $Ca(OH)_2$, is an alkali used by gardeners when their soil is too acidic. Both of these products would be harmful if you swallowed

FIGURE 2.4.3b: Which alkali does baking powder contain?

them. Magnesium hydroxide is the weak alkali found in many indigestion remedies.

4. What is the common feature of all alkalis?

5. Which elements are contained in:

   a) calcium hydroxide?

   b) sodium hydroxide?

6. Suggest what the chemical formula for magnesium hydroxide is.

Dangerous alkalis »»»

Many of the alkalis in our homes are dangerous. The most dangerous alkalis include oven cleaners and caustic soda (to unblock drains). These substances are corrosive – they both contain the alkali sodium hydroxide.

FIGURE 2.4.3c: Which alkali do both of these products contain?

Other alkalis are classed as an irritant, rather than corrosive. Examples are bleach and disinfectant.

Alkalis are often more dangerous than acids given the same hazard classification. This is because it can be hard to rinse an alkali from the skin because it becomes soapy.

7. Bleach often has 'irritant' written in braille on the bottle. Suggest why this is important.

8. Draw the hazard symbol that would be found on a bottle of bleach.

9. Bleach contains sodium hydroxide and another chemical, sodium hypochlorite. Bleach is dangerous, but caustic soda is even more dangerous. Suggest why.

Did you know...?

In the past, stale urine was used as a source of the alkali ammonium hydroxide. It was used to bleach and clean clothes – it was even used in toothpaste!

Key vocabulary

alkali

soapy

hydroxide

Using indicators

We are learning how to:

- Use indicators to identify acids and alkalis.
- Analyse data from different indicators.
- Compare the effectiveness of different indicators.

The traffic indicators on a car tell other vehicles when the car is going to turn. Indicators in science can show us whether a substance is an acid or an alkali. Nature is full of natural indicators and we can make use of these indicators in many ways.

What are indicators? ⟫

An **indicator** is a substance that has different colours in an acid and in an alkali. One example of an indicator is **litmus**. Litmus solution turns *red in acid* and *blue in alkali*. If a solution is neither an acid nor an alkali, we say it is **neutral.**

Litmus paper is sometimes easier to use than litmus solution. Blue litmus paper turns red in an acid; red litmus paper turns blue in an alkali.

FIGURE 2.4.4a: What colour is litmus in a neutral solution?

FIGURE 2.4.4b: Litmus paper is easy to use.

1. Describe what an indicator is.

2. Describe the colour changes of litmus solution in an acid and an alkali.

3. Draw a table to show the colours in acid, alkali and neutral of:

   a) red litmus paper   b) blue litmus paper.

Uses of indicators

Most flower, fruit and plant parts that are red, blue or purple can be used as an indicator. This is because these parts of a plant contain chemicals called anthocyanins that change colour in acids and alkalis. The real purpose of these chemicals is to preserve nutrients in the winter. However, we can use these chemical indicators in other ways.

Gardeners can use indicators to test soils. This is useful because some plants prefer acidic soils while others prefer alkaline soils. Home swimming pools should be kept at around neutral. Indicators can be used to check that water has not become acidic or alkaline. Industries can use indicators to check that the liquid waste that they dispose of is not acidic or alkaline. For example, photographic industries use indicators in this way.

4. Describe three uses of indicators.

5. Explain why most red, purple or blue flowers can be used to make indicators.

FIGURE 2.4.4c: Most red and purple flowers can be used to make an indicator.

What does the indicator show? »»»

A group of students made indicators from different plants. They then checked the colour change of each indicator in acid and alkali. They recorded their results.

TABLE 2.4.4: Which is the most useful indicator?

Plant used to make indicator	Colour of indicator	Colour in acid	Colour in alkali
red cabbage	purple	red	green
beetroot	red	red	purple
cherries	red	red	blue

6. An indicator made from red cabbage turned green in an unknown liquid. Explain what this tells us.

7. An indicator made from beetroot stayed red when added to another unknown liquid. Does this mean that the unknown liquid is an acid?

8. Compare the results given by each of the indicators. Suggest which is the most useful indicator.

Did you know...?

Baking powder can also be used as an indicator. It does not show any colour change but it does fizz when added to an acid, but not when added to an alkali or to water.

Key vocabulary

indicator

litmus

neutral

Using universal indicator

We are learning how to:

- Describe what the pH scale measures.
- Measure and record pH values.
- Identify the advantages of universal indicator.

Some acids, such as sulfuric acid, are corrosive and can burn the skin. Other acids, such as orange juice, are so weakly acidic that we can drink them. Sometimes we need to know how strong or weak an acid is. We cannot make a strong acid weak by diluting it – even dilute sulfuric acid, which we use in school laboratories, is still a strong, harmful acid. But concentrated orange juice is not corrosive or harmful!

FIGURE 2.4.5a: Orange juice contains a weak acid.

Are all acids the same?

If oven cleaner got on your skin, it would burn. This is because it contains a **strong alkali**. Soap also contains an alkali but you can of course put this safely on your skin. This is because soap contains a **weak alkali**.

Sulfuric acid is used when preparing skeletons because it can remove flesh from bones – it is a **strong acid**. Ethanoic acid is found in vinegar – it is a **weak acid**.

1. Give an example of a:

   a) strong acid   **b)** weak acid

   c) strong alkali   **d)** weak alkali.

2. Explain why we can put vinegar and orange juice in our mouths, but not sulfuric acid.

FIGURE 2.4.5b: Oven cleaner contains a strong alkali, sodium hydroxide.

Using universal indicator

Most chemical indicators just tell us whether a substance is an acid or an alkali. **Universal indicator** turns a range of different colours. The colour depends on whether the substance is an acid or an alkali *and* on how strong or weak it is. Each colour is given a **pH number**.

On the pH scale:

- neutral solutions are pH 7
- acidic solutions are lower than pH 7
- alkaline solutions are higher than pH 7

Did you know…?

The pH scale was invented in 1909 by a Danish chemist, Søren Sørensen. It is thought that 'pH' may stand for 'power of hydrogen', linked with the fact that all acids contain hydrogen.

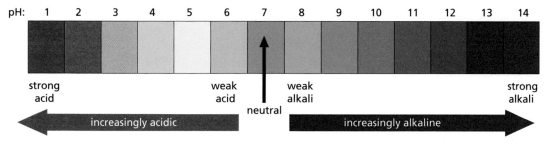

FIGURE 2.4.5c: The pH scale ranges from pH 1 to pH 14.

3. Universal indicator is added to a liquid and it changes to yellow. State the pH of the liquid.

4. Describe what happens to the strength of an acid as the pH number decreases.

5. Describe what happens to the strength of an alkali as the pH number increases.

Comparing indicators

Litmus indicator turns red in acid and blue in alkali. Red cabbage indicator turns red in acid and purple in alkali.

Universal indicator is a mixture of several different indicators. This means that it gives a full range of predictable colours, depending on the strength of the acid or alkali.

TABLE 2.4.5: Universal indicator shows the strength of different acids and alkalis.

Substance	pH	Acidic or alkaline?
hydrochloric, nitric and sulfuric acids, and car battery acid	0–1	strongly acidic
phosphoric acid	1–2	acidic
citrus fruit, such as lemons and oranges; vinegar	4	acidic
distilled water	7	neutral
egg, hand soap	8	alkaline
ammonia	11	alkaline
oven cleaner	12	alkaline
caustic soda, paint stripper	13–14	strongly alkaline

6. Describe what colour litmus indicator would turn if added to:

a) hydrochloric acid

b) vinegar.

7. Explain the advantages of using universal indicator over litmus or red cabbage indicator.

Key vocabulary

strong/weak alkali

strong/weak acid

universal indicator

pH number

Exploring neutralisation

We are learning how to:

- Describe examples of neutralisation.
- Use indicators to identify chemical reactions.
- Explain colour changes in terms of pH and neutralisation.

The pain of a nettle sting can be eased by rubbing the sting with a dock leaf. Nettles contain a weak acid and dock leaves contain a weak alkali. The alkali 'cancels out' the acid. This is called neutralisation and there are many other examples around us.

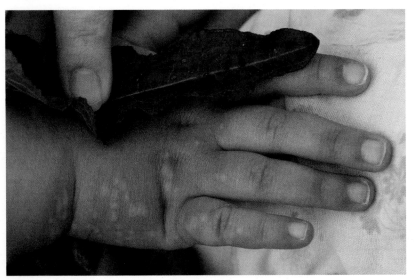

FIGURE 2.4.6a: Why does a dock leaf help with a nettle sting?

> **Did you know...?**
>
> Bee stings are acidic and are treated by neutralising the acid with a mild alkali, such as bicarbonate of soda. Wasp stings are slightly alkaline and are treated by neutralising with an acid, such as vinegar. Therefore, it is important to know what has stung you.

Mixing acids and alkalis

As we add an alkali to acid, the molecules in the acid and alkali react. The resulting solution becomes less acidic (the pH increases) as we add more alkali. It is almost as if the alkali 'cancels out' the acid. This reaction between acids and alkalis is called **neutralisation**.

If we add just the right amount of alkali, the solution will become exactly neutral.

1. Describe what is meant by 'neutralisation'.

2. Describe what happens to the pH of an acidic solution as an alkali is added. Explain your answer.

3. Describe what would happen to the pH of an alkaline solution if an acid were added.

Neutralisation in action

There are examples of neutralisation reactions all around us. Our saliva is alkaline and it neutralises some of the acid made by bacteria in our mouth. We also neutralise the acid by using toothpaste, which is also alkaline. Heartburn is caused by acid from the stomach. Antacid tablets contain an alkali that neutralises the acid. Industries such as textile and paper factories produce lots of alkaline liquid waste. This is neutralised with acid before it is disposed of.

4. Explain why alkaline waste from industries must be neutralised before it is released into lakes and rivers.

5. Summarise some applications of neutralisation in a table. For example:

Situation	Neutralised by
stomach acid	antacid tablets

FIGURE 2.4.6b: The alkali in toothpaste neutralises acid that could decay the teeth.

Demonstrating neutralisation

We can use indicators to demonstrate neutralisation in action. If universal indicator is added to an alkali, it turns purple. If some acid is then added, the colour changes. If the solution becomes neutral, the solution would eventually be green.

We can use a technique called **titration** to mix acids and alkalis precisely. This allows us the see a whole range of colour changes.

A burette allows an acid to be added to an alkali gradually. If the acid is added slowly enough, the neutral point (pH 7) can be seen. This point is indicated by the solution turning green.

6. Describe the colour changes that would be seen in the conical flask as the solution changed from a strong alkali to neutral.

7. Suggest what would be seen if more acid was added after the neutral point was reached. Explain your answer.

8. Explain the benefits of using a burette, rather than dropping pipettes, to add the acid.

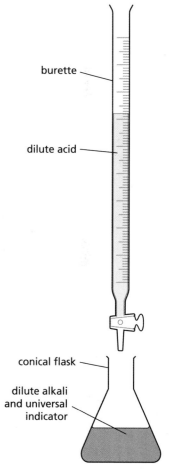

burette

dilute acid

conical flask

dilute alkali and universal indicator

FIGURE 2.4.6c: Titration can be used to carry out a neutralisation reaction precisely.

Key vocabulary

neutralisation

titration

Explaining neutralisation

We are learning how to:

- Recall the equation for a neutralisation reaction.
- Explain how water is made during a neutralisation reaction.
- Apply a model to explain neutralisation.

Acids and alkalis 'cancel each other out'. We see a change in colour of indicator when we mix them. This change is a chemical reaction, with new products being formed. A model may help us to understand what is happening during the reaction.

Making water

All acids contain hydrogen, so the symbol H will appear in the formula – for example, hydrochloric acid is HCl. All alkalis contain both hydrogen and oxygen so the formula will have both O and H. We call this combination 'hydroxide' – for example sodium hydroxide is NaOH. When acids and alkalis are mixed a *chemical reaction* takes place, with new products being formed.

The hydrogen and the hydroxide combine to form water, H_2O. **Water** is a product of neutralisation.

Acids have a low pH and alkalis have a high pH. Water is **neutral**. Therefore there is a change in pH as we mix acids and alkalis.

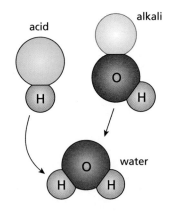

FIGURE 2.4.7a: H in acid and OH in alkali combine to form water, H_2O.

1. Name one of the new products formed when acids and alkalis mix.

2. Describe what combines from each of the acid and the alkali to form water.

3. Suggest the pH of pure water.

The neutralisation equation

Water is just one of the products of neutralisation. The other product is a **salt**. The type of salt produced depends on the acid and alkali that were reacted. We can describe neutralisation using an **equation**:

> acid + alkali → salt + water

For example, if hydrochloric acid is neutralised with the alkali sodium hydroxide, the salt produced is sodium chloride.

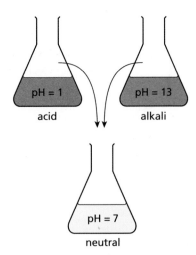

FIGURE 2.4.7b: Neutralisation

4. Write the general equation for neutralisation.

5. Name the product of neutralisation that:

   a) is always the same

   b) depends on the acid and alkali used.

6. Describe the two new products that are formed when hydrochloric acid is mixed with sodium hydroxide

A model for neutralisation ⟩⟩⟩

In science, models are often useful for helping us to understand something that we cannot see or touch. We cannot see or touch the individual molecules in an acid and an alkali – so, it can be difficult to understand the reactions that are going on.

In Figure 2.4.7c, hydrogen is shown as a red brick and oxygen is shown as a yellow brick. The rest of the acid is shown as black bricks and the rest of the alkali is shown as blue bricks.

FIGURE 2.4.7c: Which bricks represent the acid?

7. Explain why models, such as this one, are used in science.

8. Using the building bricks model, draw:

   a) the water produced

   b) the salt produced.

9. Another type of model uses circles to represent atoms and molecules. Use the model in Figure 2.4.7d to draw the products of the reaction between hydrochloric acid (HCl) and sodium hydroxide (NaOH).

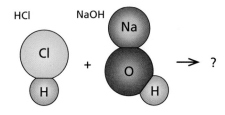

FIGURE 2.4.7d: What are the products of this reaction?

Did you know...?

Pure water is neutral. However, our drinking water is usually slightly acidic or slightly alkaline. This is because this water contains dissolved minerals and gases.

Key vocabulary

water

neutral

salt

equation

Understanding salts

We are learning how to:

- Name examples of salts.
- Describe the uses of common salts.
- Predict the reactants used in and the salts made by different neutralisation reactions.

We usually think of 'salt' as something that we add to food. The scientific name for this type of salt is sodium chloride. However, there are many more types of salt, each with different uses.

Salts and their uses

A **salt** is made in a neutralisation reaction, along with water. The most common salt is sodium chloride. It has many uses – flavouring food, treating icy roads and as a food preservative. Sodium chloride is essential in the human body. In industry, sodium chloride is used to produce chlorine, hydrogen and sodium hydroxide and each of these then have important uses.

Magnesium chloride is used in the manufacture of cement and can also be used to absorb dust in places such as excavation sites. Iron sulfate is used by gardeners to kill moss on lawns. Calcium sulfate is used to make plaster of Paris to treat fractures.

1. Describe four uses of sodium chloride.

2. List three other examples of salts and describe their uses.

3. Write a definition of a salt.

Making predictions

The salt made during a neutralisation reaction can be predicted.

The first part of the name of the salt comes from the alkali, usually from the metal in the alkali. For example, the alkali sodium hydroxide forms salts that start with 'sodium', whereas magnesium hydroxide forms salts that start with 'magnesium'.

The second part of the name of the salt comes from the acid. Table 2.4.8 summarises the ends of the salt names for each of the common acids.

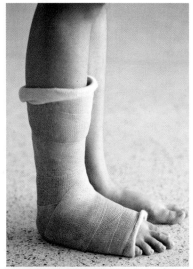

FIGURE 2.4.8a: There are many types of salts, with far more uses than making your food tasty!

TABLE 2.4.8: The acid used tells us the end of the salt name.

Acid used in neutralisation	forms salts that end in...
hydrochloric acid	chloride
sulfuric acid	sulfate
nitric acid	nitrate

So, if nitric acid is neutralised by copper carbonate, the salt formed will be called copper nitrate.

4. Suggest what the first part of the name of the salt will be if the alkali used is calcium carbonate.

5. Predict the name of the salt formed in a neutralisation reaction between hydrochloric acid and sodium hydroxide.

6. Write an equation for the reaction between hydrochloric acid and magnesium hydroxide.

Bases and neutralisation

A **base** is any substance that neutralises an acid to produce a salt and water. An alkali is a soluble base – one that dissolves in water. Therefore, all alkalis are bases, but not all bases are alkalis. Copper oxide is an example of a base. Sodium hydroxide is an example of a base that is also an alkali.

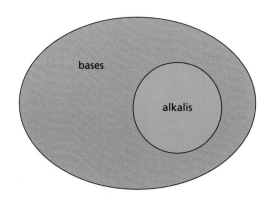

FIGURE 2.4.8b: All alkalis are bases, but only soluble bases are alkalis.

7. Explain the difference between a base and an alkali.

8. Explain why copper oxide is a base, whereas sodium hydroxide is also an alkali.

9. Write an equation for the reaction between an acid and a base. Compare this with the reaction of an acid and an alkali.

Key vocabulary

salt

base

Exploring the reactions of acids with metals

We are learning how to:

- Describe the reaction between acids and metals.
- Explain the reaction between acids and metals.
- Compare the reactivities of different metals.

Most metals react with acids. The way that a metal reacts varies, depending on its reactivity. Some metals are so reactive that we would never add some acid to them in the laboratory.

Reacting acids with metals

A **chemical reaction** is one in which new products are made. There are clues that we can look for to spot a chemical reaction. These include:

- bubbles of gas being given off
- a change in temperature
- a colour change
- a change in mass.

When we add an acid to most metals, we see bubbles. This is because a gas is produced during the reaction. We may also feel the test tube getting warmer. These observations are both evidence that a chemical reaction has taken place.

1. Describe some of the observations that tell us that a chemical reaction is taking place.

2. Describe two signs that the reaction between an acid and a metal is a chemical reaction.

3. Explain why bubbles are produced during reactions.

What are the new products?

Acids react with most metals. Just like when acids react with alkalis, a **salt** is formed. However, water is *not* formed, unlike in neutralisation. Instead, a gas is formed – gas is **hydrogen**. You can test for hydrogen gas because it burns with a 'pop'. If you put a lighted splint into the top of the test tube in which an acid and metal are reacting, you will hear a 'pop' sound. This is because the flame ignites the hydrogen and it explodes.

FIGURE 2.4.9a: How can you tell that a chemical reaction is taking place between the acid and magnesium?

We can summarise the reaction between acids and metals using an equation:

$$\text{acid} + \text{metal} \rightarrow \text{salt} + \text{hydrogen}$$

The salt produced depends on the type of acid and the metal used. For example, if you react nitric acid with copper metal, copper nitrate is the salt formed.

FIGURE 2.4.9b: Copper nitrate

4. Write an equation for the reaction between nitric acid and copper metal.

5. Write an equation for the reaction between hydrochloric acid and magnesium metal.

6. Explain why we should not put a flame near a large amount of hydrogen gas.

Comparing reactivity ▶▶▶

A group of students reacted hydrochloric acid with some different metals. They recorded their observations about the **reactivity** of the acid with the metals.

Metal	Observations when acid added
zinc	some bubbles
magnesium	vigorous bubbling
iron	a few bubbles
copper	no bubbles

FIGURE 2.4.9c: Results of reactions between hydrochloric acid and some metals

7. Order the metals in terms of reactivity, going from most to least reactive.

8. The teacher told the students that calcium was too reactive to use in this experiment. Suggest what may be seen if acid was added to calcium.

9. Write a word equation for each of the reactions.

Did you know...?

Precious metals such as gold, silver and platinum do not react with acids. They are so unreactive that they stay as pure metals. This is one reason that they are used to make jewellery.

FIGURE 2.4.9d: Precious metals are unreactive.

Key vocabulary

chemical reaction

salt

hydrogen

reactivity

Exploring the reactions of acids with carbonates

We are learning how to:

- Describe the reaction between acids and carbonates.
- Explain the reaction between acids and carbonates.
- Write word equations for the reactions between acids and carbonates.

Some rocks, such as limestone, contain a metal carbonate – limestone contains calcium carbonate. Limestone reacts with acids in a predictable way, and as new products are formed the limestone is eroded.

FIGURE 2.4.10a: Limestone is mainly calcium carbonate.

Evidence for a reaction »

If an acid is mixed with a metal **carbonate**, fizzing is seen. This fizzing is caused by bubbles of a gas made during the reaction.

The gas produced when acids react with a metal carbonate is **carbon dioxide**. You can carry out a test to prove that this gas is carbon dioxide. Carbon dioxide gas turns **limewater** cloudy. If the gas produced during a reaction between an acid and a metal carbonate is bubbled into limewater, the limewater turns cloudy.

1. Name the most common metal carbonate found in rocks.

2. Explain why some rocks fizz when some acid is added to them.

3. Describe how you can prove that the gas made when acids and metal carbonates react is carbon dioxide.

Summarising the reactions »»

Carbonates react with an acid to produce a salt and water. The reaction also makes another product – carbon dioxide gas. The reaction between acids and carbonates can be summarised in an equation.

FIGURE 2.4.10b: Limewater is used to test for carbon dioxide.

acid + metal carbonate → salt + water + carbon dioxide

As with neutralisation and acid–metal reactions, the type of salt produced depends on the types of acid and metal carbonate reacted. For example, if hydrochloric acid is reacted with calcium carbonate, the salt produced is calcium chloride. If hydrochloric acid is reacted with copper carbonate, the salt produced is copper chloride. Water and carbon dioxide are always produced during these reactions.

FIGURE 2.4.10c: Would pure calcium carbonate react faster or slower than pieces of rock?

Did you know...?

Shells contain a high proportion of calcium carbonate. An acid will react with these shells and erode them. You can test this by leaving egg shells standing in vinegar.

4. Write an equation for the reaction between hydrochloric acid and calcium carbonate.

5. Write an equation for the reaction between sulfuric acid and copper carbonate.

6. Suggest how the reaction would change if you used powdered calcium carbonate, rather than a lump of rock. Explain your answer.

A changing mass ⟫⟫

When an acid and a metal carbonate react in an open container, the carbon dioxide produced escapes into the air. The mass in the container decreases. You can plot a graph to show how the mass changes over time.

The reaction is fastest at the start and the mass falls quite quickly. As the acid and the carbonate is used up, the reaction slows down and the graph becomes less steep. When all of the acid or carbonate has reacted, the graph levels off.

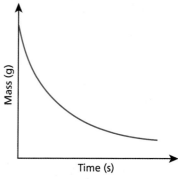

FIGURE 2.4.10d: How the mass changes over time

7. Describe when the mass is changing most quickly.

8. Explain why the graph eventually levels off.

9. Suggest what the graph would look like if the volume of gas was measured, rather than the mass.

Key vocabulary

carbonate

carbon dioxide

limewater

Applying key ideas

You have now met a number of important ideas in this chapter. This activity gives an opportunity for you to apply them, just as scientists do. Read the text first, then have a go at the tasks. The first few are fairly easy – then they get a bit more challenging.

Ever-changing urine

When we visit the doctor, we may be asked to provide a sample of urine. This sample can be used to test for the presence of substances that should not be there, such as sugar and protein. However, the pH of urine is also sometimes measured. This can give medical professionals some clues about what may be wrong with us and how to treat the condition.

The normal pH of urine ranges from 5 to 8, with pH 7.5 being the average. The pH of human urine varies during the day, typically being lower first thing in the morning than at night. Certain conditions can cause the pH of urine to be unusually low or unusually high. For example, high urine pH can be caused by kidney failure or cystitis (a urinary tract infection). Low urine pH can be caused by untreated diabetes or starvation.

The pH of a patient's urine can help to decide which treatment may be best. For example, antibiotics are more effective in treating conditions where the urine is alkaline.

The foods that we eat can affect the pH of our urine. For example, fruits such as cranberries, wine and meat lower the pH. On the other hand, foods such as bananas, chocolate and spinach increase the pH of urine. Certain medications can also affect urine pH. For example, potassium citrate, used to treat kidney stones, can considerably decrease the pH whereas bicarbonate of soda, used to treat indigestion, increases the pH.

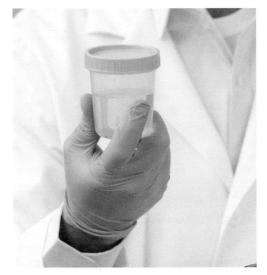

FIGURE 2.4.11a: A urine sample can provide important information about health.

FIGURE 2.4.11b: Turkey and cranberries make urine more acidic; green beans make it more alkaline.

Task 1: Considering the pH

Draw a pH chart. Label the chart to show the approximate pH of urine taken from a healthy patient, a patient with untreated diabetes or starvation, and a patient with untreated kidney failure or cystitis. What colour would a doctor expect to see if universal indicator was used with each sample?

Task 2: Preparing patients for the test

Explain why patients may be asked to stop taking some medicines before they provide a urine sample. Give some examples to explain your answer. How long before the test would you suggest that the medication is stopped? Can you identify any risks with this?

Task 3: Summarising effects on pH

Draw a table to summarise the effects of different conditions, medicines and foods on the pH of urine. Can you add any more examples?

Task 4: Considering the effects of foods

Suggest whether cranberry juice is an acid or an alkali. Explain why cranberry juice is often recommended for patients suffering with cystitis.

Suggest whether chocolate makes urine acidic or alkaline. Can you suggest a drink that could be taken with chocolate to reduce its effect on the pH of urine?

Task 5: Sizing up the effects

Explain why some foods and medicines have a greater effect on how acidic or alkaline the urine is. For example, hydrochloric acid supplements have a bigger effect on pH than wine or cranberries do.

Task 6: Representing the reactions

Wine contains citric acid. Kidney stones are solid lumps of precipitate that form in the kidneys of some people. These may then (painfully) be passed in urine. One chemical in these stones is calcium carbonate. Write a word equation for the reaction between these chemicals.

Discuss why wine may not be effective (or recommended) to remove kidney stones in the body.

Investigating the effectiveness of antacids

We are learning how to:

- Design an investigation to compare the effectiveness of indigestion remedies.
- Analyse data to identify a suitable indigestion remedy.

Heartburn indigestion is caused by acid from the stomach irritating the upper digestive tract. For those who suffer regularly, treatments are available to neutralise this acid. But are some remedies more effective than others?

The need for antacids

The human stomach contains strong hydrochloric acid, with a pH of approximately 1. The role of this acid is to enable the digestion of proteins in the stomach and also to prevent many bacteria from surviving in the stomach. Sometimes the muscle leading from the oesophagus to the stomach can open and the acid moves up along the digestive tract. A burning sensation is then felt in the chest and throat as the acid irritates the lining of the oesophagus. This is called **indigestion** or **heartburn**.

1. Describe what type of acid is found in the stomach and comment on its strength.

2. Describe two reasons why we have acid in the stomach.

3. Explain what heartburn is and what causes it.

Alkalis in action

One of the main treatments for heartburn involves neutralising the acid from the stomach. Medicines that do this are called **antacids**. Antacid remedies contain substances, such as calcium carbonate, aluminium hydroxide and sodium hydrogencarbonate (baking soda). These substances neutralise acids, as alkalis do. However, they do not dissolve in water, as alkalis do, and are known as **bases**. Bases react with acids in a **neutralisation** reaction.

acid + base   →   salt + water

Because the both salt and water are neutral, antacids reduce the acidity of the stomach acid.

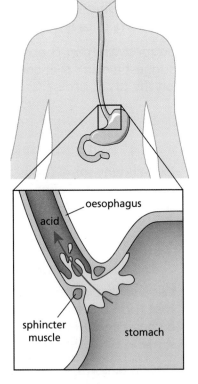

FIGURE 2.4.12a: What causes heartburn?

4. List some of the main ingredients found in heartburn remedies.

5. Explain how antacids reduce the acidity of stomach acid.

6. Suggest the effect of antacid remedies on the pH of stomach acid.

Which remedy? >>>>

A group of students wanted to compare the effectiveness of different commercial antacid remedies. They first added universal indicator to a beaker of hydrochloric acid to check that it was a strong acid (pH 1). They added the recommended dose of each antacid to the acid. The students observed any colour change and noted how long any change took.

TABLE 2.4.12: Results of tests on antacid remedies

Antacid remedy	Colour of universal indicator at end	Change in pH	Time taken for change
'Acid-ban' tablets	yellow	from pH 1 to pH 6	9 minutes
'Acid-ease' liquid	yellow	from pH 1 to pH 6	3 minutes
'Banish burn' tablets	red-orange	from pH 1 to pH 4	5 minutes

TumCalm®

Indigestion relief

Ingredients

Calcium carbonate
Magnesium hydroxide
Gelling agent
Water
Peppermint flavouring
Permitted sweetener
Colouring

FIGURE 2.4.12b: Which bases are found in this remedy?

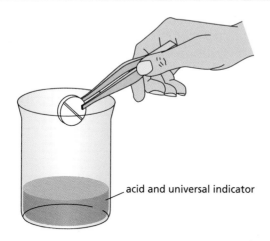

acid and universal indicator

FIGURE 2.4.12c: Antacid remedies were added to acid.

Did you know...?

Even before the chemistry was understood, acid-neutralising remedies were recommended for heartburn. One remedy was to chew limestone rock. We now know that limestone contains the base calcium carbonate.

7. Explain why it was important to start with acid of pH 1.

8. Describe which remedy is the most effective. Explain your answer as fully as possible.

9. Another student suggests that the experiment is repeated using crushed 'Acid-ban' tablets, rather than whole tablets. Suggest how this will affect the time taken to change the pH.

Key vocabulary

indigestion

heartburn

antacid

base

neutralisation

Understanding the importance of acids and alkalis

We are learning how to:

- Classify common useful chemicals as acids or alkalis.
- Explain the importance of acids and alkalis in everyday life.
- Explore common misconceptions about acids and alkalis.

Acids and alkalis are all around us. Some are useful directly, whereas others are useful in making other products in industry. Our lives would be very different without the range of acids and alkalis that we have access to.

More unusual uses of acids and alkalis »

Acids and alkalis are important in ways that are not always obvious. Hydrofluoric acid is used to etch glass. It is suitable for this because the acid dissolves glass without changing the colour of the glass.

Citric acid is commonly used to make medicines taste nicer. It is also used in cigarette papers to make them burn more slowly. Many face cleansers are slightly alkaline, as are soaps. Skin toners, which are designed to be used after cleansers, are slightly acidic. This returns the skin to its preferred pH.

1. Describe two uses of citric acid.

2. Explain why hydrofluoric acid is a suitable choice of acid for glass etching.

3. Describe the type of reaction taking place on the skin when cleanser is used followed by toner.

FIGURE 2.4.13a: Hydrofluoric acid is used to etch glass.

Acids and alkalis in industry »»

Acids and alkalis are an essential part of many industries.

The most common use for nitric acid is in making **fertilisers**. However, nitric acid can also be used to make explosives and nylon. Sulfuric acid is also used on a large scale to make fertilisers. Sulfuric acid has many more industrial uses than any other acid.

Alkalis, such as sodium hydroxide, are used as a reactant in making many other products including soap, paper and ceramics.

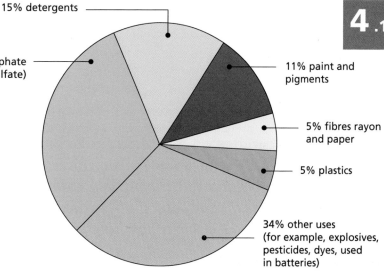

15% detergents

30% fertilisers (ammonium phosphate and ammonium sulfate)

11% paint and pigments

5% fibres rayon and paper

5% plastics

34% other uses (for example, explosives, pesticides, dyes, used in batteries)

4. State the biggest single use for sulfuric acid in industry.

5. Describe a use that both sulfuric acid and sodium hydroxide have in common.

6. Suggest why the production of fertilisers is so important.

FIGURE 2.4.13b: Sulfuric acid has more applications than other acids.

Exploring common misconceptions ⟩⟩⟩

You can see the results of some reactions of acids and alkalis, such as a change in the colour of an indicator or the production of some bubbles of gas. However, you cannot actually *see* what is going on in the reactions in terms of the particles in the acids and alkalis. With abstract concepts like this there are usually **misconceptions** – common ideas that people share that are actually inaccurate.

TABLE 2.4.13

Idea	Why this is a misconception…
All metals react with acids to produce hydrogen gas	This is not true because copper metal does not react with some acids
Acids are corrosive	This is not true because we eat some acids, such as citric acid and ethanoic acid
A gas is always produced in a chemical reaction	

7. Explain what is meant by an 'abstract' idea.

8. Explain why the third idea in Table 2.4.13 is also a misconception.

9. Explain how models may help to understand abstract ideas.

Did you know…?

Boric acid is used in nuclear power stations as a medium in which to store waste. Used rods from the plant are cooled in boric acid as the acid absorbs some of the dangerous radiation.

FIGURE 2.4.13c: Boric acid is used to store nuclear waste.

Key vocabulary

fertiliser

misconception

Exploring combustion

We are learning how to:

- Explain the terms fuel and combustion.
- Recall what is needed for combustion.
- Analyse the fire triangle and apply it to putting out fires.

When you burn candles on a birthday cake or sit around a campfire, you do not often think about the science behind it. Burning is a chemical reaction, forming new products. If you understand the process, you can also learn how to put out fires.

What is combustion?

When you burn wood or coal, new products are made. The reaction is also irreversible – you cannot get the wood or coal back. This means that burning is a **chemical reaction**.

In order to start a fire, you need a **fuel** to burn. A fuel is any material that can be burned to release energy. Examples of fuels are wood and coal. Burning also needs oxygen. Without oxygen, a fire would go out.

The scientific name for burning is **combustion**.

FIGURE 2.4.14a: Coal and wood are examples of fuels.

1. Describe two reasons why burning is a chemical reaction.

2. Describe what is meant by:

   a) combustion   **b)** fuel.

3. Explain why a fire burns more brightly if you fan the flames with air.

Did you know...?

You could not light a fire on the Moon. This is because there is no oxygen gas on the Moon.

The fire triangle ▶▶▶

We can summarise what is needed for combustion using the **fire triangle**.

If any of the three components of the fire triangle are missing, combustion cannot happen. You can use this information when you are trying to light a fire or put a fire out.

When lighting a barbeque, a match may be used as the source of heat to start the fire. The fuel used in a barbeque is often charcoal (made from charred wood). As long as oxygen is available, the charcoal will then burn. When you need to put out the barbeque fire, you could:

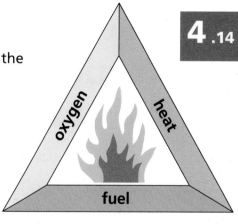

FIGURE 2.4.14b: A fire triangle shows us the things that are needed for burning.

- prevent oxygen from reaching the fire by covering it with a blanket
- remove the heat by throwing water over the fire
- not add any more charcoal.

4. If a camper builds a fire using wood and starts the fire by rubbing flint and steel together, describe the:

   a) source of heat **b)** fuel.

5. Use the fire triangle to explain why the following actions put out a fire:

   a) turning off the gas supply to a Bunsen burner
   b) throwing water on a campfire.

Applying the fire triangle ▶▶▶▶

If you float a candle under a jar in water, the water forms a seal. The candle is in a closed environment. The candle burns but eventually goes out. This is because the oxygen in the jar is used up in the burning reaction and cannot be replaced.

FIGURE 2.4.14c: Why does the flame go out?

6. Identify the fuel in this candle experiment.

7. Predict what will happen to level of water both inside and outside the bell jar after the candle goes out.

8. Suggest how the size of the jar would affect how long the candle burns for.

Key vocabulary

chemical reaction

fuel

combustion

fire triangle

Understanding combustion and the use of fuels

We are learning how to:

- Identify applications of combustion reactions.
- Identify fuels used in different applications.
- Compare the energy content of different fuels.

We use combustion reactions every day, from cooking the food that we eat to heating the homes that we live in. Even the electricity that we use often relies on combustion.

FIGURE 2.4.15a: We use combustion for cooking.

Applications of combustion

Combustion is an **exothermic** reaction. This means that the reaction releases **energy**. This energy is usually transferred as heat and sometimes also light.

Combustion is important for transportation – for example in steam engines and in the engines of cars and trucks. Fireworks are another good example of combustion in action.

Usually when you use electricity, you are relying on combustion. In power stations, fuel is burned and the heat given off is used to boil water. The steam produced is then used to drive a turbine to generate electricity. This means that you rely on combustion when turning on your lights, playing on a computer and charging up a games console.

> Did you know...?
>
> 'Spontaneous human combustion' is a phenomenon in which humans are thought to burst into flames. Some scientists believe that a spark must act as the source of heat for the burning, with fat in the body then acting as the fuel for the reaction.

1. Describe what an exothermic reaction is.

2. Draw a table to summarise the different uses of combustion.

3. Explain how combustion is involved in generating energy.

In situations such as burning logs on a fire, it is easy to identify the fuel as wood. However, in other situations, such as using an electric fire to heat a room, it is not as obvious.

Electricity is not a fuel, but it is sometimes generated using a fuel. If the electricity was generated in a coal-fired power station, then the fuel used to heat the room was coal. Traditional steam engines also usually use coal as fuel.

Traditional cars use petroleum or diesel as a fuel – these both come from crude oil. Biofuels, such as ethanol, can also be used in some cars. This is an **alcohol** made from grains like barley and maize. Space rockets can be fuelled by liquid hydrogen.

FIGURE 2.4.15b: Biofuels, such as ethanol, are made from grains.

4. State the fuel used in a:

   a) a steam engine
   b) a log-burning fire.

5. Suggest what the fuel source is for electrical appliances such as TVs and a washing machines.

6. Many biofuel cars can only run on a mixture of ethanol and petrol in a ratio of 1:9. Explain what this means.

The best fuel for the job »»»

A group of students wanted to compare the energy in different alcohols. They burned each alcohol and used the energy released to heat up water in a conical flask above the burner.

FIGURE 2.4.15c: How can we measure how much energy we get from this fuel?

7. Suggest what the students should measure to compare the energy released by each alcohol.

8. Explain why alcohols would not be a good choice of fuel on an open fire.

9. Suggest another factor that people may consider when deciding which fuel to use.

Key vocabulary

exothermic

energy

alcohol

Exploring the effects of burning

We are learning how to:

- Summarise combustion using an equation.
- Compare complete and incomplete combustion.
- Explain what is meant by the conservation of mass.

For combustion to take place, there needs to be oxygen. Without enough oxygen, only a partial reaction may take place. This type of reaction can be a problem because it produces more pollution.

FIGURE 2.4.16a: Complete combustion occurs when there is plenty of oxygen.

The combustion equation

Many fuels like coal, oil and gas contain the elements hydrogen and carbon – they are called **hydrocarbons.** We can summarise combustion using an equation:

hydrocarbon + oxygen   →   carbon dioxide + water

This reaction is called **complete combustion**. This means that there is enough oxygen to react with all of the fuel. This is an example of an **oxidation** reaction because the fuel reacts with oxygen.

Carbon dioxide is known as a 'greenhouse gas'. Any excess gas that is not used by plants forms a blanket around the Earth. Most scientists believe that burning fossil fuels is contributing to the 'greenhouse effect'.

1. Describe what is needed for complete combustion to take place.

2. Explain why combustion is also known as an oxidation reaction.

3. Describe a problem linked with production of carbon dioxide.

Did you know...?

Carbon monoxide gas can enter the blood and stop oxygen from getting to the body's cells. This can be fatal. Carbon monoxide is difficult to detect because it is odourless and colourless but carbon monoxide detectors can be used to check for leaks of the gas.

FIGURE 2.4.16b: Why do we test for carbon monoxide gas?

Incomplete combustion 〉〉〉

If there is not enough oxygen available to react with all of the fuel, **incomplete combustion** takes place. Water is still produced, but carbon monoxide and carbon are produced instead of carbon dioxide. We can summarise incomplete combustion in this equation:

hydrocarbon + oxygen   →   carbon monoxide + carbon + water

Carbon monoxide is a poisonous gas. The carbon formed this way is soot. Soot is a fine black powder that can irritate the lungs and airways. Incomplete combustion also releases less energy than complete combustion.

4. Name the product that is the same in both compete and incomplete combustion.

5. Describe three reasons why complete combustion is preferred to incomplete combustion.

6. Construct a table to compare the products of complete and incomplete combustion.

Conservation of mass 〉〉〉〉

A group of students investigated what happens to mass during a combustion reaction. They put steel wool into a test tube, covered the tube with a deflated balloon and then measured the mass. The balloon prevented gas from moving in or out of the tube. The tube was heated to burn the steel wool. The mass was then measured again.

Mass before: 43.48 g

Mass after: 43.49 g

The teacher told the students that the Law of Conservation of Mass says that mass can neither be created nor destroyed.

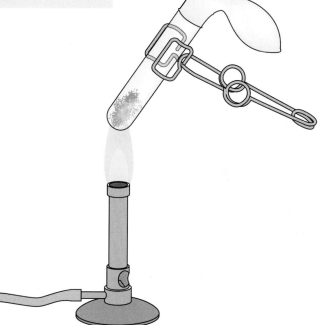

FIGURE 2.4.16c: Steel wool being heated in a closed environment

7. Explain whether the students' data supports the Law of Conservation of Mass.

8. Suggest how the students could show repeatability of the experiment.

9. Suggest what would have happened to the mass if the balloon had not been used in this investigation.

Key vocabulary

hydrocarbon

complete combustion

oxidation

incomplete combustion

Understanding acid rain

We are learning how to:

- Describe how combustion can cause acid rain.
- Describe the effects of acid rain.
- Explain the effects of acid rain.

Normal rain is slightly acidic, with a pH of approximately 5.6. However, other polluting gases can reduce the pH to 4 or lower. This is acid rain, which can damage plants, animals and even buildings. This is a worldwide problem.

How does burning affect rain? 》

Combustion pollutes the air with chemicals such as carbon dioxide, **sulfur dioxide** and nitrogen oxides. Sulfur dioxide is formed when the sulfur found in some fossil fuels (such as coal and oil) is oxidised during combustion. Nitrogen oxides are formed when nitrogen from the air is oxidised during combustion.

Both sulfur dioxide and nitrogen oxides are extremely soluble gases. They rise up into the atmosphere and dissolve in water to form sulfuric acid and nitric acid. These acids can then fall as **acid rain**.

Rain clouds can travel huge distances and so pollution in one part of the world may cause acid rain in another country.

FIGURE 2.4.17a: This shows how acid rain is formed.

1. List three chemical pollutants caused by combustion.

2. Describe how sulfur dioxide gas and nitrogen oxide gases form acids in the clouds.

3. Explain how pollution produced in the UK could cause acid rain in another country.

Acid rain can kill whole trees or even whole sections of forest. This is because:

- Acid rain can damage the leaves of plants – this means that photosynthesis cannot happen efficiently.

- Acid rain dissolves some useful nutrients from the soil and they then wash away before the plant has had time to absorb them.

- Acid rain can cause harmful chemicals, such as aluminium, to be released into the soil, which are then absorbed by the plant.

Acid rain looks and feels like normal rain. However, the chemicals that cause acid rain can be harmful to humans. This can cause respiratory diseases such as asthma and bronchitis.

Acid rain can even damage buildings and statues. This is because the acid reacts with the stone and wears it away.

FIGURE 2.4.17b: Acid rain damages the leaves of plants and they may drop off.

4. Describe the effects of acid rain on:
   a) plants
   b) humans
   c) buildings.

5. Suggest why forests are usually damaged slowly by acid rain.

Treatment and prevention 〉〉〉〉

Acid rain would be reduced by burning less fossil fuel. To do this, we could reduce the amount of electricity that we use. We could also use alternative energy sources such as wind or solar power.

FIGURE 2.4.17c: Acid rain reacts with limestone in statues.

Power stations can also clean the gaseous emissions to remove sulfur dioxide. This is called 'scrubbing' and the process uses an alkali to neutralise the gas. Lakes affected by acid rain can be treated using quicklime (calcium oxide). This is an alkali that neutralises the acid rain.

6. Explain why we cannot easily stop burning fossil fuels.

7. Suggest some reasons why wind power and solar power are not used more widely.

8. Suggest how you could test the effectiveness of calcium oxide on acid rain.

Key vocabulary
....

sulfur dioxide

acid rain

Checking your progress

To make good progress in understanding science you need to focus on these ideas and skills.

Identify some everyday substances that contain acids and alkalis.

Explain what all acids have in common and what all alkalis have in common.

Evaluate the hazards posed by some acids and alkalis and know how these risks may be reduced.

Give an example of an indicator and state why indicators are useful.

Explain what an indicator is and analyse results when using an indicator.

Compare the effectiveness of different indicators.

Describe some examples of neutralisation.

Describe the changes to indicators when acids and alkalis are mixed.

Explain the changes to indicators in terms of pH when acids and alkalis are mixed.

Recognise that water is one product of neutralisation.

Explain the formation of salt and water during neutralisation, giving some examples of common salts.

Predict the reactants or products of different neutralisation reactions.

☐ Describe the observations of reactions between acids and metal, and acids and carbonate, that tell us that a chemical change is taking place.

☐ Explain the general reaction between an acid and a metal, and between an acid and a carbonate, using equations.

☐ Summarise specific reactions between acids and metals and between acids and carbonates using word equations and particle drawings.

☐ Describe what indigestion remedies are and explain how they work.

☐ Design an investigation to compare the effectiveness of indigestion remedies.

☐ Analyse data about indigestion remedies to decide which remedy is the most effective.

☐ Summarise the reactants and products of complete combustion.

☐ Compare the reactants and products of complete and incomplete combustion.

☐ Explain the Law of Conservation of Mass and how it can be proven.

☐ Describe how combustion contributes to acid rain.

☐ Describe the effects of acid rain.

☐ Explain, using an equation, the effects of acid rain.

Questions

Questions 1–7

See how well you have understood the ideas in the chapter.

1. An example of an alkali is: [1]

   a) fruit juice   b) vinegar   c) nitric acid   d) bleach

2. All acids contain the element: [1]

   a) hydrogen   b) oxygen   c) chlorine   d) hydroxide

3. What is the pH of a neutral solution? [1]

   a) 1   b) 14   c) 7   d) 10

4. The reaction between an acid and an alkali is known as: [1]

   a) neutralisation   b) oxidation   c) burning   d) combustion

5. Write a word equation for the reaction between an acid and an alkali. [2]

6. Explain why heartburn is treated using an alkali. [2]

7. Explain, using a diagram if you wish, how acid rain is produced from fossil fuels. [4]

Questions 8–14

See how well you can apply the ideas in this chapter to new situations.

8. Which salt is formed when sulfuric acid and magnesium react? [1]

   a) magnesium chloride   b) magnesium sulfate

   c) sulfur dioxide   d) hydrogen

9. Some students add drops of an acid onto a rock sample. They observe bubbles. What is the gas given off? [1]

   a) hydrogen

   b) oxygen

   c) carbon dioxide

   d) calcium chloride

FIGURE 2.4.19a: Dropping acid on a rock

10. A student weighed a crucible containing steel wool. He then burned the steel wool and reweighed the crucible. The mass after burning would be: [1]

   a) less than before   b) more than before

   c) the same as before   d) zero

11. A student wanted to prove that carbon dioxide was produced during the reaction between hydrochloric acid and calcium carbonate. What chemical could they use to show this? [1]

12. A chemical is described as feeling 'soapy'. When tested with indicator, it is shown to have a pH of 9. Explain what type of chemical this is. [2]

13. A student notices that a concentrated acid gave a more vigorous reaction with a metal than a dilute acid with the same metal. Explain why, using the idea of particles. [2]

14. A group of campers need to put a campfire out before they go to bed. Use the fire triangle to explain how they could do this. [4]

Questions 15–16

See how well you can understand and explain new ideas and evidence.

15. A student reacts different metals with hydrochloric acid. The observations are recorded in Table 2.4.19a. One of the metals is not labelled.

TABLE 2.4.19a

Metal	Observations
unknown metal	Bubbles seen, test tube became warmer
calcium	Lots of bubbles produced very quickly, test tube became very hot
zinc	Few bubbles seen

Compare the reactivity of the unknown metal with that of calcium and zinc. Explain your answer. [2]

FIGURE 2.4.19b: Zinc metal reacting with hydrochloric acid

16. A group of students tried to make some indicators from different plant materials. They tested each of the solutions that they made. The results are shown in Table 2.4.19b.

TABLE 2.4.19b

Indicator	Colour in acid	Colour in alkali	Colour in neutral
A	red	blue	blue
B	red	blue	purple
C	yellow	yellow	yellow

Arrange the indicators in the order of most useful to least useful for testing the pH of a variety of different chemicals. Explain your answer. [4]

Exploring Contact and Non-Contact Forces

Forces and what they do

Forces can be pushes, pulls or turning forces. They can be 'contact' forces – when objects are touching – or 'non-contact' forces – when the forces act at a distance.

Force arrows drawn to scale show the size and direction of forces.

A newtonmeter allows us to measure the size of a force.

When forces on an object are not balanced they can cause a stationary object to move or a moving object to change speed or direction.

Large objects, like planets, exert strong gravitational forces on other objects. These objects are attracted towards the planet.

Electricity and magnetism

Electricity can flow through materials that are conductors.

Some materials are attracted to a magnet.

A magnet has a north pole and a south pole.

Like poles, such as two north poles, repel each other.

Unlike poles attract each other.

States of matter: solids, liquids and gases

Materials are made of particles.

Materials can be classified into three groups, or states – solids, liquids and gases.

In this chapter you will find out ⟫

Gravity and space travel

- Gravity is a non-contact force that acts between all masses.

- A planet, like the Earth, has a gravitational field.

- The gravitational fields of the Earth and other objects in the Solar System affect space travel.

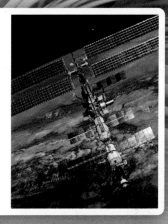

Electrostatic and magnetic forces

- Electrostatic charges have many effects. We can make use of these, but there are also dangers.

- A force field exists around a magnet, which affects certain materials.

- Magnetic fields can be drawn as lines of force.

- There are similarities and differences between magnetic fields and other types of field.

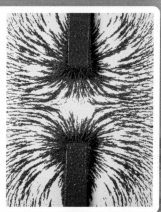

Pressure, floating and sinking

- Pressure can act in solids, liquids and gases.

- Pressure is the force acting on a certain area.

- Some objects sink in liquids and others float.

- An upthrust force affects all objects that are submerged in a liquid.

- The volume of an object affects the amount of upthrust it experiences in a liquid.

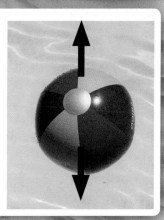

Exploring magnets

We are learning how to:

- Explain magnetic attraction and repulsion.
- Apply the concept of poles and the laws of attraction and repulsion.
- Predict the effects of arrangements of magnetic poles.

Magnets have many effects, sometimes surprisingly strong. They have many uses including computer hard drives, loudspeakers, credit card strips, magnetic fasteners and compasses for navigation. Even though satellite navigation is very effective, ships and aircraft still carry navigation compasses.

Magnetic forces

Magnetism is an example of a **non-contact force**. Magnets exert a force on the region around them. A magnet will **attract** any magnetic materials that are close enough. They do not need to be touching to have an effect.

There are three magnetic elements:

- iron
- nickel
- cobalt.

Many alloys of iron are also magnetic, including most types of steel.

Magnets have two ends, called **poles**. These are the north-seeking pole (N) and the south-seeking pole (S).

1. What type of force is magnetism?
2. List four magnetic materials.
3. Name the two poles that magnets have.

Attracting and repelling

If two magnets are brought together, the effect will depend on their positions:

- north to north **repels**
- south to south repels
- north to south attracts.

FIGURE 2.5.2a: Uses of magnets

A useful way to find out whether materials are magnetised or un-magnetised is by how they behave when another magnet is brought close. The unmagnetised material will be attracted by either pole of the magnet; the magnetised material will be either attracted or repelled, depending on the orientation of the poles. There will be no force from a magnet on non-magnetic materials.

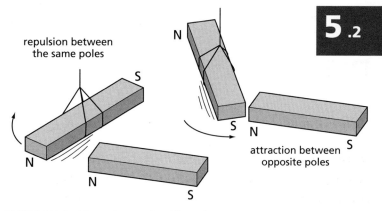

repulsion between the same poles

attraction between opposite poles

FIGURE 2.5.2b: Like poles repel, unlike poles attract.

5 .2

4. Describe the rules about magnets attracting and repelling each other.

5. Describe what will happen in each of these situations:

   a) The N pole of a magnet is brought towards the S pole of another magnet.

   b) The S pole of a magnet is brought towards a piece of magnetised iron.

   c) The N pole of a magnet is brought towards a piece of copper.

6. Explain why a magnet hanging on a thread will respond to magnetic forces more easily than a magnet laying on a bench.

Did you know...?

The Earth's North Pole behaves as a magnetic south pole S, because it attracts the N end of a compass. Changes in the Earth's core mean that its magnetic poles move. For accurate compass navigation this has to be accounted for.

Effects of magnets ▶▶▶

Magnets exert a force in the region around them and the effect can be detected with a magnetic compass. Normally, a compass needle orientates itself in line with the Earth's magnetism, but close to a magnet the force exerted is greater than the Earth's magnetism. As a magnet is brought towards a compass from a distance there comes a point when the needle is no longer in line with the Earth's magnetism. The stronger the magnet, the larger the region around it that will be affected.

7. Explain, using examples including magnetism, the differences between contact and non-contact forces.

8. Someone states that 'magnets stick together'. What would be a better explanation of the behaviour of magnets?

9. Explain the similarities and differences between the Earth's gravitational and magnetic forces.

Key vocabulary

non-contact force

attract

pole

repel

Understanding magnetic fields

We are learning how to:

- Describe magnetic fields.
- Explore the field around a magnet.
- Explain the shape, size and direction of magnetic fields.

Magnetic materials in the region around a magnet experience a magnetic force. The Earth behaves as a gigantic magnet that attracts particles from outer space towards the North and South Poles. As these particles enter the Earth's atmosphere they cause an amazing natural light display.

FIGURE 2.5.3a: The Aurora Borealis over Iceland

Magnetic fields

A **magnetic field** is the space around a magnet where its magnetic field works. Within the field, magnetic materials such as iron are attracted. Other magnets can be attracted if unlike poles are close enough or repelled if like poles are close enough.

Sprinkling iron filings around a magnet shows the magnetic field. Each of the filings becomes a tiny magnet that lines up with the field, because of magnetic forces acting on it. The arrangement of the filings shows the magnetic **field lines**. The closer the lines of magnetic force are to each other, the higher the **strength** of the magnetic field. The direction of the field lines is the direction in which a magnetic north pole would move if placed in the field – from north (N) towards south (S). This is the way a compass would point.

1. What does the pattern of iron filings around a magnet show? What does it not show?

2. Why are the lines of force closer together near the magnet poles?

3. Tiny fragments of substances other than iron could be used to show the force lines in a magnetic field. Choose which ones would work from this list: scraps of paper, steel, pepper, plastic, sawdust, nickel, house dust, copper, carbon.

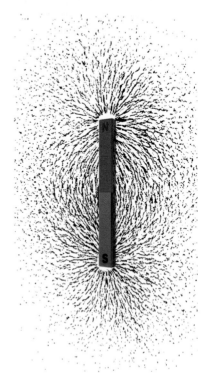

FIGURE 2.5.3b: The iron filings show the shape and strength of the magnetic field.

The Earth's **core** contains materials that are rich in iron. Around a solid inner core is a molten outer core. Scientists believe that currents within the molten core create a magnetic field as they flow around.

Two well known effects of the Earth's magnetic field are:

- Magnets line up in a N to S direction, if they are free to turn. This is how a compass works.

- The Aurora Borealis (Northern Lights). Charged particles entering Earth's atmosphere are attracted to the magnetic poles. As they collide with the gas particles in the atmosphere an amazing natural light display is created.

The Earth also has a gravitational field, which is the region around the Earth where the force of gravity acts. The gravitational field attracts all masses, whereas only particular materials are affected by the magnetic field. You will learn more about the Earth's magnetic field in Chapter 6.

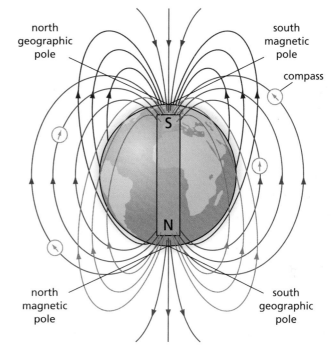

FIGURE 2.5.3c: The Earth's magnetic field. The geographic and magnetic poles do not exactly coincide.

4. Why does the Earth have a magnetic field around it?

5. Describe similarities and differences between magnetism and gravity.

6. How can evidence be collected to find out whether other planets have magnetic fields?

The magnetic field model »»»

Scientists often use models to try to represent things that are hard to see or understand. A model can be a simplified version, a description or a picture. Figure 2.5.3c shows a model that represents the Earth's magnetic field. It is useful because it helps us to understand something we cannot see. Many models do not represent reality exactly and scientists need to be aware of the weaknesses of the models they use.

7. Explain, using examples, why scientists use models.

8. Evaluate the Figure 2.5.3c as a model of Earth's magnetism. What are its strengths and weaknesses?

Did you know...?

You can magnetise a piece of steel by stroking it many times in the same direction with a magnet. When a magnet is heated or hammered its magnetism becomes weaker.

Key vocabulary

magnetic field

strength

field lines

core

Investigating static charge

We are learning how to:

- Recognise the effects of static charge.
- Explain how static charge can be generated.
- Use evidence to develop ideas about static charge.

Static electricity is a common and sometimes spectacular phenomenon. You may have noticed that after walking across a carpet, you sometimes get a small electric shock when you touch a door handle. This happens when your body has become electrically charged. Lightning is a demonstration of static electricity at work on a grand scale.

Static charge

Electrical charge can either flow or be gathered in one place. **Charge** that is flowing is called a current and when it is not flowing it is called **static electricity**.

Electricity flows through conductors, such as a copper wire. However, when a charged material is not connected to a conductor, the electricity cannot flow away and so the charge stays in place.

When a charged object comes close to a conductor the electricity jumps across as a spark. If your body has become charged by walking on a carpet, you feel the charge flowing away through your fingers when you reach for the door handle.

FIGURE 2.5.4a: When a person's hair becomes charged the individual strands repel each other.

1. Name some materials that are good conductors of electricity.

2. What does the word 'static' mean?

3. How could a material that conducts electricity become charged?

Attraction and repulsion

When an object becomes charged with static electricity a **field** of electrostatic force exists around the object. This is a non-contact force. This force can **attract** other materials and may be strong enough to lift them. A charged balloon brought close to someone's head can attract strands of hair and lift them up without the balloon coming into contact with the hair. Scraps of paper can be made to jump off a table and stick to a charged plastic comb held a few centimetres above it.

FIGURE 2.5.4b: Static electricity can cause attraction.

When two objects of the same material become charged they **repel** each other.

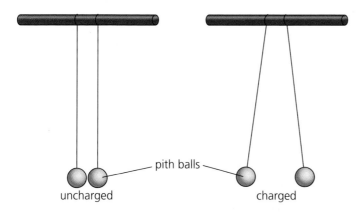

FIGURE 2.5.4.c: Repulsion between two identical charged objects

4. What could small pieces of dust and paper experience when a charged object is brought close?

5. What evidence supports the idea that static electricity exerts a non-contact force?

6. How could you find out if two charged combs repel each other?

Comparing static electricity and magnetism

Fields around charged objects and magnets result in forces of attraction and repulsion. Magnetism is restricted to iron-based materials plus nickel and cobalt. Static electricity can affect a much wider range of materials provided that there is no opportunity for the electrical charge to flow away. Magnetic effects are capable of producing much larger forces. Magnets vary in strength but can exert large forces on magnetic materials. Charged objects can attract objects around them, but in most circumstances the force is small.

When an object becomes very highly charged with static electricity the charge usually escapes through contact with other objects or into the air. Lightning occurs when a large charge escapes quickly from clouds that have become charged during a storm.

7. Thinking about forces, in what ways are magnetism and static electricity similar?

8. Devise a method for finding out which can give the greater force of attraction – magnetism or static electricity.

9. Suggest why TV screens often attract more dust than walls that are close by.

Did you know...?

Some items of clothing become charged so easily that when you take them off, the cloth crackles and sparks as the charge escapes. This occurs in dry weather and a dark room is needed to see the effect.

Key vocabulary

charge

static electricity

field

attract

repel

Explaining static charge

We are learning how to:
- Explain static charge in terms of electron transfer.
- Apply this explanation to various examples.

In ancient Greece, people started to put forward ideas about atoms. They thought that atoms were the most basic particles and that they could not be split further. It was not until the 1800s that ideas really developed beyond this. Scientists have developed a much better understanding of what atoms are like inside. These more modern ideas form the basis of our understanding in many areas of chemistry and physics, including static electricity.

Atoms and electrons

The simplest modern model of an atom is a nucleus being orbited by **electrons**. The nucleus has a **positive charge** because it contains positively charged **protons** – along with neutrons, which have no charge. Electrons have a **negative charge**. Overall an atom is **neutral** because the positively charged protons are balanced by an equal number of negatively charged electrons.

If some electrons get transferred from one object to another the charges no longer balance. This is what happens when an object becomes statically charged.

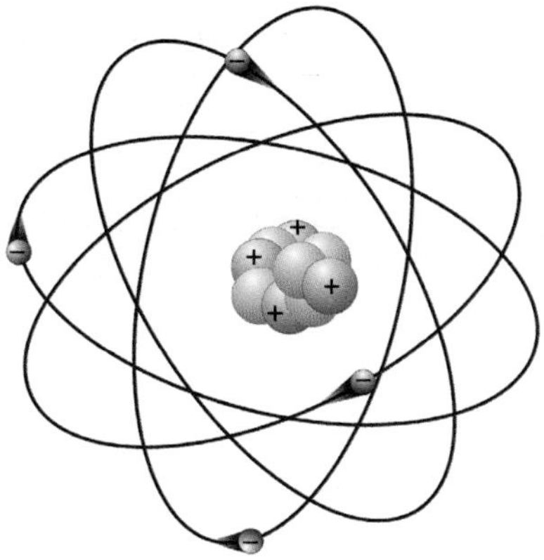

1. What are atoms made up of?
2. Why do atoms have no charge overall?
3. How can an object become negatively charged?
4. How can an object become positively charged?

FIGURE 2.5.5a: Atoms contain a balance of positively charged protons and negatively charged electrons.

Positive and negative charge

When a nylon rod is rubbed with a cloth, electrons are transferred from the rod to the cloth. Because electrons are negatively charged this makes the cloth negatively charged. The rod has lost electrons so the positive charge of the protons is no longer balanced – its overall charge is now positive.

Other materials behave differently. A polythene rod, for example, gains electrons when rubbed with a cloth.

It becomes negatively charged and the cloth, which has lost electrons, becomes positively charged.

5. Describe what happens to a cloth when it is rubbed on a nylon rod.

6. Explain how different materials behave differently when rubbed with a cloth.

Loss of charge ▶▶▶

Static charge depends on electrons being unable to flow into or out of an object. If a charged polythene rod is connected to a conductor, such as a wire, electrons will flow away from the rod. The rod loses its charge and becomes neutral.

Air is not a good conductor, but it can transfer some electrons, so charged objects gradually lose their charge. In wet weather, the water vapour in the air can transfer more electrons so charge is lost more quickly.

FIGURE 2.5.5b: Rubbing transfers electrons.

When a van de Graaff generator is turned on, the globe becomes positively charged. It can be neutralised by touching it with the earthing sphere. The earthing sphere is connected to a conductor so that electrons can flow freely to and from it.

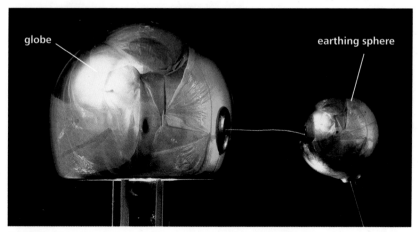

globe   earthing sphere

FIGURE 2.5.5.c: A van de Graaff generator and earthing sphere

7. Explain why experiments with static electricity give better effects in dry weather.

8. a) When a van de Graaff generator is turned on, explain what effect it has on the electrons in a person's body when they touch the globe.

 b) Using your answer from question 8a suggest why the person's hair stands on end.

 c) Explain the process of discharging the globe of a van de Graaff generator.

Did you know...?

A desk-top van de Graaff generator, like the ones used in schools, can produce 100 000 volts. Bigger van de Graaff generators can exceed two million volts.

Key vocabulary

electron

positive charge

proton

negative charge

neutral

Understanding electrostatic fields

We are learning how to:

- Explain static electricity in terms of fields.
- Explain how charged objects affect other objects.

Charged objects can affect their surroundings even when they are not in contact. Sometimes people believe that they can 'feel' electricity in the air. The idea of an electrostatic field helps to explain this.

Rules of attraction and repulsion

An **electrostatic field** exists around a charged object that can exert a non-contact force. Just as with magnetic poles, like charges repel and unlike charges attract. There is another similarity with magnetism – a magnet can attract an unmagnetised piece of iron and a charged object can attract an uncharged one.

Water has no overall electrical charge – it has a balance of negatively and positively charged particles. Despite this, water is affected by an electrostatic field.

1. What is the area around a charged object called?

2. Looking at Figure 2.5.6a, what evidence suggests that a non-contact force is working?

3. All substances contain charged particles. In many cases they have no charge – explain why.

FIGURE 2.5.6a: The water is attracted towards a charged rod.

Charged particles moving

Within many substances, charged particles are free to move. When there is no electrostatic field present, the charged particles are spread evenly.

In Figure 2.5.6b the negatively charged balloon has electrons spread over its surface. When it is brought towards the wall, the negatively charged particles in the wall atoms are repelled. This leaves the surface of the wall with a positive charge. We say that a charge has been **induced** on the wall surface by the electrostatic field of the balloon. The opposite charges of the balloon and the wall's surface attract one another.

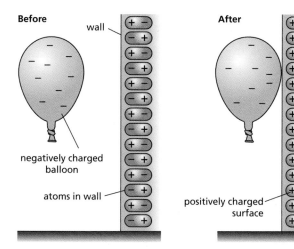

FIGURE 2.5.6b: The charged balloon has an electrostatic field around it.

4. Describe how charged particles move when an object is put in an electrostatic field.

5. Draw labelled diagrams to show how a positively charged rod can attract a trickle of water.

6. Suggest why a metal rod is unlikely to be able to attract a trickle of water.

Induced charge ⟩⟩⟩

A gold leaf electroscope allows us to explore static charge. The gold leaf is connected by a copper strip to a metal cap. This is all insulated from the rest of the electroscope and from the surroundings. Normally the gold leaf hangs downwards against the copper strip, but when it becomes charged it is repelled from the copper strip and lifts up.

FIGURE 2.5.6c: A gold leaf electroscope can detect electrostatic charge.

7. Explain why it is important for the copper strip to be insulated from the body of the electroscope.

8. In an experiment a negatively charged rod is gradually brought closer to the cap of the electroscope. At first the gold leaf hangs down against the copper strip, but the closer the rod comes to the cap, the further the gold leaf is deflected.

a) Explain why the gold leaf hangs down against the copper strip when the rod is far away from the electroscope.

b) Explain why the gold leaf is deflected when the rod is close to the cap of the electroscope.

c) Explain what you would expect to happen if the rod was taken away again.

> **Did you know...?**
>
> Lines of force exist in an electrostatic field around a charged object, in a similar way to lines of magnetic force that exist around a magnet.

Key vocabulary

electrostatic field

induced

Applying what we know about electrostatics

We are learning how to:

- Apply an understanding of static electricity to various situations.
- Explain how static electricity can be useful and can be dangerous.

Static charge leads to more than just interesting scientific effects. Our understanding has led to useful applications and also plays a big role in keeping us safe in certain situations.

Using electrostatics

In paint spraying, a mist of tiny droplets of paint are forced from a nozzle onto the surface being painted. Spraying a flat surface is easy, but when spraying a complicated shape it is hard to reach into all the corners. Furthermore, a lot of paint can end up missing its target when small objects are sprayed.

Paint spraying can be improved by using spray guns that give a positive charge to the paint. The object being painted is negatively charged. The **electrostatic attraction** pulls the mist of paint onto the object.

1. State two advantages of using electrostatics in paint spraying.

2. When paint spraying uses electrostatics, how is the paint attracted to the object being painted?

FIGURE 2.5.7a: Static charge attracts paint spray onto the car door.

Printers and photocopiers

Photocopiers work by using an electrostatic effect. Figure 2.5.7b shows how this works. Inside a photocopier a bright light is used to project the image to be copied onto a positively charged plate. The light areas lose their charge but the dark areas keep their positive charge. In the next stage the black toner ink is attracted to the positively charged areas on the plate. When paper is fed onto the plate, the toner sticks to the paper to create the image. In the final stage, the paper is heated to 'bake' the toner onto the page.

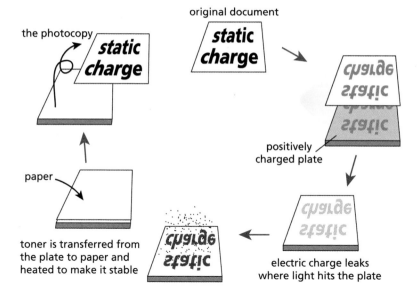

FIGURE 2.5.7b: Static charge attracts the ink to create an image in a photocopier.

3. From the information in Figure 2.5.7b, deduce what the charge on the toner in a photocopier is.

4. Suggest how a photocopier can be made to print shades of grey as well as black. Use the idea of static charge in your answer.

5. Even though printers and photocopiers use static charge, explain why it is unusual to get a shock from them.

6. Explain how an image can be copied accurately by a photocopier.

Lightning ⟫⟫⟫

Storm clouds create very strong updrafts and downdrafts. Temperatures inside the clouds can drop below −50 °C and tiny crystals of ice form. As these ice crystals fall inside the cloud, they collide with water being carried up and this causes electrons to be removed from the water. Negative charge accumulates at the base of the cloud and positive charge at the top. Eventually the difference in charge between the base of the cloud and the ground is so big that there is a massive discharge via a lightning bolt. A bolt of lightning can carry a current of 30 000 amps. Most domestic appliances, need a current of less than 10 amps.

7. What effect would you expect the electrical field from a storm cloud to have on the ground underneath?

8. Suggest why lightning strikes often happen from cloud to cloud.

Did you know...?

Lightning happens around the world many times every second. A bolt can reach temperatures over 20 000 °C. Electricity usually takes the path of least resistance, so tall buildings are fitted with lightning conductors. This protects the building and the surroundings from the damaging effects of a lightning strike.

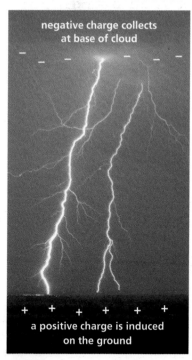

FIGURE 2.5.7c: Lightning happens when massive charge differences exist.

Key vocabulary

electrostatic attraction

lightning

Exploring gravity on Earth

We are learning how to:

- Explain the effects of gravity.
- Compare gravity to other non-contact forces.
- Use the concept of a gravitational field.

Gravity is a pulling force that exists between *all* objects. For small objects the force is tiny and unnoticeable, but when one of the objects is a planet, gravity is certainly a force to be reckoned with. The gravitational field of Earth reaches well out into space.

Gravity and weight ⟩⟩

The stronger **gravity** is, the greater the **weight** of an object. The strength of the Earth's gravity gets weaker the further from Earth you go. When scientists talk about the strength of gravity they often define the location, for example on the surface of a planet.

In space stations in orbit around the Earth, astronauts look as if they have no weight. However, the Earth's gravity is attracting them and also the space station. They fall at the same rate so inside the station it looks as if the astronauts are just floating.

> **Did you know...?**
>
> You can pay for a flight in a plane that will give the experience of feeling weightless. A plane flown in a curved path in the shape of a parabola creates a sensation similar to, but more extreme than, going over the top on a big-dipper ride.

1. Compared to standing on Earth, what would your weight be on a high-flying plane?

   a) stronger   **b)** the same   **c)** weaker   **d)** zero

2. Explain your answer to question 1.

3. Explain what would happen if an extremely heavy object was released inside the space station shown in Figure 2.5.8a.

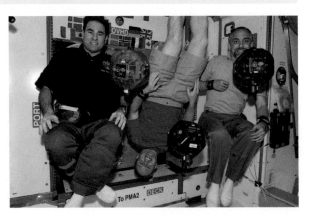

FIGURE 2.5.8a: These astronauts in the space station are falling at the same rate as the space station.

The Earth's gravitational field

The region around the Earth affected by its gravity is its **gravitational field**. The field can be represented by lines of force. Where the lines are close together, the field is stronger. The further apart the lines, the weaker the field. Gravity does not stop at the Earth's surface. If you descend into a deep mine you are still pulled towards the middle of the Earth.

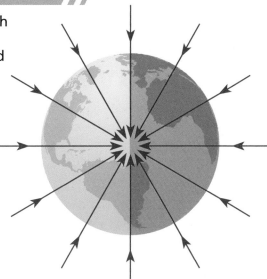

FIGURE 2.5.8b: The Earth's gravitational field

4. In what direction does Earth's gravitational force act?

5. Describe what the spacing between the field lines suggests about the gravitational field away from the Earth compared to that on the surface.

6. Describe how the Earth's gravitational field differs from its magnetic field.

Acceleration caused by gravity

Acceleration is a change in the speed or direction of an object's movement. Within the Earth's gravitational field, unsupported objects **accelerate** towards the Earth unless prevented by other forces.

Think about someone dropping an object (Figure 2.5.8c) – it starts to fall and gets faster. By the end of the first second it is falling at 10 m/s. During the next second the object continues to accelerate and by the end of that second it is falling at 20 m/s. For every one second of free fall the speed increases by 10 m/s. We say that the acceleration due to gravity (at the Earth's surface) is 10 metres per second, per second (10 m/s/s or 10 m/s^2).

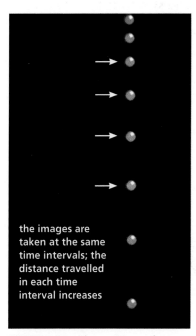

the images are taken at the same time intervals; the distance travelled in each time interval increases

FIGURE 2.5.8c: The positions of a falling object at equal time intervals

7. Explain why the gaps between the object's positions in Figure 2.5.8c get bigger each time.

8. Imagine a situation where gravity on Earth could be magically turned off. Explain what would happen to the movement of an object if it was allowed to drop for one second and then gravity was turned off.

Key vocabulary

gravity

weight

gravitational field

accelerate

Applying our understanding of gravity to space travel

We are learning how to:

- Apply ideas about gravity on Earth to other places.
- Explore how gravitational fields vary.
- Consider the effects of these changes.

Spaceships have travelled to far-off destinations in the Solar System, but the distance is tiny compared to outer space. Manned spaceships have travelled a fraction of the distance travelled by unmanned missions. Gravity is just one of the many obstacles that make space travel so challenging.

Voyager spacecraft

Two spacecraft, Voyager 1 and 2, were launched in 1977 and have been travelling ever since. In 2012, Voyager 1 left the Solar System and is now travelling through interstellar space (the region between the stars). Throughout their flights both spacecraft have been transmitting information and pictures back to Earth.

The Voyager spacecraft were launched aboard a Titan-Centaur rocket. This carried the fuel and the rocket engines needed to escape the Earth's gravity. It also protected the delicate Voyager craft from **air resistance**.

1. Describe the forces involved during the launch and flight of a space rocket.

2. State two benefits of carrying Voyager inside a rocket.

3. Explain why Voyager did not need to be streamlined.

Escaping the Earth's gravity

To lift the mass of a rocket from the surface of the Earth takes a large and sustained force. It has to overcome the pulling force of gravity and the friction caused by air resistance in the atmosphere.

As the rocket climbs away from Earth, the pulling force from Earth's gravity gets weaker and eventually drops to zero. Similarly, air resistance also decreases until the rocket has left the Earth's atmosphere, then there is none.

FIGURE 2.5.9a: Voyager 1

4. Explain why the forces of gravity and friction reduce as a rocket climbs away from Earth.

5. What would happen to the motion of a space rocket after it had left the region affected by gravity from Earth or other bodies in space?

Keeping Voyager on track 》》》

As the Voyager spacecraft travel through the Solar System, they still experience weak gravitational fields from other planets and the Sun. Signals from the scientists on Earth allow Voyager 1 and 2 to be controlled by tiny thrusters that provide enough force to keep the spacecraft heading in the right direction. The thrusters are tiny jet engines that burn fuel, and the waste gases ejected from them provide the pushing force. They use very small amounts of fuel, but because there is no chance of refuelling, Voyager spacecraft will eventually drift uncontrolled through space.

6. Explain why Voyager spacecraft only need very weak thrusters to keep on track.

7. Suggest what might happen to the Voyager spacecraft if they had no thrusters.

8. Suggest why the Voyager spacecraft have jet engines rather than propellers.

FIGURE 2.5.9b: Rockets are used to deliver delicate spacecraft into space.

FIGURE 2.5.9c (not to scale): The regular orbital motion of the planets is evidence for the existence of gravitational fields throughout the Solar System.

Did you know...?

The Voyager 1 and 2 missions are due to end, after 43 years, in 2020. By this time they will no longer be able to generate enough electrical energy to run the scientific instruments on board. The electrical needs are provided by plutonium (a nuclear fuel), which is continually decaying.

Key vocabulary

air resistance

Applying key ideas

You have now met a number of important ideas in this chapter. This activity gives an opportunity for you to apply them, just as scientists do. Read the text first, then have a go at the tasks. The first few are fairly easy – then they become a bit more challenging.

Exploring Earth's atmosphere and beyond

The Earth's atmosphere can be thought of as a protective layer around the Earth that helps sustain life. It is highly complex and constantly changing. Scientists study the atmosphere for many reasons: it helps us understand and predict the weather; we find out more about long-term changes to Earth and its climate; it is possible to learn about particles and radiation from space, which can pose a threat.

One way that scientists use to collect data is to send up balloons carrying instruments. Balloons like the one in Figure 5.2.10a are designed to go close to the edge of space – a height of 34 km above the Earth's surface. The instruments on board transmit the data they collect back to scientists on Earth.

High-altitude balloons are filled with helium, which is less dense than air. This makes it buoyant enough to overcome its weight and that of the instruments. The balloon has no propulsion or steering, so it just drifts along with the air currents.

From balloons launched in the polar regions, it has been discovered that fast-moving charged particles (protons and electrons) are held in the Earth's magnetic field. The particles spiral down the magnetic field lines towards the North and South Poles and give off harmful X-rays.

Balloons have also been very useful in the study of thunderstorms. These are one of the most dangerous weather events, not just because of the extreme wind and rain they cause but also because of massive electrical activity.

Balloons and normal aeroplanes are not suitable for exploring space, beyond Earth's atmosphere. Specially designed spacecraft need to be used.

FIGURE 2.5.10a: A high-altitude research balloon

FIGURE 5.2.10b: Cloud to cloud lightning

Task 1: Magnetic fields

Draw a labelled diagram to show the Earth and its magnetic field. Show or describe where the magnetic field is strongest. How and why would you expect different quantities of particles to strike the Earth's poles compared to the equator?

Task 2: Forces acting on a balloon

Thinking of the fields in the atmosphere, describe the forces that could be acting on a balloon – use force diagrams in your description. Suggest how these change as the balloon rises from the Earth's surface and climbs up through the atmosphere.

Task 3: Electrostatic charge

What causes electrostatic charge? A balloon climbing through a cloud may become electrostatically charged. How might this happen? How could you find out if it had become positively or negatively charged?

Task 4: Preventing lightning

Many tall structures are fitted with lightning conductors. Explain how lightning conductors help to prevent damage.

Task 5: Protecting the instruments

Scientists were worried that the expensive instruments suspended from a balloon could be damaged. They suggested three ways of protecting them: wrapped in foam; surrounded by a metal cage; surrounded by a plastic insulator. Evaluate the benefits and drawbacks of these suggestions.

Task 6: Exploring beyond the atmosphere

What are the challenges of sending instruments into space to collect data for scientific research? Consider the different methods of carrying the instruments. How can these challenges be overcome?

Task 7: Electrostatic charge in clouds

It was suggested that spraying copper dust into storm clouds could help prevent lightning. Evaluate this suggestion and try to suggest alternatives.

Exploring pressure on a solid surface

We are learning how to:

- Explain how pressure can be applied on a solid surface.
- Describe some effects of varying pressure.

Many people would think that lying on a bed of nails would be very painful and dangerous. The whole force of a person's weight would be acting through the sharp ends of the nails. Understanding the idea of pressure helps us to explain how such a feat is possible.

FIGURE 2.5.11a: The force is spread over many nails to make this possible.

Spreading the force

When a person lies down they can feel comfortable even on a hard surface. The force of weight is spread over a large surface. This reduces the **pressure** on the body.

If the force of weight is acting over a small **area**, the pressure is greater. Trying to lie on the point of a single nail would mean that several hundred newtons would be acting over an area of less than $1\,mm^2$ on the nail's point – the pressure would be massive. The skin cannot withstand such pressure and would be pierced by the nail.

Look carefully at the bed of nails in Figure 2.5.11a. There are hundreds of nails, so the force of weight is shared. The pressure on any one nail is small and the person does not suffer pain or injury.

1. What unit is used to measure the downwards force of weight?

2. Complete this sentence: 'The greater the area that a force acts over, the …'

3. Explain why sitting on a drawing pin can be painful.

Reduced pressure; increased pressure

Looking at Figure 2.5.11b you can see how the large area of a camel's feet helps to stop it sinking into the sand. Similarly, a tractor's tyres spread the weight of the tractor over a larger area than narrow tyres would.

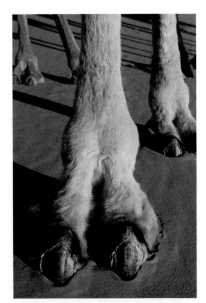

FIGURE 2.5.11b: Is it an increase in pressure or a reduction in pressure that helps in this situation?

A knife concentrates a force over the very small area of the blade's edge. The small area of the blade of an ice skate has two benefits. Firstly, the high pressure causes the ice to melt slightly underneath the blade. The thin layer of water formed acts as a lubricant. Secondly, when the skate is leaned over, there is so much pressure on one edge of the blade that it cuts into the ice, allowing the skater to turn.

4. Explain how a camel's feet allow it to walk on soft sand.

5. Explain why cutting with a sharp knife is easier than with a blunt one.

6. Suggest why roller skates would be ineffective on ice compared to ice skates.

Solving engineering problems ⟩⟩⟩

Engineers use the idea of pressure to improve designs for different purposes.

In skiing, a downhill racer uses a different ski design to someone skiing over deep powder snow. A hand-operated tin opener uses levers to multiply the force applied. This force then acts through the narrow cutting blade. The pressure is high enough to cut through the tin.

Did you know...?

Many car seats contain pressure sensors that allow them to detect if the seat is occupied. The seat belt warning sign will operate if the belt is not fastened.

FIGURE 2.5.11c: Different skis for different purposes

7. Explain the problems that a downhill ski racer and powder skier would encounter if they swapped skis.

8. Suggest how the design of a hand-operated tin opener could be improved. Use scientific ideas to explain how your improvement would work.

9. Sketch a design for a rucksack showing how its features make it comfortable to carry.

Key vocabulary

pressure

area

Calculating pressure

We are learning how to:

- Identify the factors that determine the size of pressure on a solid.
- Calculate the size of pressure exerted.

Calculating pressure is important to engineers. For example, the foundations of a building have to carry the full downwards force of its weight. There have been cases of buildings collapsing when the pressure on the foundations was too large. Engineers calculate the area needed for the foundations to support the structure.

Calculating pressure

Pressure tells us how much force is applied over an area. The **formula** used to calculate pressure is:

$$\text{pressure} = \frac{\text{force}}{\text{area}}$$

or in shorthand:

$$P = \frac{F}{A}$$

Force is measured in newtons (N) and area is measured in square metres, so the pressure is measured in newtons per square metre (N/m²). The unit for pressure is the **pascal (Pa)**. 1 Pa is exactly the same as 1 N/m².

FIGURE 2.5.12a: The bike rack exerts pressure where it is attached to the car.

1. What is the unit for pressure?

2. What is the formula for calculating pressure?

3. If we calculated pressure using force in newtons and area in square centimetres, what unit would the answer be in?

Example calculations

To calculate the pressure exerted by a box with a base of 2 m² pressing onto the ground with a force of 40 N:

$$P = \frac{F}{A}$$

$$P = \frac{40}{2}$$

$$P = 20\,\text{N/m}^2 \text{ or } P = 20\,\text{Pa}$$

Did you know...?

Engineers build in a safety margin when designing structures. This reduces the chance of a structure failing if an unexpected force is applied or if materials gradually become weaker as they get older.

4. Calculate the pressure exerted on the ground by a piece of wood with a base area of $2\,m^2$ and weighing 20 N.

5. A concrete base for a barbeque has a mass of 500 N and an area of $4\,m^2$. Calculate the pressure it exerts on the ground.

6. Which exerts the largest pressure – a crate weighing 500 N acting on a surface of $25\,m^2$ or one weighing 400 N acting on a surface of $10\,m^2$?

Solving pressure problems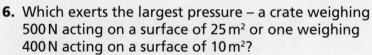

If you know what the values of two of the quantities in the pressure formula are, you can calculate the third quantity by rearranging the formula.

$$A = \frac{F}{P} \quad \text{or} \quad F = P \times A$$

An engineer can work out the strength and size of designs needed to withstand certain pressures. For example, a bridge needs to take loads up to 45 000 N. It is built on ground that can withstand 5000 Pa. To calculate the area needed for the bridge supports:

$$A = \frac{F}{P} = \frac{45\,000}{5000} = 9\,m^2$$

FIGURE 2.5.12b: How could you work out the pressure that this piano exerts on the floor?

Care must be taken to use the correct units for all quantities. The area is in square metres because the force was in newtons and the pressure was in pascals.

7. An engineer wants the floor of a car to be able to take a total force of 12 000 N from all the seats. The floor can take a pressure of 24 000 Pa. What area must the seat supports be?

8. When someone is on a trampoline they may be sitting down or on their feet.

   a) Explain whether the pressure on the trampoline is higher when sitting or standing.

   b) How could you calculate the difference in the pressures exerted when sitting or standing?

   c) Explain why the pressure exerted on a trampoline is greater when a person bounces rather than stands still.

Key vocabulary

formula

pascal (Pa)

Exploring pressure in a liquid

We are learning how to:

- Describe how pressure in a liquid alters with depth.
- Explain pressure increases in relation to particles and gravity.

Sea creatures and divers experience the effects of pressure as they swim in deep water. Whales have ribs that are joined by very flexible cartilage. This allows the rib cage to compress when they make a deep dive. Without this flexibility, the high pressure could break the rib cage.

FIGURE 2.5.13a: A whale in the deep sea

How pressure varies ❭❭

When we are on the land, the **pressure** inside our bodies is the same as the pressure of the air around us. However, when people go diving there is extra pressure from the water above – the greater the **depth**, the higher the pressure.

When you are deep in the water, the pressure results from the weight of water pressing down on you from above. The water is actually pressing all around you, so the pressure is the same all over your body.

> 1. Why would you experience more pressure at the bottom of a swimming pool than at the surface?
>
> 2. **a)** What dangers would face divers if they descended quickly to a great depth?
>
>   **b)** How can a whale descend quickly and yet face no problems?

Explaining pressure in liquids ❭❭

To help explain how pressure acts in a liquid, imagine the water particles to be represented by a large container of marbles. If you press your fist down into the marbles they push against each other and some of them are forced upwards, even though you are pressing downwards.

Imagine lying at the bottom of a deep swimming pool full of marbles. You would feel the weight of the marbles pressing down on you. The more marbles above you, the larger the force on your body.

Pressure increases with depth

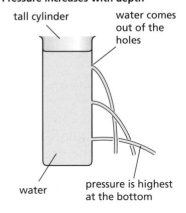

tall cylinder — water comes out of the holes

water — pressure is highest at the bottom

Pressure acts in all directions

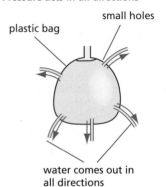

plastic bag — small holes

water comes out in all directions

FIGURE 2.5.13b: Pressure in liquids

3. Explain why the pressure in Figure 2.5.13c is greater at position B compared to position A.

4. How can the marbles model help us to understand pressure in liquids?

5. What drawbacks does the marbles model have in explaining pressure in liquids?

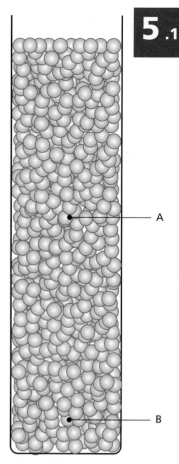

FIGURE 2.5.13c: Particles in a liquid causing pressure

Working at pressure >>>

Humans are able to explore to great depths in the oceans using diving capsules like the one in Figure 2.5.13d. Inside the capsule the pressure is similar to surface pressure, so the people inside can work normally. On the outside the pressure is many times higher so the capsule has to be built to withstand it.

FIGURE 2.5.13d: A deep-sea diving capsule with special crystal glass windows

For work at shallower depths you can wear a diving suit, but if you come to the surface quickly you can suffer from **decompression** sickness. This is caused by gases inside the body bubbling in the way that they do when a fizzy drink is opened. You must be put into a decompression chamber so that the pressure can be reduced gradually to surface pressure.

6. Suggest what features of a diving capsule enable it to withstand the very high pressure in deep oceans.

7. Suggest differences between deep-sea creatures and humans that allows the creatures to live normally at high pressures.

8. Find out about what causes decompression sickness.

Did you know...?

There have been several manned and unmanned trips to the bottom of the deepest part of the ocean – the Mariana Trench in the Pacific Ocean. Even though the pressure is around 100 million pascals, there is a thriving ecosystem.

Key vocabulary

pressure

depth

decompression

Explaining floating and sinking

We are learning how to:

- Explain why some objects float and others sink.
- Relate floating and sinking to density, displacement and upthrust.
- Explain the implications of these ideas.

The Greek physicist, mathematician and inventor Archimedes had ideas that help us to understand floating, sinking and buoyancy. Even though he lived more than 2000 years ago his principles are still used today.

Density

The **density** of a material compared to water allows you to decide if it will float or sink in water. Density is the amount of mass in a particular volume of a material. If a material is denser than water it will sink, and vice versa.

When an object is in water, the water provides a **buoyancy** force called **upthrust**. If the force of weight is bigger than the upthrust, the object will sink. Even when it sinks it is partially supported by upthrust. When an object floats, its entire weight is supported by upthrust.

1. Name three materials that are denser than water and three that are less dense.

2. Explain why people feel heavy when they get out of water after a long swim.

3. Suggest why some materials are denser than others.

Measuring upthrust

The weight of an object in air can be compared with its weight in water. The difference between the two is the difference in upthrust provided by each.

Water is **displaced** when an object is lowered into it. The weight of the displaced water is the same as the size of the upthrust force. The size of the upthrust force depends entirely on the volume of water displaced.

Neutral buoyancy happens when an object neither sinks to the bottom nor bobs to the surface. It appears to hover in the water.

FIGURE 2.5.14a: Weight is supported by upthrust.

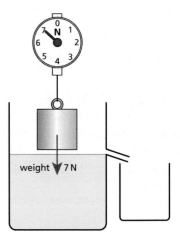

weight ▼7 N

Archimedes' principle – the upthrust force is equal to the weight of the displaced water

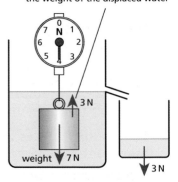

3 N

weight ▼7 N

3 N

FIGURE 2.5.14b: Water provides upthrust when it is displaced.

4. Explain what the difference between the readings on the forcemeter in the two scales in Figure 2.5.14b tells you.

5. Explain the events in each of the situations (a) to (d) using at least one of these words in each explanation: dense, buoyant, upthrust, displace.

   a) A lump of wood is lowered into water – the wood floats.

   b) The reading on a force meter goes down when a suspended piece of steel is lowered into water.

   c) A beaker full of water overflows when an object is lowered into the water.

   d) A boat made of steel floats.

Applying ideas about upthrust >>>

Modern ships are made of steel. The reason that the shape allows them to float is that it displaces a large volume of water.

The air inside the boat weighs very little compared to the water displaced.

Any object floating in water displaces its own weight in water. The upthrust is equal to the force of weight, so the object does not rise or fall.

FIGURE 2.5.14c: How does this huge cruise liner float?

6. Draw force diagrams to show the forces acting on:

   a) a lightly loaded ship floating in water.

   b) the same heavily loaded ship floating on water.

   c) a football that is being held under water.

   d) a football the moment it was released after being held under water.

7. Explain what would happen to a boat that was gradually filled with water.

Key vocabulary

density

buoyancy

upthrust

displaced

Exploring gas pressure

We are learning how to:

- Explore how the pressure in a gas varies with height above the Earth.
- Explaining the implications of this changing pressure.

The pressure of the atmosphere is not the same in all places – it varies with height. High up a mountain the atmospheric pressure is much lower than at sea level. In space there is no atmosphere and so there is no pressure.

Explaining pressure in the atmosphere

The atmosphere contains molecules of oxygen, nitrogen and carbon dioxide as well as of other gases. The force of gravity pulls all these particles towards the Earth. This causes the atmosphere to press down on the Earth and everything on it. The pressing down is called **atmospheric pressure**.

The particles in the air are constantly moving and they do not lie in a compact layer on the Earth's surface. The higher you go from the Earth's surface, the more space there is between the particles.

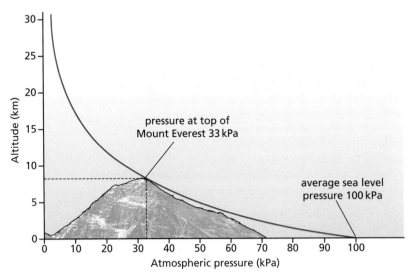

FIGURE 2.5.15a: Variation of atmospheric pressure with height

1. What causes the atmosphere to have pressure?

2. Suggest why there is no atmosphere in outer space.

3. What might limit the height that a hot-air balloon can go to?

FIGURE 2.5.15b: What challenges does mountaineering present?

Pressure and weather ▶▶▶

As well as varying with height, the atmospheric pressure is continually changing across the world. Figure 2.5.15c shows a surface-pressure chart. Where there is high pressure, the weather tends to be dry and sunny because the higher downwards force of the atmosphere reduces cloud growth. Where there is low pressure, cloud can develop more easily and it is more likely to rain. The lines are called 'isobars' and link areas of equal pressure. Where there are big pressure differences across a region, the isobars are closely packed and the winds will be strong.

Weather fronts are where warm- and cold-air masses collide. Lots of cloud usually forms at weather fronts. They are marked on the chart as lines with triangular or semicircular shapes along their length.

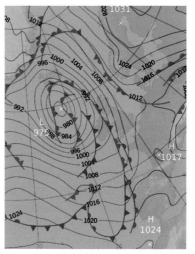

FIGURE 2.5.15c: Pressure charts help meteorologists to predict the weather.

4. What would the atmosphere be like in an area of low pressure compared to that in an area of high pressure?

5. Look at Figure 2.5.15c and suggest what the weather over Britain might be.

6. Name some areas on the map where you would expect there to be a lot of cloud.

Climbing mountains ▶▶▶

Nearly all organisms depend on a readily available supply of oxygen so that they can release energy during respiration. This energy is essential for all life processes. At high **altitude** the body struggles to take in enough oxygen to function properly and even gentle movement can be exhausting.

The part of Mount Everest above 8000 m has become known as the 'death zone'. At this height, there is about one-third of the oxygen available at sea level. In addition to this, extreme terrain, cold and wind add to the dangers. Mountaineers spend weeks acclimatising at high altitude before attempting to go to the summit. They aim to spend as little time as possible in the 'death zone' and they often carry cylinders of oxygen to breathe from.

7. Draw particle diagrams to compare the air at the top of Everest with that at sea level.

8. Suggest some problems a mountaineer using bottled oxygen may meet.

9. Suggest how a climber's body could acclimatise to breathing at high altitude.

Did you know...?

Predicting the weather is a complex process that involves modelling the atmosphere using computers.

Data about air pressure, temperature, water vapour and winds throughout the world's atmosphere are used.

Key vocabulary

atmospheric pressure

weather front

altitude

Working with pressure

We are learning how to:

- Give examples of how pressure affects our lives.
- Explain how pressure is used and managed.

A life-support machine gently increases air pressure so that air fills the lungs of a patient who is having difficulty breathing. The machine then reduces the pressure so that air leaves the lungs. Many devices use pressure differences to make them work.

Dealing with low air pressure

Most passenger jets fly at around 10 000 m above sea level, where the atmospheric pressure is low and oxygen is scarce. The cabin is **pressurised** as the aircraft climbs so that even when flying at over 10 000 m the cabin pressure is equivalent to being at around 2000 m. In case of problems with the aircraft's systems, all commercial airliners are fitted with oxygen masks that supply oxygen from a backup system.

1. Why are airline cabins pressurised?

2. Explain why some people feel a pressure change on aeroplanes even though cabins are pressurised.

3. Why are parents advised to fit their own oxygen mask before helping their children in the event of a problem with cabin pressure on an aeroplane?

FIGURE 2.5.16a: Safety talks tell airline passengers about oxygen masks.

Measuring pressure

The historical method for measuring pressure uses a **barometer**. This instrument contains a sealed, flexible container of air that expands as the atmospheric pressure decreases and contracts when atmospheric pressure increases. The flexible container is linked to a pointer that moves over a scale.

Modern pressure sensors and digital displays have taken over and are small enough to be built into a wrist watch.

FIGURE 2.5.16b: An old-style barometer

FIGURE 2.5.16c: A modern digital altimeter on a hang glider

One complication for **altimeters** is that atmospheric pressure varies from day to day and place to place. To give an accurate reading of height a pilot needs to set the altimeter to the altitude of the airport. Even with this, the pressure changes during the flight cause errors in the height reading. Aeroplanes also have GPS (global positioning system), which uses satellites to indicate position and altitude.

4. Explain how a barometer could be affected by:

   a) a leak in the flexible container

   b) a rigid container of air instead of a flexible one.

5. Explain why even a top-quality altimeter will not always be accurate.

Pressure and movement

The pressure of the air in a bicycle tyre is a lot higher than that of the air in the atmosphere. This is achieved by using a pump that compresses air inside it. The pump is attached to the tyre via a **valve**, which lets air move from the pump into the tyre, but not the other way. When the pressure is higher in the pump than in the tyre, the air moves through the valve and into the tyre.

6. When a tyre is being inflated with a pump, explain where and when you would expect the air pressure to be at its greatest.

7. Explain the role played by a valve in a tyre.

8. Draw a sequence of particle diagrams to illustrate the pressure changes when blowing up a tyre.

> **Did you know...?**
>
> A racing bike's tyres are inflated to around 6000 kPa (kilopascal), which is six times normal atmospheric pressure and over double the pressure in a car tyre. The high pressure is needed because the tyres need to be extremely narrow and rigid to reduce the friction from the road surface.

Key vocabulary

pressurised

barometer

altimeter

valve

Checking your progress

To make good progress in understanding science you need to focus on these ideas and skills.

Describe the attraction of unlike poles and repulsion of like poles; show how a magnetic field can be represented.

Identify magnetic attraction and repulsion as non-contact forces; explain how field lines indicate the direction and strength of forces.

Apply and evaluate the concept of magnetic fields in various contexts.

Describe how friction between objects may cause electrostatic charge through the transfer of electrons.

Explain various examples of electrostatic charge; use ideas of electron transfer to explain different effects.

Explain why some electrostatic charge mechanisms are more effective than others.

Describe the field around a charged object; describe some applications of static electricity.

Use the idea of fields to explain various examples and applications of static electricity.

Compare and contrast useful and dangerous instances of static charge; compare electrostatic and magnetic fields.

Describe the variation and effects of gravity on Earth and in space.

Apply the concept of gravitational fields to explain the variation and effects of gravity on Earth and in space.

Apply the concept of gravitational fields in explaining gravitational effects on Earth and in space, including acceleration.

Describe the causes and effects of varying pressure on and by solids.

Explain the effects of varying pressure on and by solids; calculate the pressure applied by a solid from the force applied and the contact surface area.

Explain how force and area can be varied to alter the pressure applied.

Describe the variation of pressure in liquids with depth and the effects of this.

Explain the variation of pressure with depth in liquids.

Identify the causes and implications of variation of pressure with depth.

Suggest why some objects float and others sink.

Use the concepts of density, displacement and upthrust in explaining floating and sinking.

Apply ideas about density and upthrust to predict the outcomes of various situations.

Describe how atmospheric pressure varies with height; state some implications of variations in pressure.

Explain why atmospheric pressure varies with height; describe how the effects of pressure are used and dealt with.

Identify some implications of pressure variation in situations such as weather patterns and high-altitude activities.

Questions

See how well you have understood the ideas in the chapter.

1. Thinking about electrostatic charge, which of these statements is true? [1]

   a) positive (+) charge repels negative (–) charge

   b) positive (+) charge attracts positive (+) charge

   c) negative (–) charge attracts positive (+) charge

   d) negative (–) charge attracts negative (–) charge.

2. Which is the correct explanation of pressure? [1]

   a) Pressure is higher when the force applied is smaller.

   b) Pressure reduces when the area that a force is applied to is decreased.

   c) When you push a drawing pin into a board, the pressure is the same on both ends.

   d) Pressure depends on the size of a force and the area over which it is acting.

3. Which of the units is correct for pressure? [1]

   a) Pa   **b)** Nm^2 **c)** N   **d)** force

4. Which of these statements is *not* true? [1]

   a) The gravitational field of a planet is stronger on its surface than 100 km away.

   b) Gravity exists throughout the Solar System.

   c) Small objects have very weak gravitational fields.

   d) The acceleration caused by gravity is larger for heavy masses.

5. Why does a wooden block float but a steel one sink? [2]

6. Explain how the pressure that a chair exerts on the floor would be affected if table mats were put under all the legs. [2]

7. Explain, with the help of diagrams, how to indicate the strength of the field around a magnet. [4]

See how well you can apply the ideas in this chapter to new situations.

8. Four identically sized boats (a–d) were floated in some water. One was left empty and the other three were loaded with equal masses of different materials:

   a) boat loaded with wood   **b)** boat loaded with aluminium

   c) boat carrying nothing   **d)** boat loaded with steel

   Put the boats in order from the one that sits lowest in the water to the one that sits highest. [1]

9. What pressure is produced by a 20 N force pressing on an area of 2 m²? [1]

    a) 100 Pa **b)** 40 Pa **c)** 10 Pa **d)** 0.1 Pa

10. In which of these examples is pressure the smallest? [1]

    a) a person standing on one foot **b)** a doctor giving an injection
    c) a person lying on the floor **d)** a knife cutting an apple

11. Which of these statements about the atmosphere is *not* true? [1]

    a) Atmospheric pressure is one of the factors that affect the weather.

    b) Somebody with asthma is likely to have more difficulty breathing at the seaside than on a high mountain.

    c) Car engines usually run better close to sea level than in high mountains.

    d) There are more carbon dioxide molecules at low altitude compared to high altitude.

12. Suggest how you could find out if one charged rod has more charge than another of the same material. [2]

13. Describe how a magnet could be used to find pieces of buried metal. [2]

14. Figure 2.5.18a shows the path of a piece of debris travelling through space in the region of three planets. Explain why it takes the path it does at each part of the journey. [4]

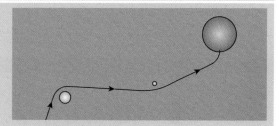

FIGURE 2.5.18a: Path of a piece of debris in space (sizes of planets to scale but distances reduced)

Questions 15–16

See how well you can understand and explain new ideas and evidence.

15. 'Powder' coating is an alternative to painting. Charged powder is sprayed onto an object of opposite charge. It is then heated to bake on the powder. What advantages does powder coating have over conventional painting? [2]

16. Using your knowledge and the data in Figure 2.5.18b to explain the challenges that face a high-altitude mountaineer. [4]

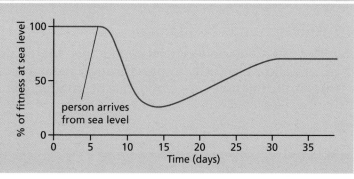

FIGURE 2.5.18b: Graph of a mountaineer's fitness against time when time is spent at 4000 m altitude.

Magnetism and Electricity

Magnets

Magnetic materials are attracted by a magnet. There are only a few different magnetic materials, including iron and steel. Most metals are not magnetic.

Using electricity

Many objects need electricity to run them. We call these 'appliances' – examples include washing machines and mobile phones. All appliances either use the mains electricity supply or a battery to make them work.

Circuits

A simple electric circuit consists of cells, wires, bulbs, switches and buzzers – these are called components; they have specific symbols.

Components in a circuit only work if the circuit is complete and contains a power supply. When the switch is open, the circuit is not complete and none of the appliances will work. If more cells are added to a circuit, the brightness of bulbs or the loudness of buzzers in the circuit will increase.

Insulators and conductors

All metals are good electrical conductors. Materials that do not allow electricity to pass through them are called insulators. Examples are wood, plastic, rubber, cloth and air.

How magnets work

- People used magnets for over a thousand years without understanding how they work.
- The domain theory explains what happens in magnetic materials and why only certain materials are magnetic.
- The Earth is magnetic because its core contains molten iron.
- We can make and test magnets using different methods.

Electromagnets

- When a coil of wire is placed in a magnetic field and a current is passed through it, the coil moves. This is because the coil of wire acts as a magnet itself – an electromagnet.
- In an electromagnet it is possible to switch the magnetic field off. Metal-recycling plants use electromagnets to separate iron and steel from aluminium.
- Electromagnetism is the basis of the motors used in power tools, mixers and cars.

Explaining electric circuits

- The current is a flow of electrons. This depends on the 'push' given by the battery, known as the voltage. Components in the circuits provide opposition to the current – we call this resistance. The current, voltage and resistance are related to each other. Models are a good way of explaining what happens in a circuit.

Series and parallel circuits

- Components in circuits can be arranged in series, in parallel or in both. These arrangements have different effects on the voltage and current, and provide different applications. Circuit breakers are arranged in series, but many Christmas tree lights are arranged in parallel.

Looking at the history of magnets

We are learning how to:

- Summarise historical ideas about magnetism.
- Describe how historical ideas about magnetism have changed over time.

People have been using magnets for thousands of years. However, our understanding of how magnetism works is quite recent, and this knowledge has made new technologies possible.

Early ideas and discoveries

In the history of scientific discovery, evidence has often become tangled up with superstitious ideas. This happened in the development of our understanding of **magnetism**.

It is reported that about 4000 years ago on the Greek island of Magnesia there was a shepherd named Magnes. The nails in his shoes and the metal tip of his staff became firmly stuck to a large, black rock. He dug up the ground and found special stones called lodestones.

Chinese people wrote about the mariner's compass in the 11th century. This consisted of a splinter of lodestone floating on top of some water. They realised the lodestone pointed in a north–south direction.

FIGURE 2.6.2a: Lodestones were the first magnets observed.

> ### Did you know...?
>
> The Earth itself is a huge magnet. The magnet's north pole is near the geographic South Pole, and the magnet's south pole is near the geographic North Pole. The magnetic field is very weak but it extends beyond the Earth for many thousands of kilometres.

At first, some people were superstitious about lodestones and believed they had healing powers. Many medicines were made of lodestone because people thought that it had a soul.

1. Give two pieces of evidence that describe the properties of lodestones.

2. Why do you think people developed superstitious ideas about lodestone?

The impact of evidence »»

Centuries passed with people using **magnets** as a means of navigation, but it was not until 1600 that a doctor called William Gilbert discovered a connection between magnetism and the Earth. He recorded different ways of magnetising steel, either by touching it with lodestone or by long exposure in a north–south direction. He concluded that the Earth itself must be magnetic.

Gilbert's finding came about through scientific testing, ignoring many historical ideas, and drawing conclusions specifically from experiments. He presented his results clearly in a scientific paper, so other scientists could repeat his investigations and debate his work, developing the idea of **peer review**. However, in those days published papers were shared only among a select group, often chosen by the scientist conducting the work.

In 1820, Hans Christian Oersted observed that a current flowing through a wire would cause a magnet to move the wire. After publishing his findings, many scientists of the time became very excited and began their own research. Eventually links between current and magnetism were made and the first electromagnet was produced. Finally, in the late 1800s, through experiments conducted by Michael Faraday, magnetism was used to generate electricity.

FIGURE 2.6.2b: The magnetic compass has been used by navigators for about a thousand years. By taking bearings of visible objects with a compass, navigators can work out the position of their ship.

3. In what ways did the approach to magnetism differ from the 1600s to the 1800s compared with that in earlier times?

4. What impact did these new approaches have?

New applications of magnetism »»»

With the use of models and improved knowledge of atoms, the way magnetism works is now understood better. Research is published worldwide and peer reviewed on a global scale. In the 1970s, this enabled research into new materials called rare-earth magnets. These are now used in many technologies, including computers, medical equipment and renewable energy. They are much stronger than conventional iron magnets, resulting in energy savings across the world.

FIGURE 2.6.2c: Without an understanding of magnetism, research into these rare-earth metals would not have been carried out.

5. What factors do you think have contributed to the increased speed of technological developments in today's world compared to the speed in the Middle Ages (1000 to 1500)?

6. How could scientists in the Middle Ages have worked differently to improve the speed of their developments?

Key vocabulary

magnetism

magnet

peer review

Exploring magnetic materials

We are learning how to:

- Investigate magnetism in materials.
- Explain magnetism using the domain theory.

We know that magnetic force can attract and repel. But why can some materials behave as magnets while others cannot?

Permanent and temporary magnets

A **permanent magnet** keeps its magnetism for a long period of time – in the case of lodestone, this can be for thousands of years. Permanent magnets have their own magnetic field, which arises from the properties of the material they are made from. Iron, cobalt and nickel are the only common elements that can show permanent magnetism.

Most permanent magnets we use are man-made from alloys (mixtures of metals, such as steel), which produce a stronger magnetic field. Fridge magnets, compasses, computers and loudspeakers all use permanent magnets.

A **temporary magnet** is one that is attracted by a magnet and shows magnetic properties in the presence of a magnetic field. For example, when a paper clip is attached to a magnet, it is able to attract another paper clip. Remove it from the magnet, and magnetic properties are no longer observed. **Electromagnets** are special types of temporary magnets. They are only magnetic when an electric current passes through them.

1. Are all materials affected by a magnetic field?

2. Predict what you could do to improve the strength of a temporary magnet.

The domain theory of magnets

In magnetic materials like iron, steel, cobalt and nickel, groups of atoms bind together in a magnetic **domain**, aligned in the same magnetic direction. If the material is unmagnetised, these domains are arranged randomly in many different directions. The magnetic effect cancels out.

When the material is magnetised, the domains line up and point in the same direction. This causes one end of the material to become a magnetic north pole (N) and the

FIGURE 2.6.3a: Which of these magnets is temporary and which is permanent?

other end a south pole (S). The greater the alignment of the domains, the stronger the magnet.

3. Use the domain theory to explain why materials such as copper and aluminium are non-magnetic even when placed in a magnetic field.

4. Explain what happens, in terms of domains, to a steel paper clip when it is placed in a magnetic field.

Making permanent magnets ⟩⟩⟩

Iron and steel items can be made into permanent magnets using a variety of methods:

- Stroke a steel rod with a permanent magnet up to 20 times in the same direction.
- Place a steel rod next to a strong permanent magnet for a short length of time.
- Put a steel rod in a long coil of wire that has a direct current passing through it.
- Place a steel rod in a magnetic field, heat it to a high temperature and then hammer it, holding the steel rod in the same direction, as it cools.
- Hold a steel bar vertically and strike it with a hammer several times.

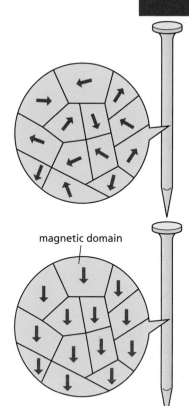

magnetic domain

FIGURE 2.6.3b: Which is the magnetised nail?

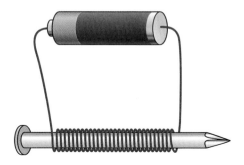

FIGURE 2.6.3c: One way to make a magnet

To remove the magnetism from a permanent magnet, the domain alignment must be disrupted, returning to a random arrangement. This can be done by dropping, hammering, heating or stroking the magnetised material randomly with another magnet.

5. Explain, using the domain theory, why stroking a steel rod with a magnet is likely to make it magnetic, but hammering it randomly will remove its magnetism.

6. Summarise and explain all the factors that affect the domains within a magnet.

Did you know...?

The world record for the strongest pulse magnet (in which the magnetic field lasts for a short period only) was set in 2012 in the USA. It is two million times stronger than the Earth's magnetic field!

Key vocabulary

permanent magnet

temporary magnet

electromagnet

domain

Testing the strength of magnets

We are learning how to:

- Compare different methods of testing magnets.
- Collect data to investigate the strength of magnetism.

There are different ways to test the strength of magnets. Do all these methods give the same results, or are some better at comparing magnets? How can you evaluate each method to determine which is the most effective?

Ways to measure magnetic strength ▷▷

The strength of a magnet can be tested simply by the following methods:

- Measure the number of objects, such as steel paper clips, that a magnet can hold, adding one at a time – the stronger the magnet, the more paper clips it will hold.

- Investigate the distance at which an object, such as a paper clip, is attracted to a magnet – the stronger the magnet, the farther the distance from which it will attract an object.

- Investigate the magnetic field using iron filings to 'see' the field lines. The closer the iron filings bunch together, the stronger the field. A diagram can be used to represent the field – the stronger the magnetic field, the closer together the field lines are drawn.

FIGURE 2.6.4a: Testing the strength of a magnet

1. Which method in Figures 2.6.4a and 2.6.4b is likely to provide the most reliable results?

2. Which method involves making the most accurate measurements?

Comparing methods ▷▷▷

Table 2.6.4 shows the results from two different ways to compare the strengths of magnets: counting the number of paper clips the magnet can hold, and measuring the distance from which a paper clip can be attracted to the magnet.

Some methods of making measurements are, however, **subjective**. This means that different people may interpret the results differently. Examples of this are judging the distance between magnetic field lines with the eye, or estimating the number of paper clips held by a magnet simply by looking at

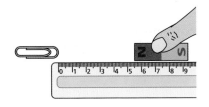

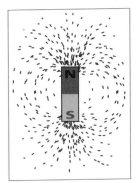

FIGURE 2.6.4b: Two other ways of testing a magnet's strength. Which method is best?

them instead of counting them. In a scientific method, it is better to choose some kind of measurement that provides a reading. This improves the **reliability** of the data.

TABLE 2.6.4: Results of two different ways of comparing the strengths of magnets

	Number of paper clips held	**Distance from which it attracts a paper clip (cm)**
Magnet 1	100	20
Magnet 2	100	25
Magnet 3	100	28
Magnet 4	100	30

3. What is wrong with subjective measurements in science?

4. Can you think of at least one reason why the results in one column of Table 2.6.4 are the same but those in the other column are different?

Evaluating scientific methods

To evaluate different methods of measuring magnetic strength, we need to compare the **repeatability**, **reproducibility**, **accuracy** and **precision** of the data from the different methods

Repeatability

The same person carries out repeat tests of the investigation. The closer the readings are to each other, the more repeatable the data. Ideally readings should be taken, outliers identified and eliminated, and then the mean calculated from three close values.

Reproducibility

If the method can be repeated exactly and the same results can be obtained by another person, then it is reproducible.

Accuracy and precision

Data close to the true values are accurate. This depends greatly on the way you conduct your investigation and the type of equipment used. Taking readings of finer measurements can result in greater precision. For example, using a metre rule marked in centimetres to measure the distance over which an object is attracted by a magnet will not be as precise as using a measurement ruler marked in millimetres.

5. Look at the data in Table 2.6.4. How repeatable do you think this investigation is?

6. Is a repeatable investigation always reproducible? Explain your answer.

> **Did you know...?**
>
> The strongest magnetic force in the Universe is produced by a type of neutron star. It has a magnetic field of about 10^8 tesla (about 10^{11} times that of a fridge magnet).

Key vocabulary

subjective

reliability

repeatability

reproducibility

accuracy

precision

Describing the Earth's magnetic field

We are learning how to:

- Explain evidence for the Earth's magnetic field.
- Explain the impact the Earth's magnetic field has on our planet.

Without the Earth's magnetic field there would be no life on this planet. It protects us from deadly charged particles carried in solar winds from the Sun. How does it do this and what causes the Earth's magnetic field to exist?

Evidence of the Earth's magnetic field

All compasses respond to magnetic fields. The fact that they all line up in a north–south direction (when not near a magnet) is evidence that the Earth must have its own magnetic field.

The N pole of a magnetic compass needle points in a geographical north direction, wherever it is on Earth. This is evidence that the Earth's geographic North Pole is actually the Earth's magnetic S pole, or very close to it (look back at Figure 2.5.3c in Chapter 5).

We also know from magnetic rocks that the poles of the Earth's magnetic field are not fixed, but reverse every few hundred thousand years.

1. Summarise the evidence for the Earth's magnetic field.

2. Use your understanding of how magnets are made to suggest how lodestone (see Topic 6.2) was first magnetised.

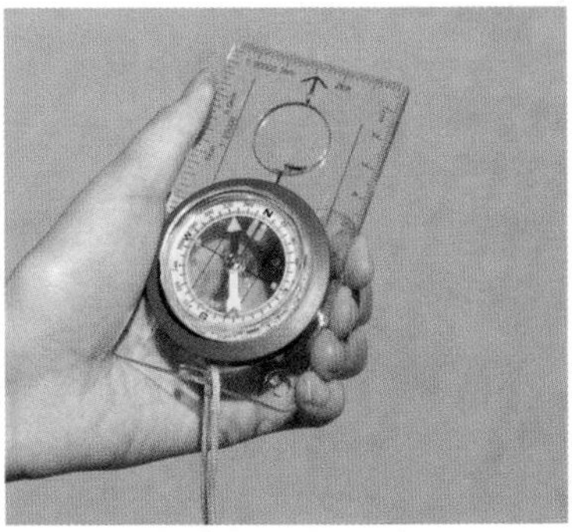

FIGURE 2.6.5a: Using the Earth's magnetic field

The geodynamo theory

Evidence about the structure of the centre of the Earth has largely come from earthquakes, volcanoes and rocks.

Scientists believe the centre of the Earth is made from a core of solid iron, surrounded by a liquid core of iron and nickel. The spinning action of the Earth causes the liquid core to spin in a regular way. This movement causes charged particles to move, forming small currents. Electric currents produce magnetic fields and so magnetic domains within the liquid develop, lining up to create a weak magnetic field. This is called the **geodynamo theory**.

3. Why can we not be certain about how the Earth's magnetic field works?

4. Draw a diagram to show how the magnetic fields in the Earth might arise.

Impact of the Earth's magnetic field ▶▶▶▶

The **magnetosphere** is the magnetic field around the Earth. It extends out into space and is shaped by the **solar wind** caused by the Sun's activity. Figure 2.6.5b shows this.

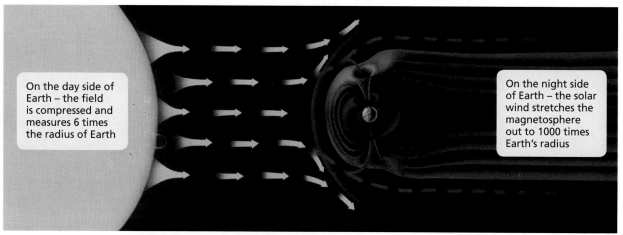

On the day side of Earth – the field is compressed and measures 6 times the radius of Earth

On the night side of Earth – the solar wind stretches the magnetosphere out to 1000 times Earth's radius

FIGURE 2.6.5b: The effects of the solar wind on the shape of the Earth's magnetosphere

The magnetosphere prevents deadly cosmic rays and the highly charged particles in solar winds from reaching the Earth. Without this protection, it would be impossible for life to exist here.

Energy and highly charged particles from the Sun create magnetic storms in the magnetosphere. Most damage is deflected by the magnetosphere, but sometimes the storms are so strong they disrupt GPS systems and other satellites, and cause the need for aircraft to find alternative routes.

Geologists study rocks in different layers in the Earth. The deeper the rocks are, the older they are. By testing the magnetic field of magnetic rocks, scientists can determine which is the N pole and which is the S pole. Evidence for over 170 pole reversals in the past 71 million years has been reported. A reversal occurs roughly every 400 000 years – the most recent took place 780 000 years ago and geologists believe another is due in the next few thousand years.

5. Why is the magnetosphere larger on the night side of the Earth?

6. Describe an experiment you might carry out to test the magnetic polarity of different rocks.

Did you know...?

The planet Mercury also has its own magnetic field. However, it is not as strong as the Earth's and, because it is closer to the Sun, solar winds cause much more damage to its surface.

Key vocabulary

geodynamo theory

magnetosphere

solar wind

Investigating electromagnetism

We are learning how to:

- Describe what an electromagnet is.
- Investigate the factors affecting the strength of electromagnets.

If you pass a current through any wire, a weak magnetic field is produced. This link between electricity and magnetism has been thoroughly investigated, enabling us to make very powerful, controllable electromagnets.

What is an electromagnet?

In 1820, a Danish scientist, Hans Oersted, passed a **current** through a single wire. Placing a compass near the wire, he noticed that the needle moved, proving that a **magnetic field** was present. When the current was switched off, the needle returned to its normal position. Oersted had taken the first steps towards understanding electromagnetism.

Any wire with a current passing through it will produce a magnetic field. When the current is switched off, the magnetic field disappears. Any magnet that uses electricity to produce a magnetic field is called an **electromagnet**.

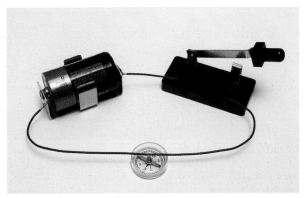

FIGURE 2.6.6a: When the switch completes the circuit, the compass needle moves – the current in the wire is acting like a magnet.

1. How is an electromagnet different from a permanent magnet?

2. Describe two different ways to prove that an electromagnet is magnetic.

Making electromagnets stronger

Oersted made a very weak electromagnet because he used a single wire and a small current.

The strength of an electromagnet can be increased by:
- increasing the current passing through the wire
- making the wire into a coil
- increasing the number of coils in the wire
- putting an **iron core** in the centre of the coil.

Did you know...?

There is a limit to how strong you can make an electromagnet. Once all the domains within the iron core are lined up, the strength of the magnet cannot be increased, no matter how much more current is applied.

Figure 2.6.6b shows a simple electromagnet consisting of a battery and a coil of wire surrounding an iron nail. The wire is covered by electrical insulation so that it does not connect electrically with the iron nail. When a current is passed through the wire, it causes the iron nail to become magnetic.

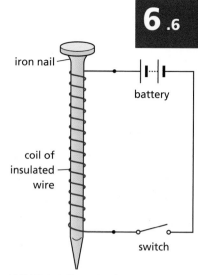

FIGURE 2.6.6b: A simple electromagnet, here made using an iron nail

3. Remind yourself of the domain theory described in Topic 6.3. How do you think the current affects the domains in the iron core?

4. Draw an electromagnet you might use to attract a steel paper clip. Explain how you could modify your electromagnet so that it could attract and lift a car.

5. How would you drop the car?

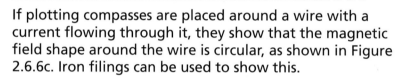

Magnetic fields around electromagnets

If plotting compasses are placed around a wire with a current flowing through it, they show that the magnetic field shape around the wire is circular, as shown in Figure 2.6.6c. Iron filings can be used to show this.

The shape of the magnetic field around a long coil of current-carrying wire is similar to that of a bar magnet, as shown in Figure 2.6.6d. One end of the coil is the N pole and the other end is the S pole. Reversing the direction of the current reverses the magnetic field – the S pole becomes the N pole and vice versa. Increasing the number of coils increases the magnetic field around the loops, resulting in a stronger field. Using a magnetic material, like iron, as a core strengthens the field.

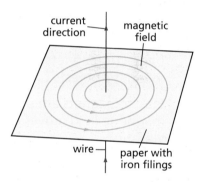

FIGURE 2.6.6c: The shape of the magnetic field around a wire carrying a current

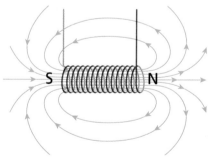

FIGURE 2.6.6d: Coils with many turns of wire are used in electromagnetic devices.

6. What would happen to the magnetic field lines if the current in Figure 2.6.6d was increased?

7. Why are the coils of an electromagnet placed in line and not in a random way?

8. Explain the advantages of an electromagnet over a permanent magnet for devices that require a magnet.

Key vocabulary

current

magnetic field

electromagnet

iron core

Using electromagnets

We are learning how to:

• Describe different applications of electromagnets.

The main advantage of using electromagnets over ordinary magnets is that the magnetic field can be switched on or off at will, making them easier to control. This has resulted in a wide range of applications.

Common uses of electromagnets

Electromagnets are used in many different devices.

• In your computer hard drive, tiny electromagnets are used to help store information on a disk.

• Separating iron and steel from non-magnetic metals, such as aluminium and copper, is one of the main uses of electromagnets. Switching the current off allows the magnetic objects to fall from the electromagnet.

• Electromagnets are used in loudspeakers – the magnetic field moves a diaphragm to amplify the sound vibrations.

1. Give two advantages of using electromagnets.

2. Give one disadvantage of using an electromagnet compared to an ordinary magnet in the applications listed above.

FIGURE 2.6.7a: How is this electromagnet being used?

The electric bell

The circuit inside an electric bell is shown in Figure 2.6.7b.

When the switch is closed at A, a current flows. The iron core of the electromagnet at B becomes magnetised.

The iron bar, called the **armature**, at C is attracted to the electromagnet and moves towards it. The hammer, connected to the armature, moves to strike the gong.

The springy steel strip at D moves away from the **contact** screw as the hammer strikes the gong, breaking the circuit.

Because the current no longer flows through the electromagnet, it loses its magnetism. The armature is no longer attracted and moves back to its original place.

Did you know...?

Electromagnets are used to remove tiny pieces of metal that accidentally enter the eye. They offer greater control than ordinary magnets, so there is less risk of injuring the eye.

The steel strip is once again in touch with the contact screw and the circuit will complete again as long as the switch remains pushed.

3. What must be done to stop an electric bell from ringing? Explain your answer.

4. What would happen if the electromagnet in an electric bell was replaced with an ordinary magnet?

The circuit breaker

A **circuit breaker** is designed as a safety device. It breaks a circuit if too much current is drawn from the mains, and so protects appliances. Household appliances and lighting are protected with circuit breakers.

Figure 2.6.7c shows how a circuit breaker works. In normal operation, a low current passes through the appliance and the electromagnet. Because the current is low, the electromagnet is weak and so is not strong enough to separate the iron contacts. If the appliance malfunctions and too much current passes through the wire, the electromagnet becomes stronger, attracting the iron contacts. This breaks the connection between the iron contacts and breaks the circuit, protecting the appliance. The spring prevents the contacts from reconnecting.

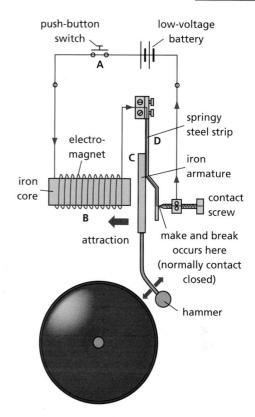

FIGURE 2.6.7b: How an electric bell works

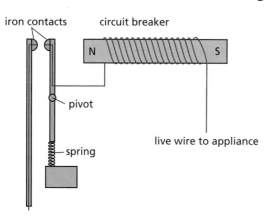

FIGURE 2.6.7c: How an electromagnetic circuit breaker works

5. In a circuit breaker, why is it important for the contacts, once broken by the electromagnet, to remain unconnected?

6. What advantages do circuit breakers have over ordinary switches?

Key vocabulary

armature

contact

circuit breaker

Exploring D.C. motors

We are learning how to:

- Describe the magnetic effect of a current and how this is applied to D.C. motors.

In certain applications, magnetic energy can be harnessed and transferred to energy by movement. The world of motors relies on this energy transfer. Motors are used in many ways, from small electric drills to giant stone cutters in deep mines.

Uses of electric motors

Electric motors are devices that use electromagnets or permanent magnets. They transfer energy by electricity and use a magnetic force to cause movement and do useful work.

Electric motors are used in many common appliances, such as food mixers, vacuum cleaners, cars, washing machines and electric drills. Every electrical device that transfers energy by electricity to energy by movement uses an electric motor.

1. Name three other devices that use electric motors.

2. Draw an energy transfer diagram to summarise the energy transfer in an electric motor.

Discovering the motor effect

We have learnt that a wire with a current passing through it produces a magnetic effect. In 1831, after the discovery, Michael Faraday found that when a wire carrying a current was placed in a magnetic field, it moved. It moved in a direction at right angles to both the field and the current. If the direction of the current was reversed, the direction of the movement was also reversed. The magnetic effect of a current was being transferred to energy by movement.

FIGURE 2.6.8a: Which appliance does not have an electric motor?

In Figure 2.6.8b, when the permanent magnet is placed over the wire and the current passes through, there are two magnetic fields – one from the permanent magnet and one from the wire. These two fields will attract or repel, causing the wire to move. This is called the **motor effect**.

A 'D.C. motor' works using the motor effect arising from a **direct current (D.C.)**, which means a current that always flows in one direction.

3. In Figure 2.6.8b, when the current is switched on, the wire moves downwards. What would happen if the battery were connected the other way around?

4. Can the set-up shown in Figure 2.6.8b produce any useful work?

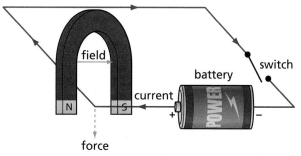

FIGURE 2.6.8b: The motor effect. What happens if the battery is disconnected?

Stronger electric motors ⟩⟩⟩

The amount of movement of the wire can be increased by:

- Increasing the current, which increases the strength of the magnetic field around the wire. This causes a bigger repulsion or attraction.

- Increasing the strength of the magnetic field of the permanent magnet. This can be done by using a stronger magnet, or changing the material the magnet is made from, so more domains within the material are lined up.

- Making the straight wire into a coil with many turns. This increases the strength of the magnetic field around the wire.

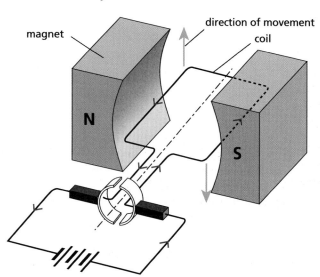

FIGURE 2.6.8c: A simple D.C. motor

Figure 2.6.8c shows how these measures work. The permanent magnet (or electromagnet) surrounds a coil of wire. The coil is able to spin freely. When a current passes through the coil, a magnetic field is produced. This interacts with the magnetic field of the magnet, which causes the coil to turn upwards. In order to allow the coil to spin, the poles of the magnetic field must be reversed. The brushes reverse the polarity of the current and so reverse the magnetic field due to the coil. In this way, the coil is able to keep spinning, enabling useful work to be done.

5. What would happen if the magnetic poles due to the coil were not reversed?

6. Motors can have different speeds. How can the speed of the motor be controlled?

> **Did you know...?**
>
> The tiniest motor built works on the atomic scale, enabling atoms to be moved.

Key vocabulary

electric motor

motor effect

direct current (D.C.)

Applying key ideas

You have now met a number of important ideas in this chapter. This activity gives an opportunity for you to apply them, just as scientists do. Read the text first, and then have a go at the tasks. The first few are fairly easy – then they become a bit more challenging.

How can magnets be used to operate trains?

Technology that uses magnets to operate trains, called Maglev trains, is in use in some parts of the world. The first commercial Maglev train ran between Birmingham airport and the railway station – it operated from 1984 to 1995. In 2004, China installed the first high-speed commercially operated train in Shanghai, followed closely by Japan in 2005. Germany has also been active in developing this technology.

Maglev trains do not have a conventional engine, which runs on diesel – they rely on the use of electromagnets. There are three main parts to the system:

FIGURE 2.6.9a: The speed reached by a Maglev train relies on electromagnetic propulsion and streamlined design.

- a large electrical power source (in China and Japan much of their electricity is produced by nuclear power, which means they do not rely on fossil fuels for their energy source)

- metal coils lining the guideway

- large guidance magnets underneath the train to cause repulsion between the train and the rail.

When a current flows through the coils in the guidance magnets, a magnetic field is produced. This field repels large magnets on the undercarriage of the train. The effect of this is to lift the train up (make it levitate) so that it no longer touches the rail underneath. It can rise between 1 cm and 10 cm. Other electromagnets in the propulsion coil, situated in the guideway walls, then propel the train forwards.

As a result of this design, when the Maglev trains are in operation there is no friction between the train and the track. With a sleek aerodynamic design, speeds of over 500 km/h (310 mph) can be reached!

A special type of electromagnet is used, known as superconducting magnets. These are made of materials such as niobium and titanium, and they must be kept at a very low temperature during operation. This enables them to transfer much higher currents through the coils compared to those transferred through normal wires. Magnetic fields of up to 15 teslas are possible with this system.

The setting up of a Maglev system is highly technical and very expensive. In addition, large amounts of electricity are needed to keep the trains in operation. These are some of the reasons why the technology is not more widespread. The advantages it holds, however, are very significant. With the ability to travel at such high speeds comfortably, the time for travelling between places is significantly reduced. As a result, there would be less traffic on the roads. The problem with noise as the air rushes past the train at such high speeds is still to be addressed.

Task 1: Types of magnets

Maglev trains use electromagnets in order to operate. Describe the main differences between electromagnets and ordinary bar magnets.

Task 2: Levitation

Draw a simple diagram, including ideas about magnetic polarity, to show why Maglev trains levitate.

Task 3: Making the magnetic field stronger

Explain the main factors that can increase the strength of an electromagnet. How has the design of the electromagnets in the Maglev trains been further modified to make the field even stronger?

Task 4: Benefits of superconducting electromagnets

You are a salesperson for superconducting electromagnets. Design a sales poster outlining all the benefits of using electromagnets to move trains compared to ordinary rail systems.

Task 5: Effect of field reversal

The Earth's magnetic field can reverse every few hundred thousand years. Use ideas about the domain theory to explain whether or not this event is likely to affect the electromagnets in the Maglev trains.

Task 6: What are the disadvantages?

Explain all the disadvantages of the Maglev system and suggest reasons why this technology has not been adopted, so far, in other countries.

Investigating batteries

We are learning how to:

- Describe the link between chemical energy and electricity.
- Investigate how fruit batteries work.

We have learnt how electricity and magnetism are linked. There is also a link between electricity and chemical energy, which we now explore.

Different types of battery

There are many different types of batteries in the world. They all have one thing in common – energy is transferred by chemical reactions to electrical energy. The amount of chemicals and types of reactions involved determine how much energy can be transferred.

The first **battery** was developed by Alessandro Volta, who placed brass and copper plates in a salty solution. The brass contains zinc, which enables the battery to work.

By using different metals and solutions, more or less electricity can be transferred.

FIGURE 2.6.10a: Alessandro Volta and his battery, in about 1800

1. Why do you think batteries become hot if they are used for long periods of time?

2. Draw an energy transfer diagram to show the changes taking place in a battery.

How do batteries work?

In Topic 5.5 you learned about static electricity – the transfer of charged particles by rubbing different materials together. The resulting force of attraction or repulsion leads to the transfer of energy by movement.

Charged particles are also involved in current electricity. In a battery, negatively charged particles, called **electrons**, move as a result of chemical changes in the battery. They build up on the negative terminal of the battery, causing electrons within the metal wires in all parts of the circuit to move away from the negative terminal. The flow of electrons forms the **electric current** – this can be used to transfer energy that makes appliances work. The bigger the difference in charge between the negative and positive terminals of the battery, the greater is the energy that can be transferred by the current.

FIGURE 2.6.10b: Charged particles move through the solution between the copper plate and the zinc plate. This creates an electric current in the circuit.

The disadvantage of using batteries, compared to generating electricity from movement energy using a dynamo, is that the energy is transferred out of the battery and the battery needs to be replaced or recharged.

3. Summarise in a bullet list how a battery works.

4. What are the advantages of using batteries, compared with a dynamo, to make an electric current?

Explaining fruit batteries

Figure 2.6.10c shows a fruit battery in operation. Two different metals are placed, a distance apart, at the same depth within the fruit. Wires connect the two metals in a circuit containing a meter that shows a **voltage** is produced. The liquid inside the fruit enables charged particles in the fruit to take part in the chemical changes – a battery will not work with dried fruit.

FIGURE 2.6.10c: A fruit battery

Different combinations of metals will produce different results. Table 2.6.10 shows the voltages from an investigation of different combinations of metals.

TABLE 2.6.10: Results from an investigation of different combinations of metals

Metal 1	Metal 2	Voltage produced (V)
copper	zinc	0.75
copper	magnesium	1.37
copper	iron	0.49
zinc	magnesium	0.67
zinc	iron	0.31
iron	magnesium	0.95

potassium	most reactive	K
sodium		Na
calcium		Ca
magnesium		Mg
aluminium		Al
carbon		C
zinc		Zn
iron		Fe
tin		Sn
lead		Pb
hydrogen		H
copper		Cu
silver		Ag
gold	least	Au
platinum	reactive	Pt

FIGURE 2.6.10d: Reactivity series of elements

5. Look at Table 2.6.10 and Figure 2.6.10d. Can you see a pattern between the metals that produce the highest voltage and their reactivity?

6. Apart from changing the metals, can you think of two other ways of increasing the voltage from a fruit battery? Explain how each one works.

Key vocabulary

battery

electron

electric current

voltage

Describing electric circuits

We are learning how to:

- Describe and draw circuit diagrams.
- Explain what is meant by current.
- Explain how materials allow current to flow.

A light bulb in an electric circuit lights up instantaneously. Even if the circuit were the size of a football pitch, there would be no time delay for the light to come on. What is actually going on in the circuit for energy to be transferred so quickly?

Components in electric circuits

An electric circuit is a loop of wire with its ends connected to an energy source, such as a battery or cell. Strictly, a 'battery' is two or more cells together.

When a circuit is complete, energy is transferred from the battery to the wires by an electric current. Devices such as light bulbs, motors and buzzers are **components** that can make use of the energy transferred from the battery.

The components in the circuit need an electric current to pass through them. If there are any gaps in the circuit, the current will not flow and energy cannot be transferred. A material that allows current to pass through it is called an electrical **conductor**. These have electrons that are free to move within the conductor. An electrical **insulator** does not have any free electrons and cannot allow a current to pass.

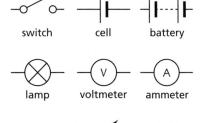

FIGURE 2.6.11a: Circuit symbols for common components

 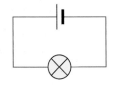  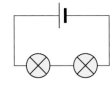

FIGURE 2.6.11b: How circuit symbols are used to represent components in a circuit diagram

1. If pencil lead is placed in a circuit with a light bulb, the bulb lights up. What conclusion can you draw about this material?

2. Draw a circuit diagram for a circuit with one cell and three bulbs.

3. Why is it important to represent components with symbols?

Current is the rate of flow of charge (electrons) in the circuit, and is given the symbol *I*. It is measured by an **ammeter** in **amperes** (symbol A), after the French scientist Andre-Marie Ampere.

Models and analogies are often used to explain complex phenomena like current. One analogy is to compare electric current to water flowing in a stream. The charges are the water particles, and the current is the flowing stream.

FIGURE 2.6.11c: In the analogies pictured in the photos, what represents the charge and what represents the current?

Another analogy used to represent current is that of a convoy of coal trucks. The trucks represent the charged particles, the movement of the trucks represents the current, and the coal they carry represents the energy they transfer.

4. Using first the water analogy and then the coal-truck analogy, draw diagrams to show the difference between a low current and a high current.

5. Which analogy is better at explaining that current transfers energy to different components? Explain your answer.

Scientific explanation of current >>>

When the battery is connected, the electrons in all parts of the wires within the circuit move at the same time, in the same direction and at the same rate. This movement constitutes the current. In this way, no matter where the components are in the circuit, they will all conduct at the same time – there is no delay because all the electrons in the circuit move simultaneously.

Current is not used up in the circuit. It has the same value before and after each component in the circuit – indeed, it is the same everywhere in the circuit.

6. Explain the strengths and limitations of the two analogies above, in light of the scientific explanation for current.

7. Explain why current is not used up in a circuit.

Did you know...?

A current of 1 amp means there are 6 250 000 000 000 000 000 electrons flowing past a point every second!

Key vocabulary

component

conductor

insulator

ammeter

ampere

Understanding energy in circuits

We are learning how to:

- Describe what the voltage does in a circuit.
- Explain voltage using different analogies.

We know that an electric circuit gets its energy from a battery. The amount of potential energy within a battery is measured by the number of volts it has. Volts are the measurement of voltage.

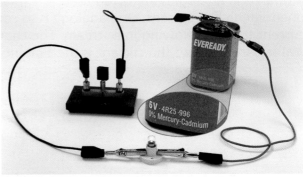

FIGURE 2.6.12a: What do we mean by voltage?

What is voltage?

We can think of **voltage** as a measure of the size of 'push' that causes a current to flow around a circuit. Because the current is a flow of charge, something is needed to make the charges move.

If there is no voltage, then there can be no current flowing because there is nothing to cause the charges to move. The larger the voltage, the bigger the 'push' and the more current that can potentially flow.

The symbol for voltage is V and the unit is **volts** (V).

The energy source for the voltage is usually a battery or cell, but it can also come from a mains socket. A large energy source, like a big car battery of 12 V, will provide more 'push' or voltage and hence more current than a small cell of 1.5 V.

If two cells are connected together side-by-side, the voltage across them is the sum of the voltage of each cell. This is because both cells are 'pushing' the same way.

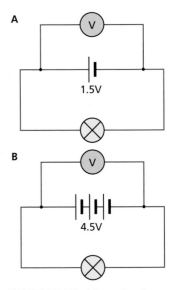

FIGURE 2.6.12b: Measuring the voltage across cells

1. Why does no current flow if there is no voltage?

2. Figure 2.6.12b shows two circuits, one with one cell and the other with three cells. If, instead, there were two cells, what reading would the voltmeter give?

Voltage and components

If there is a higher voltage, there will be more current flowing and therefore more energy being transferred to the components. A light bulb will be much brighter if it is connected to a 6 V battery rather than to a 3 V battery in a similar circuit. Voltage is measured using a **voltmeter** (Figure 2.6.12d).

Did you know...?

Electric eels can produce electrical discharges of around 500 V in self-defence.

Figure 2.6.12c shows how the voltmeter must be connected *across* a component (here a bulb) to measure the energy difference in the current either side of the component.

3. In which of the circuits in Figure 2.6.12b will the light bulb be the brightest? Explain your answer.

4. What might happen to a motor if it were connected to the 230 V mains electric supply rather than to a 12 V battery?

Using analogies to explain voltage »»»

Imagine blowing gently through a straw. The air flowing through the straw is like a current and the amount of push given to the air is like the voltage. If you blow harder (more voltage) there is more air flow (more current).

A very high waterfall is also like a large voltage. It will transfer a lot of energy to the water (charge), making the river flow very fast (a large current). The difference in height makes the river flow. In a circuit, the difference in charge across the battery provides the push for the current. This is why voltage is also known as **potential difference**.

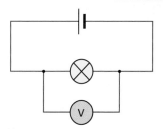

FIGURE 2.6.12c: Measuring the voltage across a bulb

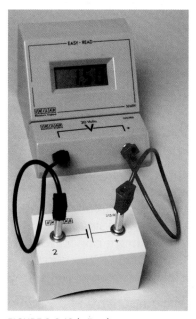

FIGURE 2.6.12d: A voltmeter connected to measure the voltage of a cell

FIGURE 2.6.12e: The difference in height makes the water move.

5. Compare a circuit with a 12 V battery and one light bulb with one that has a 1.5 V cell and one light bulb. Use the two analogies in this topic to explain how they will be different.

6. Explain one limitation for each of the analogies outlined.

Key vocabulary
....

voltage

volt

voltmeter

potential difference

Explaining resistance

We are learning how to:

- Explain what resistance is and how it affects the circuit.
- Investigate and identify the relationship between voltage and current.

All materials offer some opposition to the flow of current – we call this 'resistance'. The amount of resistance can vary widely, even in different metals. Why are some metals, like gold, better at conducting electricity than other metals, like tin?

What is resistance? >>

The word 'resistance' means to oppose. In electric circuits, electrical **resistance** opposes the 'push' provided by the voltage. The overall current flowing through the circuit, therefore, depends on both the voltage and the resistance.

If there is a high voltage and a low resistance, then a large current will flow. This is because there is not very much opposition to the 'push' given by the voltage. Imagine a motor in a circuit. The current through it causes it to spin. If the motor is swapped with one of higher resistance, there will be more opposition to the flow of charge and, for the same voltage, the current will be smaller. The motor with a higher resistance will spin more slowly.

All components in a circuit provide some resistance.

1. A buzzer is an electrical device that transfers the energy of an electric current to sound energy.

   a) A circuit, A, has a 6V battery and a buzzer. Another circuit, B, has a 6V battery and a buzzer with higher resistance. In which circuit will the buzzer be louder?

   b) Explain your answer to a) using ideas about resistance and current.

Conductors and insulators >>>

Resistance depends on the type of material an object is made from. Materials that are very good conductors of electric current have a very low resistance. Electrical insulators have a very high resistance, and do not allow current to flow easily.

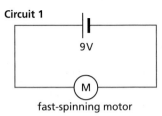

Circuit 1
9V
M
fast-spinning motor

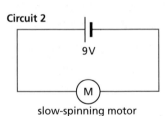

Circuit 2
9V
M
slow-spinning motor

FIGURE 2.6.13a: The resistance in circuit 1 is low, so there is a bigger current; what can you say about circuit 2?

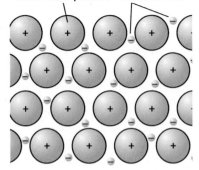

fixed metal particle   free electrons

FIGURE 2.6.13b: Conduction in metals depends on free electrons

All metals conduct electricity well because they have many **free electrons** that can move when a voltage is applied.

As the electrons move, they will collide with other atoms. This is the cause of resistance in most ordinary metals. It is why even the best electrical conductors, like platinum, will have some resistance.

In an insulator, the electrons are more tightly bound than in a conductor; far fewer electrons flow and so there is much less current.

2. As an analogy, think of an obstacle race. Which parts of a circuit do the obstacles represent? Which parts of the circuit do the people represent?

3. What would happen to a light bulb if the copper wires in a circuit were replaced with platinum? Explain your answer.

Working out resistance »»»

Resistance is measured with the unit **ohms** (Ω) and is represented by R. All the components in a circuit will have their own resistance. It is possible to investigate the relationship between voltage (V) and current (I) across a component, as shown in Figure 2.6.13c.

The definition of resistance is:

$$\text{resistance} = \frac{\text{voltage}}{\text{current}}$$

$$R = \frac{V}{I}$$

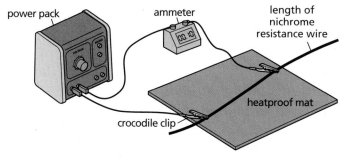

FIGURE 2.6.13c: As the voltage supplied is changed using the power pack, the current is measured using the ammeter. The resistance of the length of nichrome wire between the crocodile clips can then be determined.

4. What is the resistance of the circuit shown in Figure 2.6.13d?

5. Give two ways you might increase the resistance of the circuit. Explain your answers.

Did you know...?

Special components called resistors, with high resistance, are often made from nichrome or tungsten. They are used deliberately to transfer electrical energy to light and heat in the surroundings.

Key vocabulary

resistance

free electron

ohm

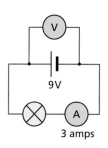

FIGURE 2.6.13d

Investigating factors affecting resistance

We are learning how to:

- Describe some uses of resistance.
- Investigate and explain factors affecting resistance.

Wires of different resistance have different purposes. High-resistance wires are used in light bulbs, whereas in some electronic applications it is essential that there is minimal electrical resistance. There are different ways in which the properties of a circuit may be changed.

Types of resistor

Increasing the resistance in a circuit reduces the amount of current passing. If too much current passes through a laptop computer, for example, it can cause damage to the circuits. Components called fixed **resistors** are used in circuits to enable a specific amount of current to pass through the components.

Other types of resistors, called **variable resistors**, allow you to change the amount of current flowing through a circuit by turning a knob or using a slider. Dimmer-light switches use this type of resistor to control the current and hence vary the brightness of the bulb.

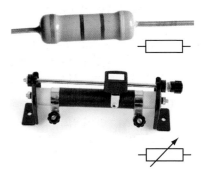

FIGURE 2.6.14a: Fixed resistor (top) and variable resistor (bottom)

1. Name at least one appliance that may contain a variable resistor and one that may contain a fixed resistor.

2. Give one advantage of a variable resistor.

Advantages and disadvantages of resistance

Resistance is the property that makes a **filament** in a light bulb work. Such a light bulb uses a very thin tungsten wire, with a high resistance. As the voltage pushes the electrons through the thin wire, there are collisions with atoms that transfer energy to heat. The tungsten wire heats up to a very high temperature and begins to glow, transferring energy to light.

In the transport of electricity across long distances, it is important for the resistance to be kept as low as possible to avoid energy losses through heating. The properties of the transporting cables enable this to be achieved.

Did you know...?

In 1910 William Coolidge invented the tungsten filament light bulb, still in use today.

FIGURE 2.6.14b: An early tungsten filament light bulb

3. Do electric heaters need a high or a low resistance in order to work? Explain your answer.

4. Mains household electricity has a voltage of 230 V. A hairdryer needs 15 A to work and another needs 12 A. Suggest one difference in the circuits of the two hairdryers.

Explaining how factors affect resistance »»»

There are three main factors affecting the resistance of a wire:

- The *material* that the wire is made from. Table 2.6.14 lists the resistance values of some materials, for the same length and cross-sectional area. This value depends on the number of free electrons that are available in the material.

FIGURE 2.6.14c: How does turning the knob affect the circuit inside the radio?

- The *length* of the wire. In a longer wire, the electrons meet with more opposition because there are more atoms to collide with during their flow. Large resistors, such as those used in electric cookers or heaters, use long lengths of wire made from nichrome – long lengths are often coiled.

  In a variable resistor, the length of the wire included in the circuit can be changed. This idea is used in the volume control of radios and televisions.

- The *thickness* of the wire. In a thin wire it is harder for the electrons to push their way through so they experience more resistance. Also, there are fewer 'free' electrons in a thinner wire.

TABLE 2.6.14: Comparing the resistance of different materials

Material	Resistance value ($\Omega \times 10^{-8}$ m)
aluminium	2.82
copper	1.72
gold	2.44
nichrome	150
silver	1.59
tungsten	5.6
iron	9.71
platinum	0.11
rubber	100 000

thin wire

thick wire

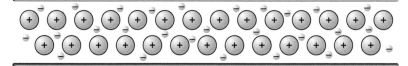

FIGURE 2.6.14d: Comparing thick and thin wires

5. Explain how the volume of a radio can be changed using a variable resistor.

6. Describe the type of wire you would choose in an overhead power cable.

Key vocabulary

resistor

variable resistor

filament

Explaining circuits using models

We are learning how to:

- Describe how the voltage, current and resistance are related in different circuits.
- Use a model to explain the relationship between voltage, current and resistance.

You have learned about what voltage, current and resistance are. Now you will see how they interact in a circuit. The 'rope model' is a useful analogy – it explains most features of current, voltage and resistance in circuits.

Relating voltage, current and resistance

The size of the voltage and the size of the resistance both determine how much current flows. Look at the three different circuits in Figure 2.6.15a.

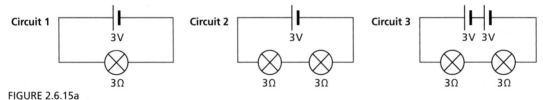

FIGURE 2.6.15a

In circuit 1, there is a voltage of 3 V and one light bulb of resistance 3 Ω.

In circuit 2, there are two identical light bulbs in series, providing twice as much resistance, but supplied with the same voltage as in circuit 1. The current flowing through the circuit is now less, because there is the same 'push' (voltage) but twice the opposition to the flow of electrons (resistance). The light bulbs are not as bright as in circuit 1.

In circuit 3, there are now two cells and the same two light bulbs, each with a resistance of 3 Ω. The light bulbs will both be just as bright as in circuit 1. This is because the resistance and the voltage are both doubled compared to circuit 1, so the current will be the same.

1. What is the voltage and the resistance of the circuit in Figure 2.6.15b?

2. Explain whether the light bulbs in Figure 2.6.15b are dimmer or brighter than in:

   a) circuit 1   **b)** circuit 2   **c)** circuit 3

   of Figure 2.6.15a.

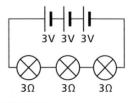

FIGURE 2.6.15b

Figure 2.6.15c shows the rope **model**. It is an **analogy** of a circuit consisting of a long rope that is held by a group of students:

- The battery is represented by one person pulling the rope round with one hand and feeding it out through the other.

- The bulb is represented by a student gripping the rope more tightly than the others. This provides resistance to the flow of current – the students feel their hands warming up as friction transfers energy from the current by heat.

- The electric current is represented by the rope moving around.

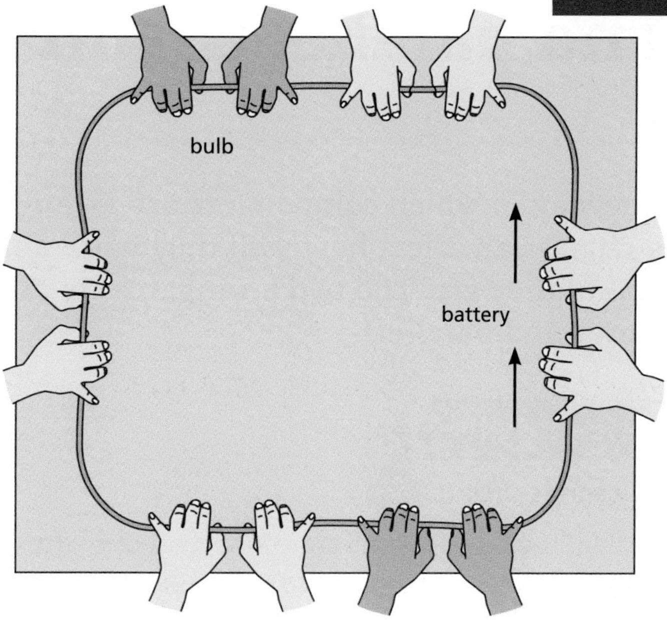

FIGURE 2.6.15c: The rope model

3. Where are the electric charges in the rope model?

4. How is gripping the rope more tightly similar to resistance in the circuit?

Applying the rope model ⟩⟩⟩

Applying the rope model can explain the way the voltage, current and resistance work in circuits. Look again at the circuits in Figure 2.6.15a.

For circuit 2, two students should be used to represent the light bulbs, gripping the rope more tightly than in circuit 1 – this represents the increased resistance. The speed of the passing rope will decrease, compared to the set-up in circuit 1, and less energy is transferred to the light bulbs.

Applying the model to circuit 3, there should be a bigger pull on the rope by the teacher. This will have the effect of increasing the speed at which the rope passes around the circuit, demonstrating an increase in current. The two students will also be gripping the rope more tightly, to provide the increased resistance. This will show that the same current is flowing as in circuit 1.

5. What needs to happen to the rope for it to represent two components with different resistances?

6. How could you use the rope model to represent a wire with less resistance?

Did you know...?

Scientists use a range of models to describe abstract ideas. By applying models we can understand what is happening more easily.

Key vocabulary

model

analogy

Describing series and parallel circuits

The way in which components are arranged in a circuit can affect how well they work and how useful they are. The two arrangements are called series and parallel.

Series circuits

In a **series circuit**:

- All the components are connected, one after the other, in a complete loop of conducting wire.

- There are no **branches** in the circuit.

- There is only one path that the current can take.

- The voltage is shared between the components.

Figure 2.6.16a shows a series circuit with two light bulbs.

1. What would happen to the components in a series circuit if one of the bulbs stopped working?

2. **a)** Draw a circuit diagram showing a motor, a light bulb and a buzzer in a series circuit.

   b) What would happen to the current in your circuit if the motor stopped working?

3. Draw two circuits – one with just one bulb, and the other with three identical bulbs in series. Both circuits should have just one cell of the same voltage. Compare:

   a) the voltage in each circuit

   b) the current in each circuit

   c) the brightness of the bulbs in each circuit.

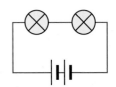

FIGURE 2.6.16a: How can you tell that the components in this circuit are connected in series?

Parallel circuits

In a **parallel circuit**:

- Each component is connected separately in its own loop between the two terminals of a cell or battery.

- There are different branches for the current to follow.
- The full voltage is supplied to each loop.
- The current from the battery is divided between the loops.

A parallel circuit is rather like separate series circuits connected to the same energy source.

The different components are connected by different wires. Therefore, if a bulb blows or is disconnected from one parallel wire, the components in the other branches keep working because they are still connected to the battery in a complete circuit.

If more bulbs are added in parallel, all the bulbs light up with the same brightness as before. There could be a hundred bulbs in parallel, all equally bright, and just as bright as if there were just one bulb. The battery, however, will not last as long!

4. a) Draw a parallel circuit with four bulbs.

   b) Explain how this is different from a series circuit with four bulbs.

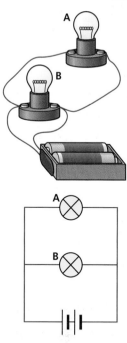

FIGURE 2.6.16b: What happens to bulb A in this parallel circuit if bulb B 'blows'?

Explaining series and parallel circuits ⟫⟫

When two light bulbs are connected in series, the resistance in the circuit is increased compared to that with one light bulb. The thin (filament) wire in each light bulb has a high resistance. The increased resistance opposes the flow of current, so fewer electrons pass per second, transferring less energy. The light bulbs are therefore not as bright as in a circuit with the same voltage but only one bulb.

However, when two light bulbs are connected in parallel, each branch behaves like a separate circuit. The resistance in each branch is the same as if there were just one light bulb in the whole circuit. The same energy is transferred to each branch from the battery, so the bulbs light up with the same brightness as in the single-bulb circuit. The battery is, however, transferring twice the amount of energy to the bulbs and will run out faster than when in a series circuit.

5. Explain the advantages and disadvantages of arranging components in series or in parallel.

Did you know...?

Most circuits used are combinations of series and parallel parts. These are called series–parallel circuits.

FIGURE 2.6.16c

Key vocabulary

series circuit

branch

parallel circuit

Comparing series and parallel circuits

We are learning how to:

- Investigate and explain current and voltage in series and parallel circuits.
- Explain the circuits in our homes.

The arrangement of components in either series or parallel affects the amount of voltage they receive and the amount of current flowing through them. Why does the arrangement make this difference?

Current and voltage in series and parallel circuits »

Figures 2.6.17a and 2.6.17b show a series circuit and a parallel circuit with light bulbs of the same resistance.

Series circuit

The ammeter shows the same readings in different parts of the circuit.

However, the voltage is divided between the components. See how the voltage across each of the components adds up to the total provided. We can write this as:

$$V_{total} = V_1 + V_2 + V_3$$

If the components have the same resistance, the voltage is divided equally.

Parallel circuit

The voltage in all parts of the circuit is the same regardless of how many branches there are.

However, the current splits up between each branch. Adding up the current in each branch gives the total current flowing from the battery. We can write this as:

$$I_{total} = I_1 + I_2 + I_3$$

If the resistance in each branch is the same, the same current will flow through each.

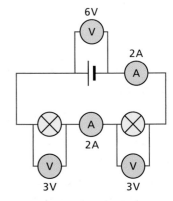

FIGURE 2.6.17a: A series circuit

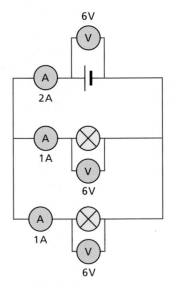

FIGURE 2.6.17b: A parallel circuit

1. If another light bulb is added to the series circuit in Figure 2.6.17a, what will happen to the voltage across the other light bulbs? Explain your answer.

2. A 12 V battery is connected in a circuit with ten identical light bulbs in parallel. Compare this with the circuit in Figure 2.6.17b. What will the current be in each individual loop?

The circuits in Figures 2.6.17a and 2.6.17b can be modelled using the rope model you used in Topic 6.15.

Series circuit

With three light bulbs, three students hold the rope more tightly than the other students. Because there is a higher resistance than with just one bulb, the current is reduced and the rope moves more slowly through the components. The speed is the same throughout the circuit.

Parallel circuit

This circuit behaves as if there were three separate circuits fed by the same battery. The rope model shows that triple the amount of charge is passed through the battery because it is feeding three branches. All the branches are given the same 'push', so the same amount of energy is transferred to each branch.

> **Did you know...?**
>
> After World War 2 there was a shortage of copper. In 1942 the ring main helped to reduce the amount of household wiring needed. This needed more length, but it could be thinner.

3. How would you change the rope model to include a fourth bulb in parallel?

4. What would happen to the current and voltage in series and parallel circuits with two bulbs that had different resistances?

Household circuits »»»

Figure 2.6.17c shows how the household electricity supply is connected in the UK. It is an arrangement known as the domestic **ring main**.

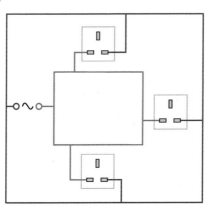

FIGURE 2.6.17c: Arrangement of sockets in a domestic ring main

FIGURE 2.6.17d: Each socket has 230 V applied to it.

All the plug sockets in the ring main are connected in parallel. This has the following advantages:

- If one of the electrical **appliances** should stop working, other appliances are not affected.

- The **mains supply** of 230 V is applied across all the sockets.

- Switches can be used to turn the current on and off within each branch.

Key vocabulary

ring main

appliance

mains supply

5. Suggest disadvantages with this arrangement.

Applying circuits

We are learning how to:

- Describe how circuits are arranged in common appliances.

We have learned about the different features of electric circuits and how they work to transfer energy. In which ways are circuits useful to us?

Common household circuits

Any object that is plugged into the mains supply or that uses a battery contains at least one electric circuit. By altering the current, voltage and resistance within a circuit, the amount of energy transferred to different components can be controlled.

Most circuits are connected in parallel, including household lighting, Christmas tree lights and overhead train cables. This is because the lights or trains all need the same voltage, and if one fails the others will still keep working. Also, using switches, the appliances can be switched on and off individually.

FIGURE 2.6.18a: Parallel circuits are very useful.

Series circuits are less common. Connecting batteries in series will increase the voltage available because the total voltage is the sum of the individual batteries. A series arrangement is used when an appliance needs to be controlled carefully. For example, **circuit breakers** are safety devices that switch off an appliance because of a fault. The appliance and circuit breaker are placed in series.

1. What would happen if household lights were arranged in series?

2. What would happen if a circuit breaker was arranged in parallel to an appliance?

More examples of series and parallel circuits >>>

Water heaters use a series circuit with a temperature control switch, called a **thermostat**. When the temperature reaches the set value, the thermostat will turn off the current. Because there are no other pathways to follow, the current is removed from the heater.

Hairdryers contain a parallel circuit, as shown in Figure 2.6.18b. In this way, if the heater needs to be switched off, the fan can still work to blow cool air instead of hot air – but the heater cannot be used without the motor working.

3. Name another appliance that needs a controlled temperature and may therefore be connected in series with a thermostat?

4. Would you use a parallel circuit or a series circuit to connect the electrical appliances in a kitchen? Explain your answer.

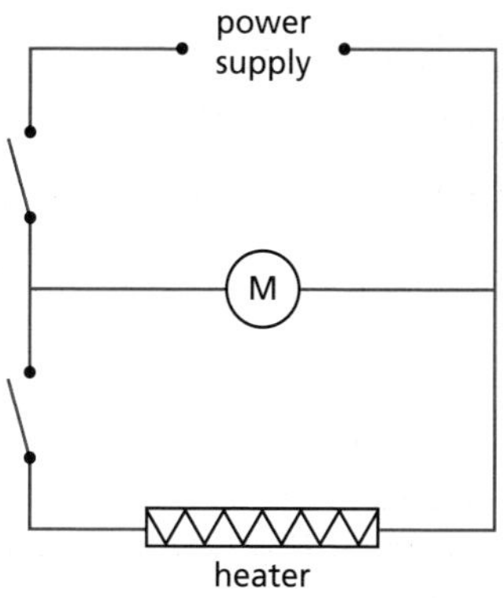

FIGURE 2.6.18b: In the hairdryer circuit shown here, why are the motor and the heater arranged in parallel?

Series–parallel circuits >>>

Most circuits are combinations of series and parallel circuits. These are called **series–parallel circuits**. Figure 2.6.18c shows an example.

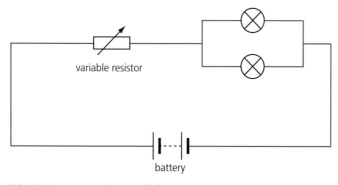

FIGURE 2.6.18c: A series–parallel circuit

This is a simple series–parallel circuit used in a car to dim the lights on the instrument panel. The variable resistor controls the amount of current that can pass. When its resistance is high, less current passes and both the lights on the panel are dimmer. To increase the brightness of the lights, the variable resistor can be turned so that it is low. More current passes and the lights are brighter.

5. Describe the path of the current in the series–parallel circuit in Figure 2.6.18c.

6. Can you think of one other application in which a series–parallel circuit might be used?

Did you know...?

In the 1920s just 10% of UK houses had an electricity supply. The main appliances in use were lights, irons and radios.

Key vocabulary

circuit breaker

thermostat

series–parallel circuit

Checking your progress

To make good progress in understanding science you need to focus on these ideas and skills.

- Describe differences between permanent and temporary magnets.
- Describe and compare different methods to make permanent magnets.
- Use the domain theory to explain how materials become magnetised and demagnetised.

- Describe some effects of the Earth's magnetic field.
- Describe the geodynamo theory.
- Explain evidence for how the Earth's magnetic field works.

- Describe how to test the strength of a magnet and an electromagnet.
- Design investigations to compare different methods of making magnets and testing the strength of electromagnets.
- Use models and analogies to explain the factors that affect the strengths of magnets and electromagnets.

- Describe different applications of magnets and electromagnets.
- Explain the advantages and disadvantages of using electromagnets.
- Compare and contrast the use of magnets and electromagnets in different applications, such as a circuit breaker.

- Describe and investigate different types of batteries, including fruit batteries.
- Analyse and interpret data to explain how to make the most effective fruit batteries.
- Explain how a battery works using ideas about charge.

Describe what is meant by current, voltage and resistance.

Apply a range of models and analogies to describe current, voltage and resistance.

Evaluate different models and analogies for explaining current, voltage and resistance.

Describe the relationship between current, voltage and resistance in a qualitative way.

Use data to identify a pattern between current, voltage and resistance.

Use data and a mathematical relationship between current, voltage and resistance to carry out calculations.

Make measurements of current and voltage in series and parallel circuits.

Use models and simple calculations to explain and compare what happens to the current and voltage in series and parallel circuits.

Use calculations to make predictions about current and voltage in series and parallel circuits.

Describe different domestic uses of series and parallel circuits.

Make comparisons between components in series and parallel circuits.

Explain the advantages of using series or parallel circuits, including the domestic ring main.

Questions

Questions 1–7

See how well you have understood the ideas in the chapter.

1. What is the unit of current? [1]

    a) volt   **b)** ohm   **c)** amp   **d)** joule

2. Which one of the following materials is magnetic? [1]

    a) copper   **b)** cobalt   **c)** chlorine   **d)** calcium

3. Which of the following uses an electromagnet? [1]

    a) a compass   **b)** a fridge magnet   **c)** a torch   **d)** a metal-sorting plant prior to recycling

4. What is the name of the magnetic material that was discovered first? [1]

    a) lodestone   **b)** iron   **c)** steel   **d)** nickel

5. Give two differences between a magnet and an electromagnet. [2]

6. Explain how a series circuit is different from a parallel circuit. [2]

7. Draw a circuit diagram to explain how a circuit breaker works – include ideas about electromagnets and why the circuit is arranged in a particular way. [4]

Questions 8–14

See how well you can apply the ideas in this chapter to new situations.

8. Figure 2.6.20a shows four circuits A–D. Which of the following shows the correct order from the circuit that gives the brightest bulbs to the one that gives the dimmest? [1]

    a) A, B, C, D   **b)** D, C, B, A   **c)** C, D, A, B   **d)** C, B, D, A

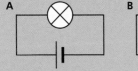 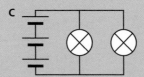 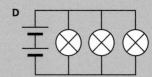

FIGURE 2.6.20a

9. A food mixer has a low setting and a high setting. Which of these is true? [1]

    a) the low setting has a lower current passing
    b) the high setting has a stronger magnet inside
    c) the low setting uses more coils around the motor
    d) the high setting has a lower current passing.

10. Which of the following will the make the strongest electromagnet?

    a) using one coil with a low current   **b)** using 100 coils with a low current
    c) using 100 coils with a high current   **d)** using one coil with a high current.

11. Venus does not have a magnetic field. Which of the following statements is false? [1]

    a) Venus does not have an iron core

    b) Venus is protected against dangerous charged particles from solar winds

    c) A compass will not work on Venus

    d) Venus does not have a magnetosphere.

12. A student drops a magnet on the floor. It no longer works. She puts it between two strong magnets for some time. Use the domain theory to explain why the magnet no longer works and how it becomes remagnetised. [2]

13. Figure 2.6.20b shows a model of a circuit. How would you change this model to show an increased voltage and resistance? [2]

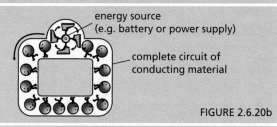

FIGURE 2.6.20b

14. Figure 2.6.20c shows a series circuit (1) and a parallel circuit (2). Calculate the missing voltages and currents. Explain the reasons for your values. [4]

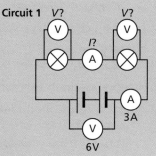

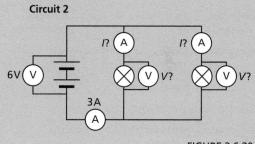

FIGURE 2.6.20c

Questions 15–16

See how well you can understand and explain new ideas and evidence.

15. Two fruit batteries are placed side by side. They are connected to identical bulbs. One bulb is much brighter than the other. What possible reasons could there be between the batteries to account for the difference? [2]

16. Table 2.6.20 gives some data from an investigation comparing the resistance of different wires. The values of resistance have been calculated using $V/I = R$. Sketch a graph of the values. A wire from an electricity distribution line is now tested. Sketch a new graph to predict how the resistance will be different. Explain the reasons for your sketch. [4]

TABLE 2.6.20

Length of wire (cm)	Average voltage (V)	Average current (A)	Average resistance (Ω)
10	0.47	0.23	2
20	0.59	0.17	3.47
30	0.64	0.13	4.92
40	0.69	0.11	6.27
50	0.72	0.09	8
60	0.76	0.07	10.9
70	0.82	0.06	13.67

Glossary

accelerate speed up

accuracy how close data is to true values

acid rain rainwater that is made acidic by pollutant gases, for example sulfur dioxide

acid substance that has a pH lower than 7

aerobic respiration respiration that involves oxygen

air resistance frictional resistance when an object moves through air

alcohol liquid chemical such as ethanol; alcohol can be used as biofuel

alkali substance that has a pH higher than 7

altimeter instrument used to measure the altitude (height) of an object above a fixed level

altitude height above sea level

amino acid joins with other amino acids to make proteins

ammeter used to measure the current flowing in a circuit

ampere unit of measurement of current, symbol A

anabolic steroid drug that increases muscle mass

anaerobic respiration respiration without using oxygen

analogy comparison between one thing and another

antacid substance that neutralises stomach acid

antagonistic muscles pairs of muscles that act against each other

appliance (electrical) device that uses electricity

area length × width; units are squared, for example m^2, mm^2

armature iron bar inside an electric bell

arthritis painful disease of the joints

atmospheric pressure the atmosphere pressing down on everything

atom basic 'building block' of an element that cannot be chemically broken down

attract pull towards; a magnet will attract any magnetic material that is close enough

Aurora Borealis collision of charged particles with air particles at high altitude; seen as green shapes in the sky in the northern hemisphere

barometer instrument used to measure pressure

base (in chemistry) solid alkali

battery energy is transferred by chemical reactions to electrical energy

bicep muscle in the arm

bioaccumulation increase in the concentration of a chemical as it is passed from one organism to another up a food chain

biodiversity range of different organisms in an area

blood cells there are two types – white blood cells and red blood cells. They are found in the blood, together with plasma and platelets

boil when a liquid changes state to a gas

boiling point the temperature at which a pure substance boils or condenses

bone made of hard minerals, for example calcium, on the outside and inside has marrow surrounded by a spongy layer

branch (in electricity) loop within a circuit

breathing system takes oxygen into the body and passes carbon dioxide out

brewing cereal grains are soaked in water and fermented with yeast

Brownian motion movement of solid particles caused by collisions with liquid particles

buoyancy upward force on an object in a liquid

calcium hard mineral found in bone

captive breeding animals are bred in zoos, wildlife reserves etc., often to try to conserve species

carbon dioxide gas in the air used by plants to make food; animals breathe it out; it is produced when fossil fuels burn and when a metal carbonate reacts with an acid

carbonate type of base; reacts with an acid to give a salt and carbon dioxide

catalyst substance that speeds up a chemical reaction

cellulose large sugar molecule made by plants for cell walls

charge electrical energy that is positive or negative

chemical change/reaction one or more substances are permanently changed into others, by their atoms being rearranged

chemosynthesis energy from chemicals is used to make food

chitin tough, protective substance made from glucose

chlorophyll green pigment in plants used in photosynthesis

chromatography process used to separate soluble substances

circuit breaker device that breaks a circuit when too high a current is drawn from the mains

circulatory system the heart and blood vessels that transport essential substances around the body in blood

co-exist different species of the same organism live successfully in the same community

collagen stretchy fibre in ligaments and tendons

colloid different states of matter are dispersed together; for example in an aerosol there are particles of liquid or solid dispersed in a gas

combustion the process of burning

commensalism type of symbiosis where one organism benefits and the other does not

compass lines up in a north–south direction (when not near a magnet) showing that the Earth has its own magnetic field

competition struggle between different organisms for survival

complete combustion when there is enough oxygen to react with all of a fuel during combustion

component part of an electric circuit, for example a light bulb

compressed squashed with a force

concentrated high number of solute particles

concentration gradient difference in concentration

concentration the number of particles packed in a certain volume

conduct transfer of heat or electrical charge by passing on energy to nearby particles

conductor (electrical) material that transfers electric charge by passing on energy to nearby particles

contact (electrical) point at which a circuit is made, for example at a switch

contract when a muscle pulls it contracts, i.e. it gets shorter and fatter

core (of Earth) centre of the Earth, contains materials rich in iron

core (of electromagnet) piece of iron inside the coil of an electromagnet which makes the magnetic field stronger

corrosive reacts with materials and makes them dissolve

current see *electric current*

cuticle waxy, waterproof, protective outer layer of a leaf

DDT pesticide used in 1960s

decomposer organism that breaks down dead plant or animal tissue

decompression lowering of pressure to below normal atmospheric pressure

deficiency lack of something, such as nutrient

density mass of a material per unit volume

dependent variable variable that is measured in an investigation

depth distance below the surface of a liquid

diatom type of algae, usually unicellular

diffusion particles in a liquid or gas move from an area of high concentration to an area of low concentration

digestive system group of organs that together enable digestion of food

dilute low number of solute particles

direct current (D.C.) current that always flows in one direction

displace when an object is put into water it displaces some of the water

diurnal animals or plants that are active in the daytime

domain groups of atoms bound together that are aligned in the same magnetic direction

earthing an earth wire in an electrical appliance that allows a safe route for current to flow through

ecology study of the interactions between organisms and their environment

ecosystem a habitat and all the living things in it

efficiency a measure of how well something transfers energy to useful outcomes

electric current flow of negatively charged electrons

electric motor transfers energy by electricity and uses magnetic force to cause movement and do useful work

electromagnet type of temporary magnet that is magnetic only when an electric current passes through it

electromyography (EMG) a medical test to check that muscles are working

electron small negatively charged particle in an atom that orbits the nucleus

electrostatic attraction attraction (pulling together) of opposite charges (positive and negative)

electrostatic field this is set up when two objects near each other have different electrical charges

element substance made up of only one type of atom

emulsion mixture of two liquids (one water-based, the other oil-based) that do not normally mix

endangered when there are so few of a species left that it could disappear altogether and become extinct

endothermic (reaction) chemical reaction in which heat energy is taken in

energy something has energy if it has the ability to make something happen when the energy is transferred

enzyme substance that speeds up a chemical process in the body

epidermis single-cell thick transparent layer in the upper surface of a leaf

equation (in chemistry) a way of summarising a chemical reaction; reactants are on the left of the arrow and products are on the right

equilibrium (in chemistry) a stable state, in which no change is occurring

equilibrium (in ecology) balance between predators and prey in an environment

evaporation change from a liquid to a gas at the surface of the liquid

evidence information gathered in a scientific way, which supports or contradicts a conclusion

exothermic (reaction) chemical reaction in which heat energy is given out

extinct when a species of organism has died out

facial muscles muscles in the face

fermentation type of anaerobic respiration that produces ethanol and carbon dioxide

fertiliser chemical put on soil to increase soil fertility and allow better growth of crop plants

field area of electrostatic force around an object charged with static electricity

field lines show the shape and size of a magnetic field

filament (in electricity) thin length of wire in a light bulb

fire triangle model to show the three things needed for a fire – heat, fuel and oxygen

foam mixture of gas bubbles trapped inside a liquid

food chain flow diagram showing how a living thing gets its food

food security availability of food and the ability to obtain it

food web flow diagram showing how a number of living things in a habitat get their food

force a push, pull or turning effect

formula chemical symbols and numbers that show which elements, and how many atoms of each, a compound is made up of

fossil fuel coal, natural gas and crude oil, that were formed from the compressed remains of plants and other organisms that died millions of years ago

fracture broken bone

free electrons negatively charged particles that move freely within a metal

fuel material that is burned to release its energy

gasohol mixture of gasoline (petrol) and alcohol (ethanol) used as a vehicle fuel

gel mixture of liquid particles floating in a solid

generalist organism with a broad niche

geodynamo theory magnetic domains within a (core) liquid line up to create a weak magnetic field

germinating when a seed is beginning to grow

glucose small sugar molecule

glycogen glucose molecules linked in a long chain; does not dissolve in water so can be stored in the body, especially in the liver

gold leaf electroscope instrument used to detect electric charge on an object

GPS (global positioning system) space-based satellite navigation system

gravitational field attractive force between objects (dependent on their mass); measured in newtons per kilogram, N/kg

guard cells leaf cells either side of each stoma that control the opening and closing of the stoma

hardness a measure of how easy it is to scratch a solid

heartburn acid from the stomach irritates the upper digestive tract

hydrocarbon molecule made up of hydrogen and carbon; fuels such as coal, oil and gas contain hydrocarbons

hydrogen atom present in all acids

hydrothermal vent forms on the sea floor where there is volcanic activity

hydroxide particle present in all alkalis

hypothesis idea that explains a set of facts or observations, and is the basis for possible experiments

incomplete combustion when there is not enough oxygen available to react with all of a fuel during combustion

independent variable a variable in an experiment that affects the outcome

indicator chemical that is a different colour in an alkali and in an acid

indigestion disruption of the digestive process, often resulting in too much acid being produced

induce a charge is induced in an object by the electrostatic field of a nearby charged object

insecticide chemical applied to crops to destroy insects and small creatures that damage crops

insulator (electrical) does not allow a current to pass

interdependence relationship between several organisms that depend on one another

intermolecular forces forces between molecules

involuntary something you cannot control

iodine orange-coloured liquid used to test for starch

iron core the centre of an electromagnet

irritant something that reddens the skin

isobar line on a map connecting places with the same atmospheric pressure

joint where two bones meet; allows movement

kinetic theory theory that all matter is made of particles

lactic acid substance produced in anaerobic respiration; builds up in muscles during vigorous exercise and causes an aching or burning feeling in the muscles

latent heat heat energy needed to change the state of a substance

Law of Conservation of Mass in a chemical reaction, the total mass of the reactants is the same as the total mass of the products; also applies to changes of state and dissolving

ligament connects bone to bone; made of stretchy fibres called collagen

lightning electrostatic discharge between electrically charged clouds or between a cloud and the surface of Earth

limewater turns cloudy when carbon dioxide is passed through it

litmus indicator solution

lubricant substance used to reduce friction

macroelement major mineral that plants use in large quantities

magnet material or object that produces a magnetic field

magnetic field space in which a magnetic material feels a force

magnetism effect of magnet poles on magnetic materials

magnetosphere magnetic field around the Earth

mains supply household alternating-current electric power supply

malleable can be hammered into shape without being broken

manure waste organic material

marrow soft substance in middle of bone; makes blood cells

mass amount of matter in an object, measured in kilograms (kg)

mean average

melting point temperature at which a pure substance melts or freezes

membrane thin layer enclosing a cell; allows substances to pass in and out

microbe tiny organism that cannot be seen with the naked eye; includes bacteria, viruses and fungi

misconception common ideas that people share that are inaccurate

mitochondria sausage-shaped organelles found in most plant and animal cells where respiration is carried out providing the cells with energy

model diagram or three-dimensional object that makes an idea easier to understand

monoculture when a single crop is grown in a huge field

motor effect a wire carrying a current moves when placed in a magnetic field

muscle tissue made up of many fibres that have the ability to contract (shorten)

mutualism type of symbiosis where both organisms benefit

negative charge the type of electric charge carried by an electron

neutral when a substance is neither acidic nor alkaline

neutralisation when an acid 'cancels out' an alkali or vice versa

newton (N) unit of force

niche role of an organism in its ecosystem

nocturnal active at nightime

non-contact force force that arises although objects are not touching, as in magnetism

ohm unit of measurement of electrical resistance, symbol Ω

osteoporosis disease in which the density of bones drops below a healthy level and bones become fragile, making them prone to fractures

oxidation reaction that increases the amount of oxygen in a substance

oxygen a gas in the air that is produced by plants, used by animals in breathing and used in combustion (burning)

oxygen debt oxygen needed to break down lactic acid produced as a result of vigorous exercise

palisade cell plant leaf cell that is long and narrow and packed with chloroplasts; found mainly in upper part of leaf

parallel circuit each component in a circuit is connected separately in its own loop

parasitism type of symbiosis where one organism benefits, but the other is harmed

particle very small part of a material, such as an atom or a molecule

particle model used to explain the kinetic theory of solids, liquids and gases

pascal (Pa) standard unit of pressure; also kilopascal (kPa); 1 kPa = 1000 Pa

peer review making scientific research available to others to repeat and debate

permanent magnet magnet that keeps its magnetism for a long time

pesticide chemical applied to crops to destroy pests

pH number number from 1 to 14 on the pH scale of acidity and alkalinity

phloem tissue made up of long tubes that transport glucose made in leaves of a plant to other parts

photosynthesis process carried out by green plants to make their food: energy from sunlight, carbon dioxide and water are used to produce glucose and oxygen

physical change change from one state (solid, liquid or gas) to another

pigment substance that gives a material its colour

pole end of a magnet; may be the north pole or the south pole

pollution presence of substances that contaminate or damage the environment

pore very small hole

porous allows water to pass through

positive charge when an atom loses an electron it becomes positively charged

potential difference difference in charge across a cell or battery

precision taking readings using a scale of finer measurements in an investigation

predator animal that preys on (and eats) another animal

pressure average force on a certain area

pressurised kept at a known pressure, for example in an aeroplane cabin

prey an animal that is hunted and killed by other animals

primary consumer organism in a food web or chain that eats the producer

producer component of a food web or chain that produces its own food (typically a green plant)

product (of chemical reaction) substance made in a chemical reaction

protect the skeleton protects the internal organs from injury

proton positively charged particle in the nucleus of an atom

quadricep muscle in the thigh

rate measure of speed or the number of times something happens in a set amount of time

reactant starting substance in a chemical reaction

reactivity how reactive a substance is

relax when a muscle relaxes it gets longer and thinner (see also *contract*)

reliability measure of how good data are

repeatability when repeat tests of an investigation made by the same experimenter give similar results

repel push away; for example, the north pole of a magnet will repel the north pole of another magnet

reproducibility when an investigation method is repeated exactly and the same results are obtained by a different experimenter

resistance (in electricity) symbol R, opposes the 'push' provided by the voltage in a circuit; unit of measurement is the ohm, (Ω)

resistor (in electricity) circuit component that opposes the 'push' provided by the voltage in a circuit

resource partitioning species with similar needs use resources in slightly different ways

respiration chemical reaction that uses oxygen to release the energy in food

reversible can also work in the opposite direction

ring main how the electricity supply in a house is connected

root hair cell specialised cell in roots of plants; the cell has long, hair-like extension that provides a large surface area

salt substance formed when an acid reacts with a base

satellite body orbiting around a larger body; communications satellites orbit the Earth to relay television and telephone signals

secondary consumer organism in a food web or chain that eats a primary consumer

series circuit circuit in which all components are connected one after the other

series–parallel circuit circuit using a combination of series and parallel circuits

skeletal system the skeleton, ligaments, skeletal muscles and tendons

skeleton all the bones in the body

soapy effect produced when an alkali is added to water

solar wind a stream of charged particles released from the upper atmosphere of the Sun

solubility the mass of solute that dissolves in a solvent at a particular temperature

soluble solid that dissolves (usually in water)

solute solid that dissolves

solvent liquid in which a solute dissolves

specialist organism with a narrow niche

spongy cell plant leaf cell that has a large surface area and large spaces around it; found near the underside of the leaf

starch large carbohydrate molecule; store of energy

static electricity imbalance of electric charges on the surface of a material

stoma (pl. stomata) tiny pore(s) on the underneath surface of a leaf through which gases can move in and out

strength ability of a solid to withstand a force

strong acid/alkali contains a lot of hydrogen atoms (acid) or a lot of hydroxide ions (alkali)

subjective different people may interpret the results of an investigation differently

sublimation a solid that turns straight into a gas; there is no liquid state

sulfur dioxide one of the main gases that produces acid rain; produced when sulfur is oxidised during combustion of some fossil fuels

support the skeleton supports the body and makes movement possible

surface area area of the outside surface of an object

symbiosis when both organisms in a dependent relationship benefit

symmetrical the same either side of an axis

temporary magnet object that is attracted by a magnet and shows magnetic properties when in a magnetic field

tendon connects muscle to bone; made of stretchy fibres called collagen

tertiary consumer organism in a food web or chain that eats a secondary consumer

thermal expansion when particles in a solid or a liquid gain enough energy to occupy more space

thermostat temperature control switch

titration laboratory method allowing accurate volumes of liquids to be measured

toxin substance that damages a living organism

transpiration movement of water in plants as it is taken up through the roots and released from the leaves as water vapour

tricep muscle in upper arm

trophic level position of an organism in a food chain

universal indicator turns a range of different colours depending on whether the solution is alkaline or acidic and how strong it is

upthrust upward force exerted on an object in water

valve controls the passage of something

van de Graaff generator generates an electrostatic force

variable resistor allows the amount of current flowing through a circuit to be changed

variation range of characteristics across individuals of the same group

viscosity ability of liquids and gases to flow

volt unit of measurement of current, unit is the volt, symbol V

voltage measure of the size of 'push' that causes a current to flow around a circuit

voltmeter device used to measure the voltage across a component in an electric circuit

volume measurement of amount of a substance

vulnerable when the number of a species drops very low

waterlogged when soil can hold no more water

weak acid/alkali contains only a few hydrogen atoms (acid) or hydroxide ions (alkali)

weather front where warm- and cold-air masses collide

weight force of gravity on an object

xylem cells plant cells that join to form a 'pipeline' through the stem of a plant; this allows water and minerals to travel around the plant

yeast single-celled organism used in making beer and bread; respires only by fermentation even when oxygen is present

yield amount of useful product

Index

Index

Acknowledgements

Acknowledgements

The publishers wish to thank the following for permission to reproduce photographs. Every effort has been made to trace copyright holders and to obtain their permission for the use of copyright materials. The publishers will gladly receive any information enabling them to rectify any error or omission at the first opportunity. (t = top, c = centre, b = bottom, r = right, l = left)

Cover and title page image © Irina1977/Shutterstock
p 8 (t) Pedro Bernardo/Shutterstock, p 8 (ct) Sebastian Kaulitzki/Shutterstock, p 9 (t) Bon Appetit/Alamy, p 9 (ct) Gelpi JM/Shutterstock, p 9 (cb) Ostill/Shutterstock, p 9 (b) Maxim Ibragimov/Shutterstock, pp 8-9 Dr Jeremy Burgess/Science Photo Library, p 11 (l) My Planet/Alamy, p 11 (r) MedicalRF.com/Alamy, p 12 Vladyslav Danilin/Shutterstock, p 13 (r) Bon Appetit/Alamy, p 13 (l) Carlos Jasso/Reuters/Corbis, p 14 Zephyr/Science Photo Library, p 16 Mark Herreid/Shutterstock, p 17 Martyn F. Chillmaid/Science Photo Library, p 18 Roibu/Shutterstock, p 19 (r) Dr. P Marazzi/Science Photo Library, p 19 (l) Age Fotostock/Alamy, p 21 Elwynn/Shutterstock, p 22 (t) Howard Klaaste/Shutterstock, p 22 (b) Itsmejust/Shutterstock, p 23 (t) Sebastian Kaulitzki/Shutterstock, p 23 (b) Fotomaton/Alamy, p 24 NASA/Science Photo Library, p 26 (t) Mike Watson Images/ThinkStock, p 26 (b) Studiomode/Alamy, p 27 Martyn F. Chillmaid/Science Photo Library, p 28 Pietus/Shutterstock, p 29 (l) Igor Zh./Shutterstock, p 29 (r) Nico99/Shutterstock, p 30 Professors P. Motta & T. Naguro/Science Photo Library, p 31 (r) Gelpi JM/Shutterstock, p 31 (l) Celia Magill/Science Photo Library, p 33 Phototake Inc./Alamy, p 34 (t) Jeff Moffett/Icon SMI/Corbis, p 34 (b) StockyImages/Shutterstock, p 35 I Love Images/Corbis, p 36 SusaZoom/Shutterstock, p 37 Cultura RM/Alamy, p 38 (t) Dr Jeremy Burgess/Science Photo Library, p 38 (bl) Dmitri Gristsenko/Shutterstock, p 38 (bc) Maxim Ibragimov/Shutterstock, p 38 (br) Paulista/Shutterstock, p 40 (t) Johanna Goodyear/Shutterstock, p 40 (b) Monkey Business Images/Getty Images, p 46 (t) KobchaiMa/Shutterstock, p 46 (b) Julian W/Shutterstock, p 47 (t) Jeanette Dietl/Shutterstock, p 47 (c) Nneirda/Shutterstock, p 47 (b) Martin Harvey/Alamy, pp 46-47 Robin Kay/Shutterstock, p 48 (t) Kosam/Shutterstock, p 48 (c) Fotokostic/Shutterstock, p 48 (b) Jerry Horbert/Shutterstock, p 49 Deborah Benbrook/Shutterstock, p 50 Ralph Loesche, p 51 (t) Cordelia Molloy/Science Photo Library, p 51 (b) Zygotehaasnobrain/Shutterstock, p 52 (t) Christopher Meder/Shutterstock, p 52 (b) Jeanette Dietl/Shutterstock, p 54 Biophoto Associates/Science Photo Library, p 55 (t) Biophoto Associates/Science Photo Library, p 55 (b) Biophoto Associates/Science Photo Library, p 56 (tl) Lafoto/Shutterstock, p 56 (tr) XLT974/Shutterstock, p 58 (t) Chris Curtis/Shutterstock, p 58 (b) Scott Prokop/Shutterstock, p 59 XLT974/Shutterstock, p 60 (t) Chris Gunter, José Garzón, and Brian Whipker/International Plant Nutrition Institute, p 60 (b) Nattio/Shutterstock, p 61 (l) Studiomode/Alamy, p 61 (r) Nigel Cattlin/Alamy, p 62 B. Murton/Southampton Oceanography Centre/Science Photo Library, p 63 (r) Interfoto/Alamy, p 63 (l) NASA, p 64 Andrea Jones/Shutterstock, p 64 (b) D. Pimborough/Shutterstock, p 68 (t) Len Wilcox/Alamy, p 68 (b) Dennis Cox/Alamy, p 69 Carlos Amarillo/Shutterstock, p 70 (t) Keith Jenkinson/Shutterstock, p 70 (b) Specta/Shutterstock, p 71 Sergey Uryadnikov/Shutterstock, p 72 (t) Alfredo Maiquez/Shutterstock, p 72 (b) Gregory Dimijian/Science Photo Library, p 73 (t) Maratr/Shutterstock, p 73 (b) Chris Fredriksson/Alamy, p 74 (t) Images of Africa Photobank/Alamy, p 74 (b) Mark Beckwith/Shutterstock, p 75 Dabjola/Shutterstock, p 76 (t) Jaubert Images/Alamy, p 76 (b) Cal Vornberger/Alamy, p 77 Kodda/Shutterstock, p 78 Chris Alcock/Shutterstock, p 79 (t) Suzanne L. Collins/Science Photo Library, p 79 (b) Chris Mattison/Alamy, p 84 (t) Achim Baque/Shutterstock, p 84 (c) James Mattil/Shutterstock, p 84 (b) Andrew Lambert Photography/Science Photo Library, p 85 (t) Clive Freeman/Biosym Technologies/Science Photo Library, p 85 (c) Julio Embun/Shutterstock, p 85 (b) Jcomp/Shutterstock, pp 84- 85 Sakkarin Chinsoi/Shutterstock, p 87 Achim Baque/Shutterstock, p 88 Africa Studio/Shutterstock, p 90 (t) Science Photo Library, p 90 (b) David Scharf/Science Photo Library, p 91 360b/Shutterstock, p 92 (t) Olga Miltsova/Shutterstock, p 92 (b) Oliver Hoffmann/Shutterstock, p 93 Jahthanyapat/Shutterstock, p 94 Phloen/Shutterstock, p 96 (t) WhiteTag/Shutterstock, p 96 (b) Steven Coling/Shutterstock, p 96 (t) Martyn F. Chillmaid/Science Photo Library, p 96 (b) Martyn F. Chillmaid/Science Photo Library, p 97 Natrursports/Shutterstock, p 99 Sdecoret/Shutterstock, p 100 Maximilian Weinzierl/Alamy, p 102 (t) Charles D. Winters/Science Photo Library, p 102 (b) Charles D. Winters/Science Photo Library, p 105 ProfStocker/Shutterstock, p 106 Brandon Bourdages/Shutterstock, p 107 Nicku/Shutterstock, p 109 Lisa F. Young/Shutterstock, p 110 Africa Studio/Shutterstock, p 111 Andrew Lambert Photography/Science Photo Library, p 112 Sheila Terry/Science Photo Library, p 113 (t) Mironov56/Shutterstock, p 113 (b) Zenphotography/Shutterstock, p 114 (t) WitR/Shutterstock, p 114 (b) Andrew Lambert Photography/Science Photo Library, p 115 Andraž Cerar/Shutterstock, p 116 Jitka Volfova/Shutterstock, p 117 (t) Science Photo Library, p 117 (bl) BORTEL Pavel - Pavelmidi, p 117 (br) Lawrence Berkeley National Laboratory/Science Photo Library, p 124 (t) Clive Freeman/Biosym Technologies/Science Photo Library, p 124 (c) Charles D. Winters/Science Photo Library, p 124 (b) Ushi/Shutterstock, p 125 (t) SciencePhotos/Alamy, p 125 (c) Charles D. Winters/Science Photo Library, p 125 (b) John Joannides/Alamy, pp 124-125 Cio/Shutterstock, p 126 (t) Signature Photos/Shutterstock, p 126 (ct) Hong Vo/Shutterstock, p 126 (cb) Steve Stock/Alamy, p 126 (b) M. Unal Ozmen/Shutterstock, p 127 SciencePhotos/Alamy, p 128 (tl) ChrisBrignell/Shutterstock, p 128 (tr) DenisNata/Shutterstock, p 128 (c) Birgit Reitz-Hofmann/Shutterstock, p 128 (b) Ffolas/Shutterstock, p 129 (l) Richard Heyes/Alamy, p 129 (r) WhiteBoxMedia Limited/Alamy, p 130 (t) Andrew Lambert Photography/Science Photo Library, p 130 (b) Art Directors & TRIP/Alamy, p 131 Kathryn Willmott/Shutterstock, p 132 (t) Aleksandr Markin/Shutterstock, p 132 (b) SeDmi/Shutterstock, p 134 Manor Photography/Alamy, p 135 Kak2s/Shutterstock, p 137 Lucy Roth, p 138 (t) Sippakorn/Shutterstock, p 138 (b) Auremar/Shutterstock, p 139 Peter Gudella/Shutterstock, p 140 Leslie Garland Picture Library/Alamy, p 141 (l) Clive Streeter/Getty Images, p 141 (r) Heritage Image Partnership Ltd/Alamy, p 142 (t) PhotoRoman/Shutterstock, p 142 (b) Trevor Clifford Photography/Science Photo Library, p 143 SciencePhotos/Alamy, p 144 (t) Imging/Shutterstock, p 144 (b) CobraPhotography/Shutterstock, p 148 Simon Bratt/Shutterstock, p 149 Jay Directo/AFP/Getty Images, p 150 (l) Sergiy Telesh/Shutterstock, p 150 (r) Cvetanovski/Shutterstock, p 151 Andrew Lambert Photography/Science Photo Library, p 152 Ulga/Shutterstock, p 153 (t) Martin Bond/Science Photo Library, p 153 (b) Leslie Garland Picture Library/Alamy, p 154 (t) Kativ/iStock, p 154 (b) Danny E Hooks/Shutterstock, p 157 (t) Karol Kozlowski/Shutterstock, p 157 (b) Photofusion Picture Library / Alamy, p 160 Charles D. Winters/Science Photo Library, p 161 Charles D. Winters/Science Photo Library, p 162 (t) Jason and Bonnie Grower/Shutterstock, p 162 (c) GIPhotoStock/Science Photo Library, p 162 (b) Silhouette Lover/Shutterstock, p 163 (t) NASA, p 163 (c) Cordelia Molloy/Science Photo Library, p 163 (b) Alex James Bramwell/Shutterstock, pp 162-163 Science Photo Library, p 164 (t) Maciej Czekajewski/Shutterstock, p 164 (c) Neyro/Shutterstock, p 164 (b) Chevanon/Shutterstock, p 166 (t) Jamen Percy/Shutterstock, p 166 (b) Imagedb.com/Shutterstock, p 168 (t) David R. Frazier Photo Library, Inc./Alamy, p 168 (b) GIPhotoStock/Science Photo Library, p 170 Friedrich Saurer/Science Photo Library, p 171 Adam Hart-Davis/Science Photo Library, p 172 Martyn F. Chillmaid/Science Photo Library, p 173 Charistoone-Images/Alamy, p 174 Jcomp/Shutterstock, p 175 Val Shevchenko/Shutterstock, p 176 NASA, p 177 Kenneth Eward/Biografx/Science Photo Library, p 178 Stocktrek Images/Alamy, p 179 (t) NASA/Science Photo Library, p 179 (b) Anteromite/Shutterstock, p 180 (t) RIA Novosti/Alamy, p 180 (b) Djgis/Shutterstock, p 182 (t) AFP/Getty Images, p 182 (b) Martin Harvey/Alamy, p 183 (tl) Salomon, p 183 (bl) IM_photo/Shutterstock, p 183 (tl) B.Stefanov/Shutterstock, p 183 (br) Salomon, p 184 Flashon Studio/Shutterstock, p 185 Marijaf/Shutterstock, p 186 Ethan Daniels/Shutterstock, p 187 RichSouthWales, p 188 Tanawat Pontchour/Shutterstock, p 189 Ruth Peterkin/Shutterstock, p 190 Galyna Andrushko/Shutterstock, p 191 The Met Office, p 192 (t) Jack Sullivan/Alamy, p 192 (b) Tobik/Shutterstock, p 193 Zolotova Sofiya/Shutterstock, p 198 (t) Ivancovlad/Shutterstock, p 198 (ct) Dzinnik Darius/Shutterstock, p 198 (cb) GIPhotoStock/Science Photo Library, p 198 (b) GCPics/Shutterstock, p 199 (t) HJSchneider/Shutterstock, p 199 (ct) Spencer Grant/Science Photo Library, p 199 (cb) Trevor Clifford Photography/Science Photo Library, p 199 (b) Seth Solesbee/Shutterstock, pp198-199 Pi-Lens/Shutterstock, p 200 Scientifica, Visuals Unlimited/Science Photo Library, p 201 (t) HJSchneider/Shutterstock, p 201 (b) Dan Hanscom/Shutterstock, p 202 (t) Kevin Mayer/Shutterstock, p 202 (c) Ivancovlad/Shutterstock, p 202 (b) MilanB/Shutterstock, p 204 SciencePhotos/Alamy, p 206 BikeRiderLondon/Shutterstock, p 208 GIPHOTOSTOCK/Science Photo Library, p 210 Spencer Grant/Science Photo Library, p 212 (t) Vereshchagin Dmitry/Shutterstock, p 212 (ct) Daseaford/Shutterstock, p 212 (cb) taelove7/Shutterstock, p 212 (b) Miroslaw Dziadkowiec/Shutterstock, p 214 AllOver images/Alamy, p 216 (t) Sheila Terry/Science Photo Library, p 216 (b) Charles D. Winters/Science Photo Library, p 217 Robert Pickett, p 219 (l) Abutyrin/Shutterstock, p 219 (r) Mostovyi Sergii Igorevich/Shutterstock, p 220 Trevor Clifford Photography/Science Photo Library, p 221 (r) SciencePhotos/Alamy, p 221 (l) Lily81/Shutterstock, p 221 (t) Krasowit/Shutterstock, p 221 (c) Andrei Nekrassov/Shutterstock, p 221 (b) Steve Wood/Shutterstock, p 222 Alexey Laputin/Shutterstock, p 229 Matthew Gough/Shutterstock, p 231 Innershadows Photography/Shutterstock, p 232 (l) Dubassy/Shutterstock, p 232 (c) Sergey Karpov/Shutterstock, p 232 (r) Seth Solesbee/Shutterstock.